Beyond Alternative Food Networks

Beyond Alternative Food Networks

Italy's Solidarity Purchase Groups

Cristina Grasseni

BLOOMSBURY

LONDON · NEW DELHI · NEW YORK · SYDNEY

Bloomsbury Academic

An imprint of Bloomsbury Publishing Plc

50 Bedford Square
London
WC1B 3DP
UK

1385 Broadway
New York
NY 10018
USA

www.bloomsbury.com

First published 2013

© Cristina Grasseni, 2013

British Library Cataloguing-in-Publication Data
A catalogue record for this book is available from the British Library.

ISBN HB: 978-0-85785-227-4
PB: 978-0-85785-228-1
ePub: 978-0-85785-229-8
ePDF: 978-1-47252-091-3

Library of Congress Cataloging-in-Publication Data
A catalog record for this book is available from the Library of Congress.

Typeset by Apex CoVantage, LLC
Printed and bound in Great Britain

To Francesca and Silvana,
Laura,
Gianna and Donatella,
and all the hard-headed women
who provide, think, and do.

'There can be no doubt that all our knowledge
begins with experience'.
Immanuel Kant

Contents

List of Figures and Tables

Tables

Acknowledgements

This book would never be what it is without the ongoing conversations and friendship with Francesca Forno and Silvana Signori, cofounders of CORES, the Research Group on Consumption, Networks and Practices of Sustainable Economies at Bergamo University.

Davide Biolghini and Giuseppe Vergani of Tavolo RES have been valid and valiant partners in research. Their achievements in enabling solidarity economies are the object of my personal admiration.

The witty, resourceful, and ingenious observations of Federico De Musso and the graduate students of the Doctoral School in Anthropology and Epistemology at Bergamo University: Oscar Biffi, Silvia Contessi, and Alberto Parovel are for me an encouraging source of motivation and hope.

To take part in the initial steps and debates of ReteGasBergamo and its working groups was a privilege and a precious occasion for reflecting on activism, engagement, and scholarship. I am particularly indebted to all those who shared their time and opinions with me, while working together for a common task—especially Alberto, Aurelio, Beppe, Francesca, Laura, Luciano, Mauro, Orazio, Osvaldo, and Paolo.

My *Gruppo di Acquisto Solidale* (GAS) in Bergamo was for me a haven— a place to provision, learn, and share. I am grateful to all its members for the friendship and thoughtfulness shown to me and my family: especially Carla, Cecilia, Donatella and Eugenio, and Gianna. I cannot believe that Sandro won't be found tinkering at his van when I come back home.

Thanks to a fellowship year at the Radcliffe Institute for Advanced Study at Harvard University and a following visiting scholar affiliation to the Harvard Anthropology Department, I benefitted from many generative conversations about food activism, alternative provisioning, and food ethnography: notably with Rachel Black, Carole Counihan, Michael Herzfeld, and Heather Paxson.

I am grateful to Giovanni Orlando for sharing ideas and readings leading up to our co-convened panel at the 2012 EASA Conference: Ethical Foods after the Global Recession: Navigating Anxiety, Morality, and Austerity.

The Community Economies Collective and the Harvard Working Group on Political Ecology provided a welcoming environment in which to read and discuss drafts of manuscript chapters. I am especially grateful to Katherine

Gibson, Stephen Healy, Andrew Littlejohn, and Oona Morrow for the comments and encouragement received.

I am grateful for the conversations and the exchanges of information that I had with Virginie Amilien, Elena Battaglini, Paolo Parigi, Juliette Rogers, Colin Sage, Mario Salomone, Giorgio Schifani, and Laura Terragni in the framework of preparing team submissions for funded projects.

The generous and constructive feedback of two anonymous reviewers made a precious contribution to strengthen the book project and manuscript. Naturally, any mistakes or misconstructions are my own responsibility.

My partner in life, Jonathan Hankins, has read, commented on, rejoiced over, and suffered through every word of this work. May this seedling bear more sustainable fruits, for us and our children.

Throughout the book, I quote informants anonymously, using pseudonyms, unless I am reporting public statements (such as conference talks or radio interviews). Hence all quotes by first name only have to be understood as pseudonyms.

Introduction

My first acquaintance with the very idea of a *Gruppo di Acquisto Solidale* (GAS; solidarity purchase group) happened through a younger colleague, an expert in agricultural history who was making a living with research projects in ethnographic museums, thanks to her experience in cataloguing items of material culture. At the time, in 2003, she was cherishing the prospect of making about 22,000 Euro per year as a museum conservator. She had a master's degree in conservation of cultural patrimony (as *heritage* is called in Latin languages). Tired of the meticulous and repetitive job of cataloging and restoring agricultural tools for ethnographic exhibitions, she found it refreshing to join a GAS in nearby Brescia, a city of just over a million people in the northern Italian plains.

She explained the GAS routine to me: each member collects orders for and buys one product for everyone else from trusted providers. Members then come to collect orders (at home or at designated meeting points) and pay their dues. My friend's duty was to buy fresh vegetables. She had just moved into a flat in a newly renovated farmstead in what was once a rural borough, but was now fully incorporated in the city's periphery. She was happy to use her spacious cellar to briefly house the collective grocery shopping. She would receive her guests and in exchange pay visits to them—to collect pasta, jam, canned food, sauces, environment-friendly cleaning materials, and so on. The visits would become occasions for tasting a Fair Trade tea, exchanging recipes, or chatting.

She liked the fact of inhabiting a rural building, however engulfed in an urban fabric, and to be able to walk to her new workplace—a newly restored water-operated iron forge converted into an iron museum. I thought it was a nice idea for a young woman (she was then thirty) to meet like-minded and cultured, and definitely *not* wealthy, purchasers of all things organic. I intuited the naturalness of the link between her passion for ethnographic conservation—which she vigorously exercised through the painstaking cataloguing of tools, mementos, and interviews with local farmers—and her almost-pastime involvement in a solidarity purchase group. Liaising with local producers and hosting and distributing fresh vegetables must have reinforced her sense of place-making. It would work as a strategy to relocate and rethink ruralness in the heart of urban sprawl.

Later on, she told me that when she moved on to direct a large ethnographic collection in a concrete exhibition pavilion located in an agricultural fair site in the middle of the foggy plains, she had pushed the administration to introduce eco-friendly cleaning materials for the exhibition spaces and nonpolluting substances for the cleaning and conservation of the collection. She had just presented to me in a nutshell the first example of crosscutting counter-epistemologies, which I believe characterize the practice of GAS. In other words, through joining a grassroots network for organic provisioning, she was exposed to many practices and tools that made her purchasing patterns more conscious, organized, and sustainable. She then applied this enhanced sensibility to her more public role of museum director to affect the institutional framework in which she worked. Her consumption choices, through socialization, had moved from the individual to the collective—from the grassroots to the institutional level. In time, she had succeeded in embedding them in a provisioning routine.

Back in 2003, I immediately sensed the potential complications of this practice: arranging for all these visits, having to pay up-front for the food orders, rescheduling the absentminded, feeling responsible for the fast-ripening produce, not being able to allocate the storage space in other ways. I thought, "Very nice, but too complicated." Six years and two children later, I was ready to embrace the GAS philosophy. I joined a GAS group in my hometown, Bergamo—in northern Italy—and, soon enough, became a delegate in a network of about sixty solidarity purchase groups.

As I write, the global financial downturn is peaking in Europe, the Eurozone trembles, and the economies of Italy and of Southern Europe are grinding to a halt. While some of the burgeoning literature on alternative food networks critically questions their actual "alternativeness" (Kirwan 2004, Whatmore et al. 2003, Fuller et al. 2010), a number of scholars are asking what's wrong with ethical consumption (Littler 2011) and raising the issue of clearly defining which objects, processes, and social actors "alternativeness" actually refers to. David Goodman, Melanie DuPuis, and Michael Goodman, on the basis of their long-term commitment to studying the new political ecologies that so-called alternative food networks may succeed or fail to establish, have recently posed a crucial question: which role will alternative food provisioning play in a global economic scenario where the era of cheap and abundant food, at least in developed countries, seems to have come to an end? (Goodman, DuPuis, and Goodman, 2012).

Due to the concurrent environmental and financial crises, we are living at the end of a global phase dominated by retail capital and cost/price squeeze to the disadvantage of marginal producers, especially in the global south (Orlando 2012)—a phase that food regimes theorist Philip McMichael has defined as "food from nowhere" (2009). However, responsible food has so far coincided with added-value, pricier food—justifying critiques of the intrinsically elitist nature of ethical consumption. Food regime scholars have debated whether "food from somewhere" can emerge within agroecology-based localism, or whether green capitalism and corporate environmentalism have already transformed place-based foods into a new regime (Friedmann 2009, McMichael 2009, Campbell 2009).

In this book I provide an in-depth ethnographic description of the evolution of a social phenomenon—Italy's solidarity purchase groups—that I would have myself described as an alternative food network (and did) until a few years ago but which, in the light of the late combination of credit crunch, recession, and austerity measures in Southern Europe, has become increasingly relevant to the current change in the food regime for the average lower-middle-class Italian family. As the title suggests, this wishes to be more than a book about alternative food networks. In fact, it is a study of a grassroots model of provisioning practice that calls into question a number of tacit assumptions about capitalism, globalized food systems, and civic participation. Through a description of food provisioning in solidarity purchase groups, it thus presents us with an ethnography of civil society and a contribution to the anthropology of contemporary Italy not only from the point of view of the anthropology of food and food activism but also from the point of view of political ecology and political anthropology.

In the current economic conjuncture, GAS enjoy widespread and increasing popularity—to the point that their own leaders find it difficult to chart them and keep updated census of active solidarity purchase groups. With the current census of 451 active GAS groups in the Lombardy region alone (Osservatorio CORES 2013)—and potentially thousands unchartered nationwide—the Gruppi di Acquisto Solidale seem no longer niche or alternative. In other words, buying collectively from proximal providers to negotiate the terms of production, price, and distribution has become a necessity for the Italian lower middle classes, and the capacity to share knowledge about food preparation and provision has become a resource. And while growing as a popular phenomenon, the Gruppi di Acquisto Solidale have shown a capacity for reflexive self-review, which is rooted in their origins in global justice activism. Thanks to the capillary diffusion of these groups, and the capacity of the coordinators to set concrete agendas while nourishing dialogue with a number of national and international networks of solidarity economy, gasistas—as GAS members call themselves—are learning to think of themselves as a movement. As they do so, media interest has exposed them to sometimes ambivalent interpretations.

For instance, in September 2012 Venice hosted the first joint conferences of the degrowth movement and the GAS national assembly. Serge Latouche's theory of degrowth denounces "growth" as the antithesis of real human progress and claims that the notion of sustainable development is deceptive and ultimately untenable (2005). According to degrowth scholars, this calls for a radical rethinking of democracy "against a more and more pervasive economic tyranny" (Deriu 2012: 553). The Conference on degrowth was devoted to "Ecological Sustainability and Social Equity," in line with the GAS assembly, "(Re) constructing Territorial Communities with a Future. Solidarity Purchase Groups and Districts of Solidarity Economy as New Actors in Territorial Economy and Policies."[1] In the run-up to the event, though, an article appeared in the magazine *Valori* (Values; issued by the Italian Ethical Bank, Banca Etica), which stirred a heated debate. The topic was "forced degrowth" and the journalist proposed solidarity purchase groups as a societal model for the "forthcoming dark ages." The new society—argued the article—would require less salaried work, less travel, and more and greener technology. But it would also require homesteading, the rediscovery of traditional self-provisioning, and female unwaged work. This greener, solidarity-driven society of GAS would be based not only on a shrinking economy but also on autarchy and ultimately on an extremely conservative and localist reinvention of the family and the community (Baiocchi 2012).

This journalistic stunt summarizes the sense of ambivalence that food activism triggers in scholars, policy-makers, and the media. It is important here to clarify what GAS are alternative to. In our contemporary consumer society, why should people spend time, resources, and efforts to deliberate collectively what to buy, from whom, and how to procure it? The answer does not lie in the *objects* of provisioning alone. It is not just healthier, cleaner, or even more just food that gasistas want. They do not trust the ready availability of these objects. The conditions for such availability are opaque or unknown, with reference to workers' rights, environmental damage, and price-making. The framework is no more transparent in the case of energy provision, the cost of healthcare, and access to nonpartisan information. These conditions and frameworks are fundamental in building trust, namely what Diego Gambetta (1990) has aptly called the "making and breaking of cooperative relations." Gasistas, like all humans, can do one thing at a time: by reappropriating food provisioning, they start regenerating trust from the fundamentals of social and individual life.

Brought back to a local level, transparency has to do with reappropriating local knowledge through proximity: reacquainting oneself with crop seasonality, remembering how to pluck a chicken, learning what grows in a specific farming landscape, and knowing who *actually* farms nearby and with what economic return. Gasistas map producers and in so doing they shift from an implicit trust in them, conveyed through commercial mediators and safety and quality certifications, to explicit trust building through community monitoring. For the farmers, this entails not only committing to quality cultivations but also actually opening the firm's doors and showing, for instance, that workers are not exploited to reap the crops. I have also witnessed the convergence and sometimes cooperation between different types of food activism, such as Slow Food and GAS, toward specific objectives, such as the reintroduction of local cultivars in short food chains, the organization of fairs and festivals of short chain foods, or specific events of solidarity economy such as markets for "clean" textiles.

This book describes these alternative foragers ethnographically based on two years fieldwork with solidarity purchase groups. GAS are difficult to define in abstract terms. In general, they are networks of families and friends that engage in collective provisioning on the basis of a solidarity principle. GAS members buy as much as they can of their food collectively and directly from farmers, generally privileging organic and local produce, and managing the associated financial and logistic tasks on a voluntary basis. Their criteria for selecting providers include respect for the environment and solidarity toward the providers but also among group members. I particularly focus on the activist notion of co-production as a transformative practice, through which gasistas come to think of themselves as more than mere consumers. I will show how food becomes a pivot around which social and economic relationships are rewoven in GAS practice. Gradually, this allows gasistas to radically rethink economic transactions in the light of their societal and political implications, to finally move beyond food, building more comprehensive provisioning networks. Food provisioning nevertheless remains the focus of most of GAS activism. The organizational and critical capacities generated in the process are profoundly imbued by this practical and relational effort.

The self-presentation of the Gruppi di Acquisto Solidale can be read on the website retegas.org:

> Usually, a purchasing group is set up by a number of consumers to buy food and other goods directly from the producers, or from big retailers, at a discounted rate. When a purchasing group doesn't search for just for the cheapest price, but instead puts people and environment before profit, the group becomes a solidarity purchasing group. This chooses the products and producers on the basis of respect for the environment and the solidarity between the members of the group, the traders and the producers. Specifically, these guidelines lead to the choice of local products (in order to minimize the environmental impact of transportation), fair-trade goods (in order to respect disadvantaged producers by promoting their human rights, in particular women's, children's and indigenous people's) and reusable or eco-compatible goods (to promote a sustainable lifestyle). Every single G.A.S. has its specific motivation, but usually all groups draw their roots from a critical approach to today's global economic model and lifestyle of consumerism; individuals that feel the unfairness in this model and are searching for a practical alternative can find reciprocal aid and advice by joining solidarity purchasing groups. Usually when some friends develop a tendency toward a less

consumerist way of life, the idea of undertaking shared purchase initiatives is quite natural. When the idea becomes more concrete, a fair amount of effort is needed for the search of some local producer that meets the solidarity criteria; the next step is the establishment of an internal structure in the group in order to collect the orders and redistribute the products, and the solidarity purchasing group is already born!.[2]

A detailed charter, *Documento Base dei GAS,* serves as guideline and as a record of how GAS came about, starting with the first group established in Fidenza (near Parma) in 1994.[3] Retegas.org functions as a portal to foster coordination among groups in a national network. Adhesion to the network (called Retegas or Rete dei GAS) is purely voluntary and consists of registering online. The Documento Base dei GAS is signed collectively by Rete dei GAS, though the contact address given on the website is personally traceable to Andrea Saroldi, one of the charismatic leaders of the network.[4] Despite the abundance of materials online, solidarity criteria are interpreted and appropriated on a strictly local basis; each GAS group being sovereign. Some only buy organic, while others prefer to support local agriculture first, and still others again invest in what is largely known in the solidarity economy movement as self-production, *autoproduzione:* namely growing and conserving staple foods at home, through home-gardening, exchanges between families, and homesteading.

In my own experience, on average GAS groups consist of twenty to forty families, though they can be much larger. There are networks of GAS and large GAS with subgroups, and so on. Unsurprisingly, the debate on how to establish a collective identity and the issue on representation are key in the movement (I dwell on this in Chapter 4). CORES, Bergamo University's research group on consumption, networks, and practices of sustainable economies, of which I am a co-founder, conducted a comprehensive survey of solidarity purchase groups in the Bergamo area in 2011/12 and is now expanding the research to northern Italy. The statistical data that I quote about Bergamo gasistas are the results of this online survey. The online questionnaires were made accessible only to local gasistas, by contacting all the GAS groups in the Bergamo area one by one. CORES collected both socioeconomic indicators and elements of network analysis through two structured questionnaires: one for every GAS member and one for each GAS coordinator. If an entire family participated in a GAS group (as is often the case), we requested that the family member that devotes the most time to GAS activities fill out the questionnaire. GAS coordinators answered detailed questions about the organization of the groups (date founded, number of members, money spent, etc.). When the survey began at the end of 2011, there were sixty-two active GAS in the province of Bergamo (more than double the number known in September 2009).

The CORES survey was carried out almost in parallel with a self-mapping process initiated by the newly founded GAS network of the Bergamo area, ReteGasBergamo. It was important to us that about half of the existing groups had either been operating without making contact or had just been set up in the momentous growth of the latest couple of years. Each GAS was individually contacted through its coordinator, known in the GAS world as a *referente* (literally "delegate" or "spokesperson"). Forty-two groups, 71 percent, accepted to undertake the survey, despite gasistas suspicion of any kind of formal investigation on their activities from what are perceived as external bodies, including research institutions. All the researchers involved, including myself, were well-known on the local scene. One CORES colleague was especially famous, as she established a seminar and study group in 2007 that later developed into a network for the promotion of solidarity economy: Sustainable Citizenship. Thus forty-two GAS coordinators filled out a detailed online questionnaire about the GAS foundation, routines, economic practice, organization, number of members, products bought, producers involved, and money spent. The second phase of the project required each member of each of the forty-two GAS groups to fill out a second online questionnaire about their individual routines, beliefs, education, motivation for joining a GAS, and so on. Two hundred ninety-nine heads of households participated in this phase—that is, 29 percent of the 1,032 families enrolled in the sixty-two GAS that were present in the Bergamo area at the time.[5]

The first statistical portrait of the average gasista in Bergamo is that she is female in about 70 percent of the cases (205 out of 299 interviewees). She has higher education (a master's degree) in about a third of the cases and is between 30 and 44 years old in about half the cases. She has a family with children over five years old in half the cases, is employed in commerce, services, teaching, or clerical jobs in more than 66 percent of the cases, and her average family income, in more than half the cases, ranges between 2,000 and 3,600 Euro per month.[6]

This statistical portrait confirms my ethnographic experience. The gasistas I met in my own solidarity purchase group were mostly middle-age women, some regularly accompanied by their husbands. They worked in schools, nurseries, social services, or as post employees, nurses, or clerks, or were retired. They wore decent but cheap clothes and lived on secure but tight family budgets. Most of them worked nine-to-five jobs, and others worked night shifts. A few came to GAS assemblies straight out of work meetings. We met monthly, in the evenings, in the public library, and we were tired. We had long lists of queries and letters to go through in every meeting. We cheered ourselves up by bringing fruit, honey, or homemade wine. But we were matter-of-fact, gave out Excel sheets of orders for Fair Trade chocolate, Sicilian oranges, olive oil from postquake Abruzzese farmers, and Parmesan cheese cooperatives. We read letters from inmates in Palermo proposing their almond sweets made in jail and from Roberto Li Calzi, the promoter of a mafia-free network of orange producers. We competed with other GAS for the only organic beef breeder and butcher in the province and hurriedly paid each other visits to pick up meat, cans, rice, and unbleached toilet paper. What do these women tell us about social class and alternative food networks? In the course of the book, I hope to show that they question facile presumptions about social positioning and elitism. As heads of households with secure jobs and the capacity to exercise selective consumer choices, they constitute a social élite. As members of a lower middle class threatened by decreasing purchasing power, they do not. However, as they carry out specific provisioning strategies in the name of solidarity with other workers and with the environment, they acquire the potential of becoming a critical social movement.

A useful comparative benchmark is provided by a survey on the styles of consumption of the average Bergamasque family carried out by CORES in 2011. Of the 155 participants, more than 30 percent had a degree. More than half went regularly to the shopping mall for food and nonfood purchases, but about 40 percent were concerned about health issues related to the food they bought and with environmental issues. Yet 96.6 percent chose by price only. Again, while 75 percent of interviewees maintained that local foods (increasingly known as "zero-mile foods") offer a good quality/ cost ratio and thought that they are tastier and environmentally friendlier, only an insignificant minority bought them. As sociologist Francesca Forno, who directed this research, rightly concludes, "Income and awareness of the risks associated with certain styles of consumption are not sufficient to adopt new lifestyles that are more respectful of the environment and of one's health" (Forno and Salvi 2012: 21). In fact, the critical economic conjuncture of 2011 meant that 41 percent of the Bergamasque interviewees had decreased the quantities of food bought, in order not to compromise with quality, and a further 23 percent claimed that they had begun to accept lower quality food, too.

This gives us a hint as to why solidarity purchase groups have been very successful in Italy in the latest decade. Their growth has become exponential during the crisis years, from 2008 onwards (see Figure 0.1). During a radio interview on November 26, 2011, one of the charismatic leaders of the movement and founder of the first Italian GAS, Mauro Serventi, announced that the number of registered groups had reached one thousand.[7] Registering with the online census is a completely voluntary and unsolicited move. Retegas estimates that up to double the number of registered GAS may be active. This is based on the observation that, where GAS were actively mapped out, such as in the province of Bergamo (Osservatorio CORES 2013) or Rome (Fonte et al. 2011), twice as many as the registered groups were found.

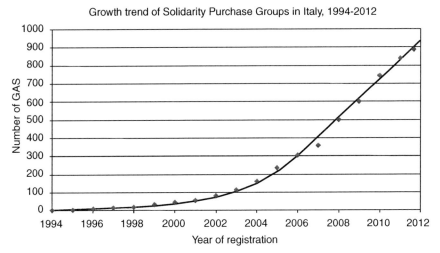

Growth trend of Solidarity Purchase Groups in Italy, 1994-2012

Figure 0.1   Growth trend of Solidarity Purchase Groups in Italy, 1994–2012, based on the number of GAS that self-registered with retegas.org. Courtesy of Davide Biolghini.

In fact, according to a national survey of the Farmers Union Coldiretti, 18 percent of Italians (about 7 million people) are allegedly involved in various forms of collective provisioning—including carpooling, condominium shopping groups, and collective agreements with farmers (Rubino 2012).[8] More conservatively, according to Retegas, about 150,000 people may be involved in solidarity purchase groups. If these numbers are confirmed, these people are purportedly shifting about 80 million Euro away from large distribution without any centralized coordination among them.[9] In this book I claim that participation in solidarity purchase groups is an entry point into alternative economies. While seeking a direct relationship with food providers for solidarity reasons, GAS practice creates opportunities for affordable quality food and reweaves relationships around the daily and mostly female task of provisioning.

GAS are an important case study for understanding the mechanisms and decisional processes through which citizens can enter into cooperative relationships among themselves, with providers, and with institutions. Networks of GAS are sometimes key in providing a survival opportunity to small farms and family enterprises, supporting short food chains and multifunctional agriculture. In some cases, networks of networks develop further projects of sustainable agriculture, green economy, and social inclusion. In particular, I recount the laborious and improbable but enthusiastic steps through which previously uncoordinated groups from disparate political allegiances gave birth to a network of GAS and a network of solidarity economy (RES) in Bergamo, between 2009 and 2011. In my description, I replicate and analyze gasista language: using reproductive metaphors from both the animal world ("a GAS is already born") and from botany (GAS proliferate by "budding" and "grafting").

I used mostly participant observation, developed over more than two years of continuous fieldwork with one solidarity purchase group and with the GAS network of the Bergamo area between January 2009 and August 2011. I was both a member of a solidarity purchase group and a delegate in the network ReteGasBergamo. I also took part in the 2010 and 2011 national GAS assemblies. Fieldwork has continued through virtual connections (email, Internet forums, and Skype conversations) and follow-up visits—and never really stopped. This ethnography was the basis of my further involvement in the CORES project to map the GAS scenario nationwide.

This quantitative research was conducted collaboratively with local gasistas and in coordination with the national Retegas, with a conscious agenda of opening up academic research to social actors. I and my Bergamo colleagues Francesca Forno and Silvana Signori, co-founders of CORES, engaged in the design, administration, and analysis of the survey as an explicit token of collaborative partnership and restitution to the GAS movement. We offered our professional skills in interpreting the movement's impact and internal structure as it evolved. The double questionnaire was devised on the basis of our firsthand knowledge of solidarity economy networks. Quantitative data acquired meaning in the light of in-depth qualitative knowledge of the very same objects. Vice versa, I could place my own ethnography against a quantitative scenario, highlighting significant aspects of it, as the CORES survey sketched an outline of many gasistas I could have never met in person.

The objective of this book is to analyze solidarity purchase groups not only as an alternative practice of provisioning but also as a distinctive social phenomenon in contemporary Italy, a lens through which to read its characteristic politics, social structure, and cultures of participation. I dwell on the internal diversity of the GAS movement itself, explaining how it is rooted in specific histories and local political cultures (Baccetti and Messina 2009). My thesis is that the limits and potentials of Italy's solidarity purchase groups to impact economies and imaginaries depend on the diversity of the associative cultures and styles of participation in which they are embedded.

In some of the examples cited, GAS activism increases civic participation in local governance by concretely addressing specific issues in the current food system (such as food quality, environmental pollution, or the fate of local small farmers). Moreover, on a national level, the GAS coordination network Retegas consistently discusses and compares the strategic problems that GAS, as a movement, encounter. During the frequent thematic workshops, yearly assemblies, and topic-driven working groups, GAS activists look for solutions to a variety of strategic issues: how to evaluate produce quality (by demanding organic certification or by accepting and aiding forms of self-certification?); how to keep GAS activities informal and supple but legal; whether to assume a specific juridical profile (such as that of a registered association or a cooperative); how to interpret and promote food sovereignty; how to move beyond food and impact larger distribution chains—for instance, in the realm of manufacturing and energy, finance and insurance.

Although I encountered and became informed on many of these issues and debates, my focus is not on the GAS overall agenda as a movement. Rather, I insist on how the projects I observed and participated in had varying organizational capacities, styles of deliberation, and efficacy of results. I do not aim to suggest ways of improving GAS practice or activist theory. Beginning with an unassuming and everyday participation in one GAS group, in time I progressed in my acquaintance with the many layers and degrees of GAS participation (potentially infinite!). My ethnographic examples and narratives aim to show how civic engagement may be the result, not necessarily the self-conscious objective, of GAS practical approaches to food provisioning and beyond. The current context of economic and political crisis spurs gasistas to rethink and bridge the rural/urban divide, starting from their own needs, aspirations, and positionality in Italian society. During my participant observation with solidarity purchase groups, a shared concern with our own health and family livelihoods co-existed with a genuine will to reshape the destiny of the landscape we inhabited. We struggled to use our own scarce spare time and resources to invent routines, reflections, and relationships that would increase our well-being, our knowledge of our own place, and our capacity to recognize seasonality and duration within and around us. All this, I maintain, was transformative of our own lifestyles and allowed us to contribute—however minimally but significantly for our contexts—to pose the problem of food sovereignty and global justice from the bottom up. By collectively purchasing and distributing our food and everyday provisions, we were reinventing time, place, and quality, treating them as nonmeasurable items and as common resources—hence, not as commodities but rather as commons. Precisely by giving our time freely in painstaking meetings and discussion, by refusing to accept the authority of certified food quality or geographical indications, by scouting our own neighborhoods and countryside to meet, map, and negotiate with our providers, we were reweaving the economy, and society with it (see Chapter 3). It was at once a humble and visionary task. Consuming more local products, reducing food miles, and favoring new local economic circuits were concrete and pragmatic objectives, but with a significant political and relational potential.

Building on interdisciplinary literature on political consumerism (Micheletti 2003), ethical consumption (Carrier and Luetchford 2012), and community economies (Gibson-Graham 2006), I draw on my own participant observations of solidarity purchase groups and networks to identify specific features and critical points of GAS groups and networks as a form of solidarity economy. This definition emerges from the French, Portuguese, and Italian literature on global justice (Laville 1994, Mance 2001, Biolghini 2007) and has established itself as a cross-disciplinary notion (Amin 2009, Kawano et al. 2010, Hart et al. 2010). Here, I critically reflect on the limits and potentials of the ways in which networks and districts of solidarity economy are built, drawing both on ethnographic experience in solidarity purchase groups and on activist scholarship (Biolghini 2007). I discuss GAS practice as an economy not only of solidarity but also specifically of trust, and I explain how this is anthropologically significant in the context of Italy's failing democracy. I hope to show how gasistas' consumer behavior is collective, innovative, and transformative, how it can be undermined by their self-perception of provisioning as an apolitical practice, and how misleading it would be to interpret it as a middle-class foodie circle. The following outlines how the book unfolds.

Chapter 1 introduces a literature review on alternative food networks, drawing mostly on social anthropology, human geography, and rural sociology. I argue that GAS justify theorizing beyond alternative food networks, as they are venturing into more comprehensive alternative models of provisioning, which include nonfood items such as textiles or energy provision. I explain the GAS agenda of co-production as one seeking a direct relationship with producers and distributors. Co-production thus moves beyond both the boycott and "buycott" strategies of individual critical consumers. In solidarity purchase groups, provisioning becomes a political activity because individuals organize themselves into networks in order to exercise agency (co-producing) in the economic system.

Chapter 2 details the field-site of northern Italy, presenting a diverse scenario of initiatives aimed at rerooting food supply in local food systems. In December 2010, according to Coldiretti, the main Italian agricultural trade union, in the province of Bergamo (about one million inhabitants) 325 farms exercised direct sales and 35 automated distributors of refrigerated raw milk were in operation, as well as 70 ecotourism farms and 4 farmers' markets. Coldiretti claimed to support "a new democracy of shopping" based on food traceability.[10] With thirty-two local GAS working at the time to set up a network and a district of solidarity economy, a veritable reinvention of local food systems seemed to be on its way (Grasseni 2011a, 2012b). By the end of 2011, the local GAS network had managed to map double that number of solidarity purchase groups, for a total of sixty-two groups. I explain how this dynamic scenario includes distinctive and competing agendas and stakeholders. GAS and especially districts of solidarity economy add a critical edge to a generalized desire for a reterritorialization of food that is voiced by many actors, from Slow Food to agricultural parks, to zero-miles restaurants.

In Chapter 3, I quote in detail from my own ethnography to present the nitty-gritty of gasista activism. What is exactly entailed in being a gasista? In my experience, GAS adherents come from all walks of life but have on the whole a higher education profile and a previous exposure to associative movements. Notably, they are not rich but come mostly from the clerical low middle class. The crux of their activity is to convene periodically and organize bulk-buying from trusted producers. Organic farming is preferred, but special care is also taken to buy locally and to promote conversions to organic farming. This means assessing the producers, organizing visits, and often holding social events to cook and share the foodstuffs. In this way, recipes are circulated and information is shared. Participating in a group thus eventually means being socialized into bread-baking, cherry-picking, grape-harvesting, chestnut-picking, and so on, turning these experiences into educational family outings. It also means being exposed to the philosophy of degrowth and voluntary simplicity. Sobriety and conviviality co-exist in the associative routines of GAS, and I argue that these are conducive to trust-building and to increased "social capital" (Putnam 2000) within solidarity purchase groups and solidarity economy networks. Participating in the meetings often involves long, drawn-out decision-making processes. Nevertheless, participation and collective action is both effective and affective, inducing lifestyles changes.

In Chapter 4, I describe how the solidarity purchase groups of the Bergamo area slowly elaborated their own identity as a network, ReteGasBergamo. If, to use gasista language, networks are born, Chapter 4 focuses on the labor and birth-pains of networking. GAS are a successful example of self-organization, but nourishing networks of solidarity economy require effort and stamina. Rather than a pool of contentment, ReteGasBergamo was a sizzling melting pot and a terrain of continuous debate. I observed and participated in the laborious first steps of ReteGasBergamo beyond its initial mapping efforts. Its beginnings and failings provide an ethnographic account of how gasista participation amounts to an alphabetization to nonviolent consensus-building. I participated in the network's Mapping Group, in two national GAS assemblies, and in occasional meetings of working groups on training, communication, and network consolidation. Pragmatic issues (shall we order potatoes as a network of GAS or as individual groups?) imposed a debate about representation, delegation, and democratic decision-making. Would the network decide by majority or by consensus? People with different interpretations and expectations about provisioning and activism had to meet and collaborate toward a course of action.

The thesis that I elaborate in Chapter 5 is that GAS aid the circulation of crosscutting counter-epistemologies across activist networks, amidst the desolate social and institutional scenario of an ever-failing state. Through newly acquired competences and practices, GAS activists learn and diffuse forms of self-help and self-training. For example, *slow-foodisti* (members of Slow Food circles) and *gasisti* (members of GAS groups), though largely coming from different social milieus, share an interest in comparable practices, such as mapping local producers, sustaining their choice of converting to organic farming, and recreating short food chains. This spontaneous convergence can be read as a symptom of a widely felt social need for new styles of consumption in conjunction with new styles of participation. I stress how gasistas' critical rethinking of provisioning in terms of solidarity is not only an economic act but also a political one. By socializing food and reweaving reciprocity, it is the fabric of society itself that is refounded. Building on a critical review of the role of familism and proximity relationships in Italian ethnography, I shall focus on the weight of trust, or lack of it, as a starting point of solidarity economy. I argue that solidarity economy activism does not only organize grassroots food provisioning but also elaborates a discourse and practice of solidarity that moves beyond consumption, rethinking, and transforming society and the economy.

In Chapter 5, I will also ask how and if my own position as a gasista eased, complicated, or hindered my research. Initially I did not conceive of my GAS membership as anything different than mere participant observation, but as I found myself participating in discussions, representing my group at assembly, and inevitably orienting the results of such discussions, I felt that my scholarship was moving toward a different terrain. Feeling the responsibility of facilitating the flux of information between different sectors of the movement, I came to categorize my research as "engaged anthropology" (Low and Merry 2010). J. K. Gibson-Graham (2006)[11] invite scholars to engage in community economies (including through action research) to voice models of noncapitalist economies. Further engaged with the mapping initiative of the CORES survey, I came to the conclusion with my Bergamo colleagues that this part of our research was in fact co-research. Social science is imbued with a suspicion of personal enthusiasm for one's objects of research: one cannot be researching objects and processes in which one is personally involved, as a dispassionate attitude is required of scientific scholarship. Nevertheless, gasista activism and academic pursuit share many traits. For instance, they both require passion and endurance. They are dissipative of personal energy while conducted in the spirit of collective advancement. Ethnographers are well-equipped to analyze and represent the gradual and ambivalent process of mutual recognition, which involves both informants (for lack of a better word) and anthropologists.

In the concluding chapter, I explain why I move beyond alternative food networks in defining the specificity of solidarity purchase groups. I argue that the complexity of GAS participation challenges and expands our understanding of solidarity-driven provisioning. Individual group members, representatives in local and national networks, charismatic leaders authoring published manifestos, and local working groups each seek a viable interpretation of food sovereignty and food justice. In a community-building movement of a non-oppositional nature such as GAS, this means changing one's own lifestyle first: networking, recruiting, studying up, using self-help and peer help, and slowly becoming visible to the institutions. While local and regional administrations begin to realize the importance of alternative economies, these actors find and support local producers, paying them more than large distribution chains. They negotiate standards of transparency and build trust. Borrowing the concept of co-production from the movement itself, I point out how this notion expresses a need for active citizenship through economic practice. An anthropological contribution to the analysis of this scenario draws on the well-established idea that our present material culture is imbued with continuous processes of commodity resignification and of affect. If Daniel Miller argues that shopping "does not merely reflect love, but is a major form in which this love is manifested and reproduced" (Miller 1998:18), this is particularly true in the case of solidarity-driven and collective purchase. We should not be surprised to find that affect is an important side of GAS practice.

Alternative Provisioning Networks

BACK TO BASICS?

In 2007 I moved back to my childhood neighborhood. It was a very different neighborhood than the one I grew up in, as I could see it now from the point of view of a mother of two. The area had gentrified in one sense, desertified in another. The number of food shops had halved—there were seven bars but only two grocery shops within walking distance, one of which was often closed and not very freshly supplied, as the elderly lady who owned it only worked an erratic part-time schedule. The other one was selling potatoes and cherries at boutique prices and was definitely well beyond my purse-power. A few steps further away was a fresh meat shop that soon closed down. For meat, we were left with the not-so-fresh supplies of a Spar chain, which served the ageing housing estate surrounding it at monopoly prices. It was a different life from the popular neighborhood of Loreto where I had lived the previous five years. There, I could go on a swift walk in between breast-feedings and forage Sicilian bread, iron-rich horse meat, fresh groceries, and feel-good patisseries for prices higher than those of the supermarket but still affordable. My second child grew fast, and we soon were ready to send him to nursery school in the new neighborhood.

It was one of the nursery school teachers, Claudia (a pseudonym), who invited me to join a GAS. It was the end of 2008. She simply said, "I am going to join the GAS group of the Time Bank.[1] We are meeting tomorrow night at the public library. Will you come?" I did. I knew my way to the unpretentious neighborhood public library, basically a place to go and read newspapers for free and entertain the kids on dated books and linoleum floors. Sitting around the spartan table in school chairs, I was greeted with no specific welcoming ritual by Gisela, the group coordinator, and briskly introduced as a friend of Claudia. I think I may have presented myself as a resident of the neighborhood, and working at Bergamo University, but there was no particular round of self-introductions. There were about twenty people present, mostly middle-age women, two (including Gisela) with their husbands. The meeting was matter of fact. Gisela had a list of issues to go through: firstly they discussed their likes or dislikes of particular products currently under trial, particularly olive oil from Lake Garda. Then the yearly schedule for circulating orders was reshuffled—I realized I had just missed a number of once-per-semester rounds (especially rice, cleaning materials, and canned food), which had happened late in the fall. Then, a couple of people explained their problems with being a product referent for one rather than the other thing: transporting rice was a problem for the current referent, who had a small car. The Parmesan producer was a long way away, and its referent had to organize a one-day car trip on purpose to go and collect orders. Arrangements were made to include the travel expenses in the rice and Parmesan price that group members would pay for their share. I wasn't particularly told what to do. I was simply reassured that after a few meetings everything would be clearer, that I did not have to take on any responsibility for now, and that I would receive invitations to join the collective orders by e-mail. I gave my e-mail address to Gisela, did not sign anything, was not even sure of everyone's name by the end of the evening, and left with Claudia when the meeting came to a close after a couple of hours. She, too, was a bit disoriented. "Don't worry, it will all fall into place in due course," she reassured me.

In time, I got to know that in other GAS groups of the Bergamo area the protocol for acceptance was stricter and more elaborate and that this had become a source of conflict specifically between my own group and a longer-established group, as a result of which the two groups decided to go each its own way. In the other group, new members were admitted only after six months of apprenticeship or coaching (accompagnamento), during which they were assigned to a supervising senior member of the group. This did not happen to me. This late realization gave me the sense of how deeply varying gasista experience must be, even at a short distance within different groups and even more so among different regions, where GAS etiquette draws on distinctive associative cultures and experiences. I acquired the sense of our anarchic difference by picking up cursory and half-chuckling references during meetings, such as, "imagine what the others would say if they knew that we buy this product through a cooperative!" The joyful anarchy was also spelled out by the freedom of each to invest what one could in the group—both in terms of time and in terms of money spent. For example, the GAS I had joined was formally the solidarity purchase group of Bergamo's Time Banks, but GAS activity was carried out separately from the Time Bank.[2] I, for instance, was an active member of the GAS but not of the Time Bank. I was asked, of course, if I wished to join, but I was too poor in time.

I debated with my husband why, in his opinion, the nursery school teacher would invite me, and not other mothers, to attend the GAS meeting. We concluded that we probably came across as alternative in our own right: we all wore secondhand clothes, did not particularly care for our appearances, did not buy the children designer clothes or electronic games, and not know what was on television; we evidently had a more-than-usual gender-balanced family ménage, with my husband doing his share of child-caring (probably much more than 50%). Nevertheless, I, not my husband, got invited to the meeting. The overwhelmingly female attendance of the GAS meeting reminded me that in my society women are still expected to be the ones in charge of provisioning for the family.

AN ANTHROPOLOGIST LOOKS AT ALTERNATIVE PROVISIONING NETWORKS

I came to position myself as a researcher of the GAS movement after prolonged research on traditional dairy farmers in northern Italy. My perspective on alternative provisioning networks did not come then from an interest in global justice grassroots activism but from participant observation of the complex processes of standardization in Alpine agriculture (Grasseni 2011a). In my research experience, I often witnessed the heritigization and patrimonialization of natural and cultural resources as part of their rediscovery and reevaluation (Grasseni 2011a, 2012a,b,c).[3] This is why I became interested in the limits and potentials of new consumer-driven networks in creating sustainable alternatives for farmers.

Over the last decade, my ethnographic research has mainly focused on community-based approaches to local development vis-à-vis the deskilling and technification of rurality, specifically in the case of dairy farming in the Italian Alps. I focused on tacit knowledge, place-making, and immaterial patrimony (2007, 2009a, 2009b) and raised concerns about the social as well as environmental sustainability of models of development based on the marketing of local foods as heritage (Grasseni 2014). The problems I highlighted were the impact of techno-scientific standardization on local practices and the market pressure to commmodify recipes, festivities, and foodstuffs. This line of research also included a critical assessment of the local impact of breed improvement programs, agricultural aid, and EU-sponsored consortia for local development such as the various editions of the Leader project and the associated local action groups (Grasseni 2004, 2007). I concluded that a great diversity of skills, local cultures, and networks required case-by-case consideration when trying to adapt local patterns of production to global standards and urban markets.

Over time, my ethnography followed the objects of the momentous transformation that my field was undergoing: namely as regarded cows and cheese, their breeders and cheese-makers. Through participant observation, I developed a research agenda on the reinvention of food. I argued that this included a significant reshaping of the ethics and politics of consumption, which involved both "consumers and producers in new market relations" (Carrier and Luetchford 2012). Reinventing food also meant drawing new boundaries and fueling fights around naming strategies, geographical indication, and niche products (Paxson and West 2012). I was observing traditional mountain farmers in the Alps as they were confronted by more and more stringent "audit cultures" (Strathern 2000): visits by the breeders' association representatives to update their herd census, perform quality checks on their milk, make assessments regarding loans for bigger sheds, so as to accommodate their bigger, "improved" cows, the introduction of milking parlors, and so on. Moreover, for my friends in the field, positioning oneself successfully within the new "global hierarchy of value" (Herzfeld 2004) required the ability to cast oneself as "modern and progressive peasants," but also as the witnesses and the "saviors" of authentic mountain traditions. This capacity did not only include a fair amount of social performance but also liaising with local politicians and trade union consultants to apply for European agricultural aid or local development projects. In the case of my fieldwork site, my hosts and friends were increasingly appearing in local, even national, media, casting their public peasant persona into the global heritage scenario while scaling up their business locally. My rural informants were, in a sense, "seeing bifocally" (Peters 1997): I was witnessing the emergence of a new local elite, the prominent testimonials of traditional cheese-making, guests of the Slow Food Salone del Gusto—the biennial food fair in Turin—as well as of the accompanying global peasant happening, Terra Madre, held under the auspices of the Slow Food Foundation for Biodiversity.

Peasant food is being discovered and gentrified in Italy at a time of significant socioeconomic decline, which is sharply felt both in urban neighborhoods and in postindustrial wastelands. Turin itself, the seat of Slow Food international events, is a city at the foot of the Alps in significant postindustrial transformation, encircled by a peri-urban helter-skelter dissemination of factory warehouses and rural pockets. Many social experiments take shape in the face of the socioeconomic challenges presented by deindustrialization, food desertification, and the pauperization of the urban working classes. I was drawn to alternative food networks as new practices of place-making at the urban/rural interface. I decided to join the circles of the "ethical" consumers to critically analyze what my rural informants interpreted straightforwardly as yet another urban fad—just another way of longing for the rural idyll (cf. Grasseni 2003). To this, some of my mountain friends quite cynically played up their own role of "authentic" peasants. Elsewhere, I tell the story of how I found myself in Turin's Slow Food Salon in October 2010, left alone selling cheese at a Slow Food Presidium stand, while my farmer friends flocked to an installation featuring themselves next door. Their voices and faces were being video-projected on a screen of fake milk, during a milk-curdling demonstration for children and families, using spotless copper cauldrons while instructions and entertainment reached the audience via headphones (Grasseni forthcoming).

These new "relationships of the market" (Strasser 2003), which urban consumers and marginalized peasants seek to establish—not without ambivalences and misunderstandings on both parts—represent an important aspect of what I am analyzing as a reinvention of food at the foot of the Alps. I increasingly came to see this conjuncture as an opportunity of establishing new economic circuits, within which each party—producers *and* consumers—could gain while redefining development on its own terms. GAS activism is key to this reinvention. My own reading of Italy's solidarity purchase groups as alternative provisioning networks comes from this ethnographic viewpoint. My thesis is that a substantial part of the relational, practical, and theoretical work done by GAS activists is that of reinventing food (Grasseni 2011a, 2012b). As David Goodman argues, the provisioning of quality food per se is by and large an elitist social phenomenon: "In short, there is a strong class dimension to the social relations of consumption of the 'organic', the 'local', the 'regional', and the 'alternative'" (2012: 189). This kind of "alternative food economy," in fact, is indistinguishable from "territorial valorization" as a "market-oriented developmental imaginary" (2012: 194). Nevertheless, in my experience solidarity economy networks such as those of GAS try to imbue critical consumption with a further transformative role, that of constituting collaborative networks with proximal farmers.

The ethnographic narrative that unfolds over the following chapters identifies solidarity purchase groups as an example of solidarity economy and locates significant nodes, layers, and emerging patterns of collaboration across different networks. A key role is played by individuals with more than one associative affiliation, sometimes with a history in political, social, or environmental activism. As an example, one such network, Cittadinanza Sostenibile in Bergamo, was initiated as a study group in December 2007 on the topic of "Shopping for Human Rights," with the aim of supporting Sicilian entrepreneurs who resist the practice of paying the local mafia rackets as a form of extorted insurance. As I argue in Chapter 5, this project offered a meeting ground for a range of activists who had seldom the opportunity of regularly sharing ideas, readings, and discussions about alternative provisioning and its significance. This forum quickly developed into a network whose first common project was that of mapping the different and nascent experiences of solidarity economy in the Bergamo area. It then developed into a self-standing network of solidarity economy (Rete di Economia Solidale [RES][4]) whose president, a gasista herself, comes from previous experience in an environmentalist association. Cittadinanza Sostenibile further generated a working group on citizenship markets, which is currently managing gasista farmers' markets in the Bergamo area.

These networks of networks coalesce around practical agendas and attempt to slowly disenfranchise themselves from consumerism as a taken-for-granted but politically loaded lifestyle (Cohen 2003). This realization will inform most of my ethnography in this book, as my own experience as a gasista revealed much more than individual attempts to buy alternative foods, and in fact moved beyond food. I propose the notion of alternative provisioning networks because it renders the idea that these networks can and wish to impact society through new practices of provisioning and are not just interested in securing quality or niche foodstuffs. Also, provisioning networks cast the provisioners neither as consumers nor as eaters but as people who are collectively engaged in the work, art and business of providing for themselves and their families. In other words, alternative provisioners take good care not only of their food but also of the relational channels that provide it.

LOCATING GAS IN THE LITERATURE AND ON THE GROUND

The relevance of provisioning systems for global sustainability has become more and more apparent in the last couple of decades.[5] Current global food styles pose a challenge to sustainability and thus set a scene in which various practices of alternative provisioning become globally significant.[6] Alternative provisioning thus offers examples of social innovation in a context marked by negative financial conjuncture, worldwide ecologic crisis, decreasing soil production, and climate change. From community supported agriculture (CSA) to farmers' markets or direct-to-customer organic farming formulas, from locally rooted associations such as the French AMAP (*associations pour le maintien d'une agriculture paysanne*) to globally successful movements such as Slow Food, many alternative foodscapes co-exist (Kneafsey et al. 2008). Sometimes they radically rethink the role of localities in energy provision, such as the Transition Towns of Ireland, United Kingdom, and beyond, while in some cases they impact local economies in important ways, as in the case of some Slow Food presidia (Berlendis 2009, Badii 2012).

In Italy, the *Gruppi di Acquisto Solidale* are a popular form of social reorganization around the issue of provisioning. Nevertheless, they are only one of a number of projects and initiatives regarding alternative food systems, nationwide and abroad. Another well-known phenomenon that currently stresses the urgent agenda of reinventing provisioning is the capillary associative and commercial enterprise of Slow Food, which originated in Italy. While GAS count probably around 150,000 people, the latter forms an international network of well-informed consumers and professionals (including producers, chefs, food journalists, and restaurant owners).

In France, since 2003, the AMAP have established a contract subscription between farmers and networks of consumers who pay in advance for organic and seasonal crops. While sharing the financial risks, they also participate in the distribution work (Lamine and Perrot 2008). According to its inventor, Daniel Vuillon, during AMAP's first year of existence in 2003, twenty-five farms provided about four thousand consumers with dairy products, meat, and vegetables in Provence alone. AMAP aim to reeducate local consumers about seasonality and to motivate vocational farming (80% of AMAP producers are allegedly young farmers).[7] Providing advance payment for crops effectively transforms producers and consumers from anonymous agents who only meet at the market into durable partners, the consumer being both stakeholder and shareowner, involved in planning and sometimes field monitoring and harvesting.

A comparable US experience is that of Community Supported Agriculture (CSA), which was established by biodynamic farmers at the end of the 1980s in Western Massachusetts (White 2013). Concerted attempts at scaling up CSA rely mainly on cooperatives and Web retail portals that make organic produce directly available to large urban areas (such as justfood.org and localharvest.com). Food relocalization in local communities, on the contrary, is one of the primary objectives of Transition Towns. The Transition movement is specifically concerned with the challenges of peak oil prices and climate change. "The Great Reskilling" (grow-it-yourself, recycling and reusing) implies achieving food and energy security locally but also lobbying local government.[8]

It is not the ambition of this book to provide a comprehensive or comparative framework regarding the role of the Italian solidarity purchase groups within the vast international scenario of alternative provisioning networks. Nevertheless, a few distinctive traits and specificities can be noted here. Unlike urban community gardeners, for example, direct food production is not one of the most popular practices of GAS. GAS seem to root in congenial social webs, typically at the intersection of urban and rural settings (in other words, in or close to peri-urban peripheries with active farmers, and sufficiently densely populated to facilitate face-to-face networking). Their main activity consists of finding local producers in alternative to large distribution chains, not so much as in substituting themselves for them. The organization of farmers markets, the mapping of sustainable farming in nearby areas, and the deliberation about how to best accompany producers toward more sustainable practices are therefore more popular activities than self-production (*autoproduzione*) through urban farming or community gardening. In other words, co-production does not mean producing food instead of or together with the farmers but rather developing pacts with existing producers, such as smallholders, social cooperatives, or agricultural cooperatives. Such models of territorial development can also involve institutional or community-based partners such as municipalities or conservation and agricultural parks. As a consumer-driven form of self-organization (Arvidsson 2008), solidarity purchase groups tend to be very different from CSA-type commercial agreements between individual farmers and an anonymous cloud of customers, who may contact the farmer and receive their products directly at home in boxes. The whole point about solidarity purchase groups is that they are groups and that transactions are managed and mediated by the group: people get together on a regular basis and hold meetings, whether in private homes or in publically available meeting rooms, to organize their provisions collectively from a range of producers with whom they are in direct contact.

The diversified scenario of alternative provisioning networks that is emerging across the Western world has attracted a growing scholarship across different disciplines. An expanding socio-scientific and economic literature has often identified alternative provisioning as alternative food networks or alternative agri-food networks. In rural sociology, the debate on alternative food networks has hinged on whether they constitute a paradigm change in European rural development. David Goodman (2004) has skeptically called for a more thorough analysis of its consumption side. Van der Ploeg and Renting (2004) on the other hand have insisted on the "creation of wealth," the "new institutional patterns," and the "shift in power relations" between agri-business and rural communities that the networks bring about. In sociology and anthropology, the consumption turn has emphasized the significance of the local scale and of the role of gender, social, and health concerns in shaping local experiences (Marsden 2000, Murdoch and Miele 2004). Placeless foods have been revealed as a political phenomenon and provenance a concept of political significance (Morgan, Marsden and Murdoch 2006).

Alternative provisioning networks have been accused of refueling an unreflexive ideology of localism (DuPuis et al. 2005, Goodman 2003, 2004), making a not-always sound connection between the relocalization of food systems, their environmental and social sustainability, and social justice. Crucially, DuPuis and Goodman point to the uncritical adoption, in the academic literature, of food activist rhetoric. They are particularly critical of European parochialism and of the food system literature that pitches short supply chains as value chains, envisioning the local as a mythical locus of resistance to capitalistic globalization. In lieu of seeking an uncritical embeddedness, they urge the researcher to pay attention to specific local alliances that take inequality and social justice into consideration. This book fully embraces this pledge and is in fact informed by a seasoned skepticism of the ideas of locality and community as symbolic investments.[9] Some of the community activism rhetoric about going back to basics does risk underwriting a localist, nostalgic, sometimes even racist notion of community. In this chapter, I show what local provisioning networks actually look like, focusing on their diversity and fragmentation, as well as on their occasional convergence on the same projects or on similar agendas.

In the sociology of consumption, consumerism is being refocused as a social, economic and political object. Leonini and Sassatelli (2008) have highlighted how many different forms of 'civic consumerism' have developed in Italy. The shift from critical consumerism to civic participation through political consumerism happens when consumers claim a new identity as members of a community or polity, not just as buyers. This book describes ethnographically what is concretely entailed in that transition, in terms of negotiations, self-representation, and effort, so that ethical responsibility may be enacted not only as preference in a market transaction but as a social connection. Michele Micheletti (2003) for instance has argued that solidarity-based purchasing is a way of developing a collective action while assuming individual responsibility. Thus food, and the act of provisioning in general, is turned into an object of political action. Recent sociological literature analyses political consumerism as a social movement and as a rediscovery of embedded economy (Castells et al. 2012). This is an important advancement in the debate on alternative provisioning networks. Consumer agency is usually associated with individual lifestyles: it is understood first and foremost as an expression of one's choice and identity which is made public through social performance. Complex and collective practices of alternative provisioning such as that of the Italian solidarity purchase groups have introduced the possibility of reading critical consumption as a collective, deliberate, and concerted effort that is at once enabled and constrained by its specific political context, existing social rules, and the actual presence of resilient communities, alternatives, and resources (Spaargaren and Van Vliet 2000). This book ethnographically tests the hypothesis that alternative food provisioning may work as a social ground in which, by meeting a basic need in new and collective ways, individuals and families move beyond their primary motivation in order to elaborate more complex political needs and agenda.

Anthropological studies of food have focused on domestic intimacy and conviviality, social memory, and the senses, highlighting the link between food and identity through ties to local communities (Counihan 2004, Sutton 2001). Recent ethnographies and theoretical reflections focus on ethical consumption and its ambivalences (Carrier 2008) and on the diversity and creativity of alternative provisioning networks in the contexts of migration and urbanization (Corrado 2006). In particular, recent ethnography in urban Tanzania has shown how "social alliances are vital to food entitlement" (Flynn 2005: 204) and how this fundamental social factor cuts across the rural/urban and rich/poor divides. For instance, in the city of Mwanda on Lake Victoria, urban agriculture is lived by the urban elite "as a new source of confidence" (Flynn 2005: 205).

Anthropologists also show how local food can be preferred and even institutionally supported because it is viewed as a way of marketing cultural heritage. Following UNESCO's drive for a global inventory and conservation of intangible cultural heritage, local foodstuffs and recipes are increasingly rediscovered and patrimonialized through quasi-ethnic forms of food revivals. The patrimonialization of traditions and localities (Vaccaro and Beltran 2009) is, in fact, part of a larger process concerning the standardization and heritagization of both foodstuffs and lifestyles. For instance, the transformation of mountain cheese from simply local to typical can be described in terms of what economic anthropologist Richard Wilk has called "structures of common difference" (Wilk 1995, Grasseni 2011a). The ethnic association of certain cuisines, foodstuffs, preparatory techniques, or modes and rituals of consumption is instrumental to what Jean and John Comaroff have identified in the case of bio-geographical knowledge as a double and joint phenomenon: the commodification of culture and the "incorporation of ethnicity" (Comaroff and Comaroff, 2009). Once food is valued as heritage, the notion of patrimony and no longer of commons is used. Heritagization has an immediate economic counterpart in patrimonialization—that is, the cultural construction of exchange value through new circuits of commodity resignification (Wilk 1995). It would be an entirely different matter if, instead of underlining ownership, property, and copyright, the language of food heritage highlighted collective access, solidarity, and reciprocity.[10] With a recent ethnography of food patrimonialization in Tuscany, Michela Badii has proposed an analysis of the positioning of Slow Food in the current food system as that of an "ethical food management agency" (2012). Badii makes reference to the heritage processes entailed in setting up the Zolfino bean Slow Food presidium. It is not banal to consider the establishment of Slow Food presidia, which are usually defended under the rubric of biodiversity conservation, as a process of heritagization. According to Badii, "Producers have supported this revival despite the difficulties of reintroducing practices and *habitus*" (2012b). This gives us a symptom of how producers manage to reposition themselves in times of recession and austerity, selling traditional foods as value-added commodities. Subsequent internal divisions between modernizers and traditionalists often ensue.[11] As Badii does not fail to observe, patrimonialization is an institutional discourse, "a political category of governmentality"—as Palumbo (2003) earlier established with his ethnography of UNESCO heritage claims in western Sicily.

The conventionalization of alternative foods is thus another relevant counter-scenario to the proliferation of alternative provisioning networks. In other words, the corporate organic market differs dramatically from small-scale organic farming, as it is conducted as a monoculture for supermarket distribution, thus losing all the difference that is assumed between organic and conventional farming: the care for context, size, and relationship (Guthman 2004, Johnston et al. 2009). The repositioning of different types of ethical actors in the food systems of advanced or postindustrial capitalist society appears just as notable as the transformation of the affect. In a context of global recession, it may be paradoxically easier for food activists to navigate the political, social, and economic constraints and possibilities that a shrinking market with increasing retail food prices but diminishing rewards for producers may grant. At the institutional level, a striking example comes from the recent invitation of Slow Food's leader, Carlo Petrini, to participate in the rediscussion of the Common Agricultural Policy (CAP) alongside more institutional stakeholders, such as the Farmer's trade unions, in Brussels.[12] The EU is displaying renewed interest in the economic potential of local agriculture and the inclusion of measures in favor of short supply chains in the CAP reform proposals for after 2013—notable is the acknowledgement of a need for cooperation between hygiene authorities and small farmers in redetermining acceptable standards for production.

Italy's solidarity purchase groups were explicitly taken as a model by Slow Food, when it embraced a more engaged and political stance toward a clean, just, and fair food (Petrini 2005). I was present at the Slow Food general assembly of May 2010 at Abano Terme, when Carlo Petrini repeatedly praised gasistas for their pioneering efforts to establish new relationships with the peasantry in the name of co-production (Slow Food Italia 2010). Nevertheless, this does not obscure Slow Food's ambition to position itself against an institutional backdrop—that is, as interlocutor of national governments as much as of local municipalities, as well as of the European Union. The most common criticisms raised against Slow Food among the ranks of GAS activism, apart from its pricy elitism, is that because of its selective practice of niche, artisanal, and authentic productions, it represents yet another form of urban domination over rural food systems, social organization and symbolic capacities. In other words, the managers, town councilors, gastronomic experts and sommeliers that Badii observes in the Slow Food movement would not aptly represent the symbolic workforce—the peasantry—that Slow Food wishes to speak for.

This disenchanted view of the reciprocal positioning of social and economic actors within alternative food networks allows us to rethink and better articulate what critical consumption actually entails. If it entails enhanced purchasing power (paying higher prices in exchange for added value, whether this is quality, heritage, or "doing the right thing"), then the solidarity economy evoked by solidarity purchase groups is something different than mere critical consumption. First, within solidarity economy networks there are many different types of motivation and means of paying for added value. GAS run on volunteer work, and the scarcest resource among its activists is time. Being a gasista is not about paying a higher price for organic food. It is about putting in the time to sit with peers at endless meetings, to deliberate whether to purchase organic, from whom, and how to go and pick it up and redistribute it. Second, in a time of recession, austerity policies, and the consequent loss of jobs, people can think creatively about how to produce and exchange value. For instance, by devoting more time in collective provisioning and securing fresh produce at lower prices directly from farmers (who get paid more for their produce in return). If alternative provisioning networks succeed—as they do—during crisis and recession, then they obviously respond to economic needs as well as those of social distinction. In my own experience, the opportunities for bartering, gifting, or procuring free and excess food within a network of peers, once access is granted, greatly exceed the higher expenditures that one undergoes, strictly speaking, in order to buy through a GAS. For instance, I was given free meat, I was offered secondhand bikes for my children, and I met people who kept garden patches and orchards, who were liberally sharing their crops. Third, if affect plays a role in determining value, it may well play a role in motivating collective buying, as this is not only a matter of logistics and accounting but of relationality.

Solidarity might not mean the same for everyone and unsurprisingly, these differences have important class connotations, drawing our ethnographic attention on how added value is or can be construed and on how and if post-recession food activists are in fact different from the ethical concerns of the commonly construed middle-class critical consumer. My own ethnography leads me to believe that academic scholarship on alternative food networks might cast stereotypical views on what "alternative" means and on what kind of social actors we find engaged in such networks. In other words, ethnographic observation with alternative provisioning networks records not only the foodie or the farmers' market goer, but also the precariously balancing head of household of the lower middle classes.

In the light of this, we should locate solidarity purchase groups vis-à-vis ethical consumption, alternative food networks, and solidarity economy. I do so ethnographically by asking who is involved, through which economic circuits, and via which social networks? James Carrier maintains that ethical consumption is an ongoing collective commentary on economy and society, on their distinction from one another, and on their relationship. As such, he concludes, it "is inherently, if not always overtly, political" (Carrier and Luetchford 2012: 3). A number of possible connotations are entailed in solidarity purchase groups, and I would suggest that a paramount one is that of responsibility: from responsibility to agricultural workers (paying a fair price) to concerns about the unsustainable practices of intensive agri-business (negotiating clean products with low ecological footprints, short chain, etc.), to responsibility to one's own peers and family (buying locally, supporting local producers, or self-produce, or buying cheaply though seeking the best available price/quality ratio). There is also responsibility to one's own and one's neighbors' health. In general, what ethical consumption reminds us of is that food, and provisioning in general, is not a private phenomenon, that it has only partially to do with taste, distinction, and self-crafting. It is political and economic.

The advancement that GAS propose vis-à-vis other examples of alternative provisioning networks is their self-understanding as a form of political activism and not just as an ethical choice of the individual consumer. In the rest of this book, I will argue that Italy's solidarity purchase groups produce novel social networks. As such, they cannot be analyzed as a sum of individual consumers' preference, which could be equally exercised in a supermarket as in a local shop or in a farmers' market. GAS display the complexity of relational and associative life. They have a proactive agenda in that they attempt to reconfigure the ways in which food and services are planned and distributed in supply chains, empowering themselves in the process. Thus GAS activity should not be interpreted as the sum of individual actions motivated by responsibility, liberal guilt, or environmental awareness but as an associative lifestyle wishing to trigger important economic, institutional, and environmental effects.[13]

Human geographers focusing on community economies read alternative provisioning networks as postcapitalist relations (Gibson-Graham 2006). According to this approach, academic analysis should not simply unveil the workings of biopower[14] but also be proactive in voicing and constructing viable alternatives. Transforming economic subjectivities would be a precondition to challenging orthodox forms of economic practice, ethics, and politics, as the work of resubjectification is an important prelude to new forms of governance (Gibson-Graham et al. 2013). As we shall see in Chapter 3, the idea of learning to be affected through a collective (Roelvink 2010) is relevant to this ethnography: in GAS activity, voluntary activity and the gift of one's time to organizational tasks affects relationships among gasistas by imbuing them with the moral obligation of reciprocity. In addition to the positive but superficial emotions of doing the right thing, of securing quality food, or of enjoying festive conviviality,[15] my ethnographic experience suggests that GAS affect is about reciprocal responsibility, conscientious participation, and collective learning. In this sense, affect becomes a practice of active citizenship and to this extent GAS activism can be read as a form of bio-political militancy.

In sum, a number of disciplines have taken alternative provisioning networks as their intense object of scrutiny, interpreted as a new political arena by some and as a new space of relational reinvention by others. It is open to debate whether market-based political action is an actual alternative to capitalism: does alternative provisioning effectively transfigure market relations? In order to answer that, the present study distinguishes between networks of individuals and networks of networks. These are two levels at which GAS reorganize the market economy and reweave it in the relational fabric of society. We shall see how GAS and their networks create districts and networks of solidarity economy (*Distretti e Reti Economia Solidale;* DES and RES). Some examples of DES and RES are mentioned in the following chapters as innovative forms of economies of trust (Sage 2007) and of regard (Offer 1997). By establishing a direct relationship of cooperation, trust, and sometimes shared risk between producer and consumer, they transcend the anonymous transactions of formalist economy. Nevertheless, they do live in the capitalist market and share its rules, for instance, of price formation and competitiveness (trusted producers should be transparent about price but cannot afford to go bankrupt, for instance). The thesis of this book is that what we observe in GAS is not an exit from capitalism altogether but rather a painstaking, reflexive, and collective endeavor to transform sectors of it into economies of trust, in which reciprocal respect, solidarity, and co-production shift economic practice away from the sole consideration of profit maximization.

BEYOND ALTERNATIVE FOOD NETWORKS

At first sight, GAS might appear as just another form of ethical consumerism, characterized by secondary and radical chic concerns with consumer issues such as the social, environmental, and economic sustainability of production and distribution (Meyer 1989). In fact, the thesis of this book is that they are more than that: they represent a dynamic laboratory that approaches social, economic, and political issues in a holistic way. Consumer movement activism is usually limited to purely economic action such as boycott and "buycott" initiatives or the organization of consumer cooperatives. Contemporary social research has nevertheless argued that active citizenship and political engagement may well be expressed through collective consumer behavior (Scammell 2000, Forno and Gunnarson 2010). Especially in contexts—such as Italy—in which the state is perceived as an absentee regulator that abdicates its normative role vis-à-vis the market, provisioning may thus become a politically significant practice with a transformative impact on lifestyles and policies. This, not just strictly regarding consumer issues such as price and quality but also the wider ecological and civil rights issues that capitalist globalization has rendered more pressing and evident (Barnett et al. 2005). In other words, considering ethical consumerism as a phenomenon that regards individual choice and motivation alone would underestimate the growth of organized forms of collective action that involve citizen-consumers in associations and social networks. Which role do these social actors play in creating new economic circuits? How do they act in order to privilege sustainable agriculture—in terms of economic durability, respect for the environment, and respect of the workers?

My thesis is that in contemporary Italy, GAS display dynamics of self-organization not only in economic terms but in relational and political terms. GAS groups have not only flourished in the rich northern Italian regions, endowed with a lively and capillary associative fabric, but also in some southern regions challenged by the mafia. According to Mauro Serventi, about 200 solidarity purchase groups were founded in the wake of the 2008 GAS assembly which took place, significantly, in Sicily. There, GAS meet specific local needs: not only provisioning quality food at affordable prices but also supporting a clean, mafia-free local economy in a context of tragically high unemployment.[16] Furthermore, recent research (Forno 2011a, Forno and Ceccarini 2006) has shown how the expansion of solidarity economy networks in the north and center of Italy has favored new nationwide economic circuits, involving tight collaboration between northern Italian consumers and southern Italian farmers (especially organic farmers from Sicily seeking to break loose from mafia-ridden distribution circuits).

As we shall see in detail in Chapter 2, solidarity purchase groups describe themselves as networks that wish to involve both producers and consumers in practices of co-production. Responsible consumers, who are prepared to pay "the right price" in solidarity with producers, organize themselves into a collective and collaborate with farmers, associations, and public institutions to plan, buy, and distribute provisions. In some cases, co-production entails the negotiation in advance of part or the whole of a farm's crops including types, quantities, and cultivation methods (from certified organic farming to ad hoc compromises about using specific weed killers or animal diet integrators).

Co-production is thus an important concept in Italian solidarity economy activism (and also used by Slow Food). It conveys an explicit step beyond mere purchasing and ethical consumerism to define the collaborative effort of consumers and providers, the former actively enabling production rather than simply indicating preferences on the market. The term is both evocative and ambivalent, as it has many interpretations in different scholarly and activist contexts. In rural sociology, co-production denotes that both natural and social resources are co-constituted in the farming practice (Van der Ploeg and Renting 2004): thus, for instance, local agronomic knowledge and composted soil are co-produced in a process of mutual refoundation (Van der Ploeg 2007: 200). In Science and Technology Studies, co-production indicates the simultaneous and reciprocal definition of nature and culture as terms of normative discourse and epistemic practice (Jasanoff 2006). Finally, in feminist geography co-production expresses the active collaboration of scholars with postcapitalist activists to map, voice, and empower a variety of community economies that would remain otherwise uncharted as a globally emerging pattern (Gibson-Graham 2006). The activist literature that makes use of this term encompasses the issue of achieving sustainability in food production, a new

logistics and politics of supply, and nonviolent group dynamics within the activists' networks (Biolghini 2007; Biolghini et al. 2008; Servettini 2008).[17]

In this regard, an ethnographic description of GAS activity shows its differences and distinctions from the Global Justice Movement—the latter having
developed a more oppositional stance through repertoires of public protest
(see Juris 2008) and the former investing more on community building to
realize sustainable provisioning styles on a local, sometimes ad hoc basis.
Nevertheless, as I wish to show in Chapter 2, the underlying common themes
and concerns with capitalist globalization, and sometimes the life histories
of activists and leaders themselves, suggest that the Global Justice Movement and especially Italian pacifist and missionary activism has acted as a
political think tank for solidarity economy in Italy. It is nevertheless important to avoid a naive contrast between GAS, seen as nonoppositional mi-
croactivism that eschews confrontation with corporate capital, and the more
oppositional public stance of social movements rallying against unsustainable global policies (but often incapable of performing revolutionary change
in the commodity-dominated fabric of society). Recent scholarship on social
movements has highlighted the processes of contamination—that is, cross-
fertilization—in the making of the Global Justice Movement in 1990s Italy.
Della Porta and Mosca stress how different types of organizations, such as
trade unions and solidarity associations in particular, found themselves coop-
erating and trusting each other through "the combination of structural, cognitive and affective mechanisms" (2007: 1). In other words, it is the act itself
of networking that performs "multiple belongings, flexible identities and the
construction of another politics" (Della Porta 2004).

Issues of power and powerlessness are far from remote in GAS discussions
of co-production. Peter Luetchford (2008) and Sarah Lyons (2011) have independently shown how the Fair Trade model of the smallholder as ideal counterpart for an ethically driven transaction is in fact beset by a number of power
imbalances on the ground, such as the pervasive use of underpaid immigrant
workers (in Luetchford's case, Nicaraguans in Costa Rica) or gender inequalities
within landowning farming families (Lyons and Moberg 2010), or again the ambivalences and discordances within rural cooperatives on whether to trade their
ethnic identity as part of the transaction (Lyons 2011). In other words, the
hands that pick Fair Trade coffee may well be different from the hands that
benefit from a Fair Trade cooperative relationship. Most of the activities
I became involved with as a GAS member were oriented to restoring the reciprocal dignity of buyer and seller, farmer and consumer, northerner and south-
erner. Nevertheless, as I shall show in Chapter 3, the reciprocal dynamics of
producers and consumers involved in solidarity purchase and co-production
were not definable as one of paternalistic charity. As Amanda Berlan has
revealed in the case of cocoa growers for Fair Trade circuits in Ghana, the

assumption that farmers are inevitably powerless victims of global supply chains and distribution networks is simplistic (2008). GAS provisioning practices introduce a political element of innovation and creativity in urban neighborhoods, whether food deserts or gentrified. They also take into account the ingenuity and innovation-driven strategies of local farmers to disenfranchise themselves from unequal partnerships, often adopting the very discourse of food heritage and reevaluation of locality that drives critical consumers.

The convergence of local strategies of food reinvention (Grasseni 2011a, 2012b) with sustainable and participative practices of provisioning is in itself a novel social phenomenon. Nevertheless, an apt theoretical framework is needed to account for the complex practice and multifaceted agenda of solidarity purchase groups. GAS networks sometimes involve local Fair Trade shops or corner shops in their deliveries of groceries, for instance, to facilitate contact and reciprocal recognition of the local shopkeepers and Fair Trade circuits. In other cases, the GAS collectively mobilize to rescue their trusted providers from bankruptcy—as in the case of the Tomasoni organic dairy (see Chapter 2) but also Abruzzese farmers struck by earthquake in 2009 and Parmesan producers struck by another earthquake in 2012. Locally, alternative provisioning networks display distinctive associative routines. They encounter differing reactions in local institutions and administrators. Nevertheless, much of their capacity to impact local communities and economies is due to the structure and modality of their internal and external relationships. The next chapters offer an empirically grounded analysis of GAS workings, management, relational qualities, and ambitions within a seminal but growing phenomenon that is attracting much media attention. The observational material that I have gathered has underlined the level of interconnection between producers and consumers, the ways in which their members cooperate within the network, and the practices and discourses of mutual trust enacted within and across networks. My aim is to highlight both the optimistic attitude of a diverse range of voluntary actors who are engaging in producing new forms of sociability and innovative economic solutions and their orientation to the future: envisioning solidarity purchase groups as seeds of trust which will hopefully yield crops.

The reevaluation of local foods and short supply chains is not at all an exclusive trait of GAS, and in fact it converges at least partially with other strategies of promotion of short food chains as an added value for marketing local products (Grasseni 2014). The next chapter familiarizes the reader with the context of many different types of relocalization strategies in northern Italy. How does solidarity economy then interact with the patrimonialization of local foodstuffs as a form of heritage? Do the relevant social networks overlap, at least partially? Do they contribute together to a logic and a rhetoric of local identity? Does this create contradictions or tensions? Can the two trends converge on implementable models of socially and environmentally sustainable development? To answer these questions, the recommendation of rural sociologists such as Jan Douwe van der Ploeg, Gianluca Brunori, and Roberta Sonnino is that one should make explicit which sustainable rural development paradigm is adopted and if it includes provisions to reconstitute multifunctional agriculture. They propose an analysis of the webs of rural regions in terms of "the pattern of interrelations, interactions, exchanges and mutual externalities within rural societies" as a new driving force for rural development (van der Ploeg et al. 2008: 2). In my own description of solidarity purchase groups, on the other hand, I focus on interrelated and mutually reinforcing processes of cross-fertilization within networks of consumers whose ambition is to co-produce with farmers and providers.

–2–

The Reinvention of Food

On a Friday night, April 9, 2010, I took part in the first public meeting of the district of solidarity economy (DES) of Val Brembana. The open invitation had come through the mailing list of Sustainable Citizenship, a network for the promotion of solidarity economy in the Bergamo area. The nascent DES of Val Brembana was offering a series of public seminars and discussions on solidarity economy networks, alternative agriculture, and alternative economy. Municipal representatives, farmers' unions, local entrepreneurs, school principals, and administrators in charge of local governance were invited. Val Brembana being a mountainous area, it is served by a Mountain Community Council (Comunità Montana Valle Brembana) and by the steering committees of influential EU-funded development projects such as the Local Action Group managing Leader II and Leader Plus projects for mountain agriculture and ecotourism. Val Brembana covers about one-fifth of the province of Bergamo but is inhabited by only about 43,000 people (in a province of about 1 million) scattered over thirty-eight municipalities, the most populous of which, Zogno, S.Giovanni Bianco, and S.Pellegrino Terme, respectively have about 9,000; 5,100; and 5,000 residents. Due to acute outmigration from the higher reaches of the valley, the smallest municipalities have fewer than 100 inhabitants.[1]

The first meeting was led by Davide Biolghini, author of *Il Popolo dell'Economia Solidale* (*The People of Solidarity Economy*), followed by an open discussion on how to organize and run a DES in Val Brembana. The DES main promoter and coordinator, Ovidio (a pseudonym), introduced himself as a representative of a minority farmers' union (Union of Smallholders) and explained that the district was a project for local development in a marginalized rural territory. The goal was to set up a zero-mile market and, gradually, to develop food and energy sovereignty. This call was immediately appropriated in the discussion as a potential alternative to wage labor in declining local manufactures (a subsidiary of Freni Brembo, the maker of Formula 1 brakes, had just closed down, and the historical Pigna paper mill had previously closed). The San Pellegrino water-bottling factory seemed to be the only thriving local firm. A national leader in bottled water and soda drinks until it was bought out by Nestlè at the end of the 1990s, San Pellegrino is now a world-renowned brand. Few know that it owes its name to the homonymous and now declining spa resort in the Bergamasque mountains, once an art nouveau gem. Hundreds of trucks drive daily by the nineteenth-century Grand Hotel, now lying in ruins, exporting tens of thousands of bottles of mineral water. As advertised on the Nestlé site, "With a tradition of excellence and fine taste since 1889, S. Pellegrino sparkling mineral water is an extraordinary combination of exceptionally pure water and minerals. It has a distinct sophisticated taste which has helped make it the sparkling mineral water preferred by top restaurants worldwide."[2] However, neither the sales revenue nor the symbolic wealth of this brand has to be redistributed locally.

The seminar, attended by about eighty people, had a distinctly alternative style, flaunting the peace flag and hosting a Fair Trade sales desk, as well as books on nonviolent activism. The Fair Trade cooperative manager sitting next to me told me that he recognized about half of the attendees. Sociologist Francesca Forno introduced the seminar, explaining the idea of political consumption, giving the example of Nestlè boycotts. The idea of "buycott," the active support of local products and entrepreneurs through dedicated provisioning, was introduced as a form of environmental and social responsibility. The example of the Sicilian network of Addio Pizzo was mentioned: a network of consumers buying "pizzo-free" products in Palermo was reaping more sustainable effects than street demonstrations or antimafia manifestos.[3] Davide Biolghini illustrated the example of Milan's district of rural solidarity economy (*Distretto di Economia Solidale Rurale;* DESR), a network of GAS that purchase their food preferentially from farmers of South Milan's agricultural park, thus supporting a new local economic circuit that privileges seasonal and organic farming.

Of the people attending the meeting, about 80 percent disclosed that they were already members of solidarity purchase groups. The rest of the evening was devoted to an open discussion to gather information about the situation in Val Brembana, to debate its potential to become a DES, with a view to drawing a roadmap for Val Brembana. Despite the fact that local cheeses had gained several denominations of protected origin, and that about 3,500 individuals were registered farmers, it turned out that only about 200 had commercial milk quotas, which meant that all the others were not authorized to sell milk. Few orchards and fields were cultivated, as most of the flatlands had been occupied by factories, stores, or parking lots. Networking appeared fraught by political and personal competition. Training and cooperative leadership had to be provided and built. Local entrepreneurs and stakeholders had to be mapped. However, a number of projects had already focused on sustainable agriculture for cultural tourism or food heritage projects. Solidarity purchase groups were nascent and few. DES activists counted on local smallholders, breeding farm animals on free-range pastures or cultivating organic vegetables, to initiate short supply chains. But smallholders, in turn, needed a trusted pool of dedicated gasista customers to move beyond self-sufficiency and place their surplus products on local markets. There was a long path lying ahead.

Over the following meetings, it was decided that we'd begin with small and recognizable actions, supporting the existing projects of Bergamo's network for solidarity economy, Sustainable Citizenship, and the farmers' markets of the association Market & Citizenship (of which I talk at length in Chapter 5). In the following two years, under Ovidio's coordination, DES Val Brembana drew up a Charter of Principles, supported the choice of the local youth hostel to shelter twenty asylum seekers from eight African nations at war, drafted a management plan for the citizenship markets in the valley, and promoted a training course for the cultivation of chestnut trees—traditionally one of the local staple foods—increasing the visibility and economic value of local orchards and woods through the organization of fairs, collective purchase groups, and public meetings with local and regional administrators. DES Val Brembana is growing slowly but stubbornly and has placed itself on the map of Lombardy's solidarity economy. DES Val Brembana will not be the focus of my ethnography, which closely follows the workings of solidarity purchase groups and their network in the Bergamo area. Nevertheless, it played a part in many of the concurrent strategies of food relocalization and reterritorialization that I witnessed in my fieldwork. Their common agenda was a renewed interest in local food as a resource for development and sometimes for territorial marketing. While foodstuffs and geographical provenance were central to these projects, the cultural dimension of this refocalization on food provenance spanned both material and symbolic issues such as sustainability, quality of life, and identity.

FOOD RELOCALIZATION AND SOLIDARITY ECONOMY: TWO AGENDAS FOR THE SAME OBJECT

Food consumption is clearly used by many social actors a form of place-making, as suggested among others by Michael Goodman, David Goodman, and Michael Redclift (2012). Such actors may be local administrators or grassroots activists, sometimes—but not always—working in synergy with each other. In several areas at the foot of the Alps, the last ten years have seen very active campaigns in favor of local foods and short supply chains, both at the grassroots and at the institutional level. Local administrations and the farmer's main local trade union, Coldiretti, are supportive of farmers' markets and sometimes instrumental in setting them up. In Bergamo, but also the neighboring provinces of Como, Lecco, and Sondrio (all of which span mostly mountainous areas), farmers' markets are an established practice, although significant retail-oriented agricultural production is virtually absent and the agricultural labor force counts for less than 2 percent of the population. Nevertheless, these initiatives foster new and direct-marketing opportunities for marginalized smallholders. Demand for organic and traditional products, such as homemade cheese and the on-farm sale of raw milk, usually comes from relatively high-income urban residents. In this area, cheese production is also very diversified and sought after, especially high-pasture summer production (including Bitto and several goat cheeses: Corti e Mastalli 2010, Grasseni 2012c). However, local ethnographic museums and eco-museums document survival practices such as manual manure-spreading on donkey-back, chestnut- smoking, or the use of horse-drawn sledges and wooden back packs (*gerli*) for hay-making.[4] Michele Corti, on the basis of 300 self-administered questionnaires and informal interviews with the producers participating in Lecco's and Como's farmers' markets, claims that sustainable economies are being established through food reterritorialization (Corti 2009b). Moreover, Slow Food has fostered direct intervention to shorten the food supply chain to Lombard restaurants (Berlendis 2009), designing zero-mile menus that include information about locally supplied ingredients. Food heritage discourse and short supply chains hence share overlapping discourse and agendas.

According to a Milan University survey (Corti 2009b), in Lombardy raw milk automated dispensers, farmers' markets, and short chains rely heavily on neorural entrepreneurs and settlers. The latter are often retired professionals or urban youth with higher education, whose farms breed goats, make cheese, or cultivate organic vegetables and fruit, sometimes vineyards. At the foot of the Alps, declining industrial factories and winter tourism are giving way to the rediscovery of traditionally marginalized hillside agriculture, favoring multifunctional rural entrepreneurship. Long seen as uncompetitive because it was unfit for intensive maize, rice, or dairy farming, smallholder agriculture maintains the appeal of locality, vicinity, and artisanship. Thus, local food chains are viewed as a potential resource by many different actors: from farmers' trade unions and local administrations to food activists of various types. In the province of Lecco, the first farmers' market was established in 2004 in Osnago,[5] a village of scarcely 5,000 inhabitants, which five years later was also the venue for the GAS national assembly.

Several agencies thus foster short supply chains, which are sometimes celebrated as zero-mile, relocalized, or reterritorialized foods. What happens to local food in the process? My thesis elsewhere has been that it is either reinvented as an icon of typicity or that it becomes the pivot of a direct relationship between responsible consumers and food producers (Grasseni 2012b, 2014).[6] I argued that both connoisseurs and food activists cultivate a high degree of discernment and self-consciousness about food provisioning and consumption, and, to this extent, both agendas can be read under the rubric of distinction, in very broad terms. Nevertheless, this is where the parallel stops. While solidarity purchasers exercise alternative provisioning practices for ethical or political reasons, tasteful consumers practice elitism vis-à-vis the low-price, mass-available food stocks. The scenario of marginalized agriculture de facto sustains both elitist food practices and grassroots food activism, with significant overlaps and sometimes collaboration. Nevertheless, despite the fact that the same smallholders or local farmers may be sought out, rewarded, and to an extent courted by distinction purchasers as well as gasistas, the nature of the two agendas remain distinct.

Short food chains are being introduced both by GAS activists and by Slow Food *Convivia.* In the north Milanese region around Monza (Brianza) in 2009, a short chain bread project was organized by the administration of a conservation area that was protected from building interests as an "agricultural park."[7] The project, initiated in 2007 by the park's president, introduced local bread (Pane of Park Mogora or Pane Molgora) in eight bakeries of as many municipalities, using a local mill with a view to restoring the park's disbanded watermills on the river Molgora. The immediate difficulties concerned the amount of grain and flour available—enough only for baking once a week. Local farmers were involved (for a total of forty hectares of land) and flour availability raised to fifty tons (Corti 2009a). First, the relocalization of grain production made evident the impact of climate change: in 2009, sowing was late due to exceptional rains, and crops were lost due to a heat wave in May. Second, logistics was critical: once production was up at capacity, local farmers did not have storage space to take the grains to the mill in weekly installments and had to sell the stock on the market, thus losing the extra profit they could have made if they had been able to sell locally (Corti 2009a).

Between 2006 and 2007, on practically the same territory, another project for a bread short chain in Brianza was initiated by a district of solidarity economy (*Distretto di Economia Solidale;* DES). DES Brianza reintroduced wheat farming and involved an organic mill and artisan bakers to provide about 500 GAS families with fresh bread made with locally grown grain. The project, named Spiga & Madia (Spike & Cupboard), led to the distribution of 300 loaves of bread per week for a total production (and consumption) of about twenty tons of flour per year (both white and whole wheat). It involved a farmer, a landowner, a miller, and a bread baker located at a maximum distance of thirty kilometers between each other. Funding partners came directly from ethical funding cooperatives[8] and the association Nuovi Stili di Vita (New Life Styles, which developed out of the previously EU-funded project EQUAL, Nuovi Sitli di Vita, 2004–2007). By 2011, Spiga & Madia reintroduced an autochthonous variety of wheat, which displays a higher genetic diversity but requires manual harvesting. After sowing four kilogram of seeds in 1,000 square meters, about forty kilograms of new seeds were produced and reaped. Crucially, the DES Brianza project, unlike the Pane Molgora initiative, had the ambition to rethink the economics of price definition as part of the process. In fact, the combination of participatory price definition (*costruzione partecipata del prezzo;* Bocci, De Santis, and Rossi 2009) and participatory short supply chain (*filiera corta partecipata*) was the very reason for which DES Brianza became a model for the solidarity economy scenario in Italy (Tavolo RES 2010: 93–99). Because of its grassroots rather than top-down design, the Spiga & Madia project was conceived, organized, and managed by DES Brianza.

Spiga & Madia was presented in May 2009, in Monza at the conference Apprezziamolo (Let's Appreciate It), together with a number of local solutions to the issue of how to price food in a "right" way within solidarity economies. The conference motto was "towards a new market: a solidarity economy with the right price."[9] This project, called Verso il Prezzo Giusto (Toward a Right Price) was initially managed by a Padua-based agricultural cooperative and a consumers' association (El Tamiso and Associazione Bio Rekk), each supporting the other through collective, coordinated, and online purchasing of organic produce from associated producers (a dairy, a tofu and seitan producer, a winemaker, an environmentally friendly hygiene products provider, etc.; Sandon, 2009). Bio Rekk is an association for social inclusion that developed in 2004 out of a solidarity purchase group (Sandon, 2009). In the viewpoint of Bio Rekk, GAS are "those groups of 10 to 20 people who get together in each other's living room to organize food orders, and use their free time to inaugurate an informal model of consumption" (Sandon 2009: 134). Having made an organizational leap, Bio Rekk now serves 500 families through online ordering thanks to the work of about thirty volunteers. Nevertheless, Bio Rekk does not define itself and does not wish to be understood as an online grocery delivery service. Bio Rekk in fact makes a point of not offering home-deliveries and requires that customers organize themselves in groups of families to collect their online orders from the producers or from city-based collection points. It thus maintains the quality and experience of collective self-organization that distinguishes solidarity purchase groups. Furthermore, the association promotes direct encounters with the producers, through collective sowing and reaping, dinners and lunches with local products, collective production of jams and preserves, as well as bike trips, theater performances, and concerts at the producers' premises. Concerning the nineteen producers associated with the agricultural cooperative El Tamiso, Bio Rekk's role is not only one of promotion but of coordination: collective orders through a consumers' association enable long-term planning, guarantee a market outlet, and provide a stable and concerted remuneration for the crops. Bio Rekk claims that it is only in this condition of serenity that producers can be motivated to recoup traditional or nonconventional crops

(Sandon 2009: 139). The consumers' advantage is that of low retail prices, obtained through a drastic reduction of packaging and of logistics, as well as advantageous prices for collective purchase.

The expression used by Bio Rekk in this case was not co-production nor degrowth but co-growth (Sandon 2009: 143): a perspective of collaboration through innovative production relationships and light provisioning networks. Bio Rekk developed into the DES of Padua, and together with DES Brianza, DES Como, and DES Turin, initiated a collaboration on a co-energy project (Co-Energia) in 2009 to collectively produce energy from renewable sources and to distribute it to its associates. In this capacity of reframing the very premises of how goods and services flow, and how producers and consumers relate to each other, lies the core of alternative provisioning practices. In other words, it is a reinvention not just of specific products and foodstuffs but also of the food system and of the economic circuits that enable provisioning in our society. The preference for local-level projects does not shun networking as a strategy for comparing, learning from each other, and sharing ideas and solutions that aim for further encompassing objects and scale. Here lies the paramount difference between mere "territorial and identity-driven economies" (economie territoriali e identitarie; Corti 2012) and apparently identical experiments by solidarity economy networks.

Identity economy as such would not in fact be devoid of a streak of political conservatism (a return to locality, to authenticity, to territorial identities, and even to ethnic purity). For instance, Clare Hinrichs (2003) critiques the revival of Iowa foods in the Iowa-Grown Banquet Meal project as an instance of a "defensive politics of localization."[10] Lewis Holloway and Moya Kneafsey (2000) have critiqued the nostalgic rhetoric of farmers' markets as spaces that are arranged and aestheticized in such a way as to hark back to an imaginary wholesome rusticity. Similar comments can be made about the self-foklorization of food revivals in the Alps (Grasseni 2012a). Food revivals, such as food heritage short chains, do not call into question the wider food system of which they are a niche but rather position themselves as marketable alternatives. They embed the ideal of a return to the small, bounded community in a rhetoric of local development. Other projects, such as Spiga & Madia, are devoid of these conservative nuances and are conceived of as a form of "food resistance", in defense of fair prices for the farmers and for the consumers. In this case, the reconstruction of short supply chains is a self-conscious exercise of food sovereignty (De Sanctis 2006).

Price determination is a fundamental aspect for contextualizing alternative provisioning networks as solidarity economies in the current economic crisis. According to Antonio Onorati, president of Crocevia, an Italian NGO that promotes the agenda of food sovereignty in international agricultural development,[11] food consumption "eats up" a growing percentage of low and medium wages in Italy. As a result, while food expenditure remains more or less stable at a national level, it tends to decrease for people of low and medium wages. In Italy in 2009, the volume of food consumed increased by 0.6 percent but decreased in value. This means a decreasing value of the food bought by the poorest sections of the population: poorer people tend to buy more food at lower prices and of lesser quality. This, combined with the ways in which large distribution supplies are organized, puts extra pressure on the farmers to sell at even lower prices.[12]

In the case of DES Brianza, on top of the objective of introducing transparent and solidarity-based prices, the Spiga & Madia project has the further political aim of preserving agricultural land from the speculations of building lobbies. According to Edoardo Gnocchi, representative of the DES Brianza, the project included collaborative price-definition year by year, based on the costs that each actor sustained. The estimated costs were anticipated by the GAS families, in the form of committing to buy at the calculated price. DES Brianza uses the expression of *co-producer* to define a nonpassive collective consumer who assesses his or her needs and shares risks with the producer. The accounting project of Spiga & Madia included a "copyleft" trademark to protect "the intangible value of the products and the value of our work" (Gnocchi 2009: 40). To claim intellectual property of Spiga & Madia was an important passage that recognizes the value of conceptual work, organization, and volunteer resources in knowledge-gathering, planning, and the management of the project. At the same time, it encourages its diffusion, appropriation, and amelioration by other practitioners of solidarity economies, similarly to Creative Commons in the dissemination of artworks, or to Copyleft in the distribution of open access software. Co-production here meant defining the quantities to be produced in advance, as well as determining the price based on costs, rather than leaving the adjustment of price to supply and demand on the market. In fact, the distribution channels were defined and protected: the bakers were involved from the start in the project; they knew how many customers they would have and even who they would be.

Solidarity economy districts refer indirectly to the literature on the industrial districts of the "Third Italy." In the early 1990s, the family-sized but intensely connected enterprises of Lombardy and Veneto (known as the Italian Northeast) seemed to withstand the challenge of global competition without consolidating; they instead specialized in a combination of design, high-tech, and soft logistics to create districts of world-renowned manufactures (shoes, sunglasses, industrial textiles, embroidery, silk, etc.; see Becattini, 2000). Italy's industrial districts have been mapped, and forms of institutional support have been studied to sustain this kind of self-organizing (though capitalist) economy, with mixed results. DES consciously take the industrial districts model in the direction of liberating economic relations from the crunching price-making and land-eating mechanisms of the agribusiness market. In the public presentation of the DES Brianza project, three systems of relationships were mentioned: the landscape and territorial system, the relational system, and the value system. Consequently, the project results included 18 hectares of land converted to organic farming and crop rotation and 400 meters of hedge plants reintroduced, with the involvement of 2 farmers, 3 bakers, and a seitan workshop, 2,800 consumers reached, as well as 400 co-producers (namely the gasistas who invested their capital in terms of cost anticipation), and the 26 municipalities involved.[13]

SOLIDARITY IN CO-PRODUCTION

In the light of these examples, the concept of co-production becomes crucial for rethinking food justice and food heritage jointly as a political and economic problem of food sovereignty. Co-production is a notion introduced to rural sociology by Jan Douwe van der Ploeg to signal how material and natural resources are simultaneously and reciprocally co-constituted. In Italy, this literature is associated with the territorialist school in geography or with Serge Latouche's antidevelopment stance (2005). Van der Ploeg proposes valuing the diversity of rural entrepreneurship, featuring not only multiple strategies of production but multifunctional networks: "An agricultural entrepreneurial style should involve both aspects of production: the social and the material. Agriculture is a clear expression of what we call a theory of coproduction and coevolution of the social and the material" (Van der Ploeg 2007: 186). Biodiversity and product typicity (see note 6 in this chapter) are two potentially conflicting agendas (Brunori 2007), and co-production should not be understood as enhancement of local agriculture but rather as an enabling relationship. "This mutual refoundation implies the reconversion of most of the resources through a specific process of coproduction: pasture, variety, breeds, technical artifacts, knowledge, and manure—just to mention a few of the resources involved—which will result in new combinations and balances, different from locality to locality" (Van der Ploeg 2007: 200). By noting how rural development in Europe must move beyond modernization, Van der Ploeg articulates a sensibility that he has in common with degrowth activists and with alternative provisioning co-producers: agricultural modernization and its evident nonsustainability, in fact, amounts to the opposite of rural development. He interprets new multifunctional forms of labor organization as a reconstruction of rurality that guarantees not only quality food but also the social reproduction of the farm itself—including a decreasing dependence on the market and on technology and the farmers' capacity to voice defensive strategies from crushing institutional regulation (Van der Ploeg 2006).

In other disciplinary areas, co-production is mostly interpreted as a merely perfunctory collaboration between two complementary agents—typically a public and a private partner in a common enterprise or as a form of involvement of the end user in designing or enhancing a product or service. We can measure all the distance between this interpretation, which frames co-producers as subservient to a production process largely defined elsewhere, and the GAS meaning of co-production as enabling the production process itself.[14] The role of the co-producer is here equated to that of the "prosumer," whereby the consumer is enrolled in testing or customizing a product. Such a role is also taken into consideration as community involvement in areas of public interest such as health services, community safety, and crime prevention.[15]

As opposed to the corporate co-production philosophy, which casts the co-producer as a prosumer who adds value to a product that is designed elsewhere, in alternative provisioning networks co-producers redefine the entire production process, whether it's growing one's own food or enabling the farmer next door to grow and sell his or her own. In general, this move away from corporate production also includes the capacity to provide an intellectual production on one's own techniques, strategies, and networks—hence the proliferation of activist literature, websites, fairs, and seminars on alternative networks, degrowth, and voluntary simplicity. Thus, for the co-producers of DES Brianza, agreeing on a (higher) bread price beforehand meant actively enabling the farmers involved to produce almost twenty tons of high-quality wheat (at double the conventional costs) and to remunerate the 80 percent extra labor that went into their conversion to organic farming, while reducing *twenty times over* the associated supply costs. This means that the total retail price of this organic, high-quality, zero-mile bread was about 30 percent less than its market price, according to DES calculations.[16] This leaves little ground for critiquing this as an elitist practice—in the sense that this is obviously not a form of gourmet shopping. It is a self-selective practice that diverts time, effort, and money into a motivated and collectively organized effort—and is in this sense clearly political—but it is certainly not a one-off radical chic stand.

The parallel initiative Pane Molgora was supported by other social actors: the Molgora Agricultural Park, the farmers' trade union, Coldiretti, and its farmers' market project, Agrimercato, as well as the association Cooks of Lombardy (Cuochi di Lombardia). The latter, sponsored by the élite winemaker Il Calepino (of Valcalepio, in the Bergamo province), counts on a network of gourmet restaurants such as the Osteria della Buona Condotta, in the north Milanese area. These restaurants feature Medieval banquets, food-art events, and menus based on typical local cuisine (such as the controversy-ridden *alpage* cheese Bitto; see Grasseni 2012c). Cuochi di Lombardia has the mission of promoting local, quality wine and food through its restaurant network and has sponsored the reintroduction of wheat, rye, emmer, and nonstandard maize such as red maize. It is a consortium that boasts its "autonomy from political and unionist positions."[17] It features innovative logistics such as collective network purchases from locally traceable and organic producers and, through a direct link with the Ministry for Cultural Affairs, boasts a cultural mission as well as a professional commitment to serving healthy, artisanal, and local foods.

The two networks (of GAS activists organized in the DES Brianza and the alliance between the network of restaurant owners, an agricultural trade union, and a conservation park) seem to have overlapped but not to have cross-fertilized each other. The Molgora agricultural park features among the stakeholders in the 2006 project for Spiga & Madia, but a conference called in October 2010 at the alternative food festival Kuminda to promote an "encounter amongst the bread short supply chains of Lombardy" did not enlist the Pane Molgora project nor the association Cooks of Lombardy.[18] Specifically asked about this apparent lack of convergence, one of the organizers of Spiga & Madia explained that connections were sought but were laborious and finally stalled on the different project agendas: to commercialize local bread, based on the cultivation of costly wheat for baking, on the one hand, and to reengineer the whole supply chain, on the other. According to DES Brianza, in fact, the former is nonsustainable in economic terms without using institutional subsidies or applying elitist prices.[19]

In sum, the shortcoming of projects such as Pane Molgora is that they rely on the attractiveness of local foods to introduce a number of typical products, based on the premise that each locality should market a suitably varied palette of products that are indicative of the singularities of the land and the agricultural tradition of that specific territory, hoping that this will be rewarded by the market. Alternative provisioning networks on the other hand aim not just to stimulate but to rethink and reweave the local economic fabric. The case of Tomasoni, a family dairy salvaged from bankruptcy in 2009 by a network of solidarity purchase groups, is emblematic. In 2009, 200 GAS put together an emergency rescue fund for Tomasoni, a dairy farm in the province of Brescia. Tomasoni had begun serving GAS customers in 2002, converted to organic in 2004 in response to their preferences, and ran into financial trouble in 2008. In 2009, as a result of the credit crunch, the factory was about to close and sent a request for financial help to its GAS customers. These organized themselves and called for help from other GAS groups, raising an interest-free, eighteen-month loan of about 150,000 Euro within forty-five days of the e-mail campaign, partly in anticipation of payment for future orders and partly through the support of Mag 2 (a cooperative for ethical finance, which also supported Spiga & Madia) (Venturelli 2009). This was enough to pay for standing bills, and since then Tomasoni almost exclusively supplies gasistas, who in return are happy to accept higher prices.

To appreciate the uniqueness of this event, one should keep in mind that this happened in the northern Italian plains, a context where intensive farming and large dairy concerns are the norm. Milk production from the Lombardy region, which is roughly as large and populous as Massachusetts, covers 40 percent of the Italian national production and averages 4.3 million tons a year. It employs 6,000 enterprises and 12,000 people (plus 400 local packaging and transformation plants). Eighty percent of Lombard milk is transformed into cheese which brings in about 1.5 billion Euro, thus generating 23 percent of the regional agricultural income. About 40 percent of all cheese produced in this region is protected by a geographical indication (PDO), and geographical indication production uses about 50 percent of the milk transformed.[20] In this context, the critical issues for small-scale cheese producers (especially if using raw or organic milk) are the added costs of quality checks over the minimal quantity produced, then the costs of logistics vis-à-vis the generally low retail prices (33cents per liter in 2010). Direct-to-consumer provisioning through a solidarity purchase group can ease economic pressure both on small dairy farmers and on small- and medium-scale dairies. This is perceived by gasistas as a political issue and as a chance for them to rescue small-scale agriculture from the encroachment of the three main monocultures of the Padanian plains: rice, corn, and grass for dairy cows.

In purely business terms, the Tomasoni case created a novel precedent and an economic conundrum: the family firm had not turned into a co-op, nor had the funders organized themselves into an association, nor was this for the gasistas involved a form of socially responsible investment into a specific fund or bond. It was simply a new form of economy of trust—where the firm's conversion to organic first, and its financial distress partly as a result of an increase in quality and a decrease in quantity, had been understood by the gasistas as loyalty and thus repaid in a spirit of reciprocity and support. It was this relationship that resulted in the firm's resilience in the face of the financial crisis. In fact, this was viewed as just the latest step in a successful process of self-conscious downsizing, which brought the firm from a gross product of 2.5 million Euro to about 300,000 Euro per year, specializing now only in organic produce and particularly in organic Grana Padano (a mature cheese similar to Parmesan). The farm had effectively scaled down, focusing on quality and transparency over quantity. This brought it to the verge of bankruptcy, but for the gasistas the passage from customers to financial backers was swift.

Co-producing thus does not mean taking to the fields or to the renneting cauldron but doing the work of enabling those who tend the fields and make the cheese to keep on doing it on a noncorporate scale. Asked via a structured questionnaire for their reasons for anticipating money in a risky business, GAS members indicated as their main motivations the "desire to play an active role," the possibility "to do something important," and the wish "to find alternative solutions" (Signori 2010). As we have seen in the case of the DES Brianza and the reintroduction of wheat, to an extent this political ambition goes as far as wishing to reverse engineer the agribusiness landscape. In fact, as we shall see in Chapter 5, some districts of solidarity economy are developing co-production as a relationship of reciprocal trust by investing in noncertified organic producers and conventional farmers who wish to convert to organic farming. Such investment is based on the honest recognition of the difficulties, after establishing a direct contact and an onsite assessment. In other words, trust is not automatically established through a sheer transaction but requires cultivation over time.

The third and last example of co-production comes from another financial rescue: the Provenzano dairy in Sicily. A family business that had been bought out by a mafia clan in 2008, the Provenzano dairy owed 18 million Euro when it filed for bankruptcy. It transformed milk collected by 400 local smallholders and maintained the costly techniques of manual cheese-making regarded as preferable in the traditional production of mozzarella and ricotta. Once the mafia infiltration had been cleared out, the enterprise went bankrupt. The mandated administrator, instead of disbanding the firm, opted for a novel formula of co-responsibility with the firm's workers. The firm is not making a profit but slowly paying back the debt while negotiating the salaries with the workers, who were not laid off (Maselli 2010). The firms' salvage was made possible by the significant support of a network of trusted buyers, affiliated with the association Addio Pizzo (good-bye *pizzo*) where *pizzo*, literally "lace," is the money that gets regularly extorted by mafia clans from entrepreneurs and shopkeepers in Sicily and far beyond.

Founded in 2004, the association Addio Pizzo supports entrepreneurs and shopkeepers that denounce extorters and stop paying the *pizzo* (see Forno and Gunnarson 2010).[21] The association cooperates in this way with the reconversion projects of farms and lands that were expropriated from condemned Mafiosi. In turn, such projects are managed by associations of producers and farmers' cooperatives such as Libera Terra (Free Land, founded in 2006) or the cooperatives named after mafia victims Placido Rizzotto and Pio La Torre. The cooperatives are assigned this land for a symbolic rent and usually opt for producing organic wine, grains, lentils, and oranges— pledging to respect the land as well as workers' rights. Their produce, such as wine and pasta, sell well (at slightly higher prices than market average) especially if branded (such as the pasta Libera) and sold in Fair Trade shops or Addio Pizzo shops. Several northern Italian solidarity purchase groups, such as mine, and Fair Trade shops buy Libera pasta and wine. In 2011,

Addio Pizzo registered 407 pizzo-free entrepreneurs and shops, backed by 9,972 registered pizzo-free-supporting consumers organized into 18 associations. Addio Pizzo also sponsored antimafia and antiracket education projects in 112 Sicilian schools (Maselli 2010).

These are the examples of co-production that alternative provisioning activists have in mind when they talk about "shifting" portions of their family budget toward solidarity-driven objectives, or even "liberating" sections of the real economy from the alienating mechanism of profit-making. Both expressions are used frequently by the activists of districts of solidarity economy. In fact, according to Paolo Graziano, Francesca Forno, and Massimo Lepratti (2009), solidarity purchase groups of the type that I joined at the neighborhood library at the end of 2008 are themselves forms of active political participation. In other words, it is precisely because they fashion new forms of solidarity economy that GAS show how critical consumption can evolve into a form of political participation (Graziano and Forno 2012). Familiarizing oneself with alternative provisioning in Italy means becoming progressively apprenticed into a militant scenario, which is quite different and distinct from that of consumption-driven alternative food networks or reterritorialized food chains. Within this scenario, GAS and DES are not interchangeable expressions and do not represent the same kind of project, even though networks of GAS are often involved in planning and developing DES projects. GAS and DES histories have intertwined significantly and officially converged in 2011. To appreciate this, we need to contextualize the origins of solidarity economy in Italy in a fairly complex history of anticapitalist reflections.

ALTERNATIVE PROVISIONING AS A MILITANT SCENARIO

Alternative provisioning networks in Italy have important predecessors in the cooperative and workers' mutual help movements. These have a long history both in Europe and the Americas. The Italian cooperative movement is particularly relevant to the sectors of education, the organization of after-work sociality, and in general the historical regimentation of social life within the ranks of either Catholic or communist activism (Kertzer 1990, Shore 1990). At the end of the 1990s, both the breakdown of the Iron Curtain geopolitical scenario and the momentum of the global justice campaigns contributed to an innovative turn (Della Porta et al. 2006). Social movements began to focus on the global power of the capitalist market, turning away from state politics as a target of protest and inaugurating important boycott campaigns such as those against Nike and Shell (Forno 2013a). As Forno illustrated, in Italy this was the time when a number of alternative magazines started to be published (such as *Altraeconomia, Terre di Mezzo,* and *Valori;* see Forno 2013b). Terre di

Mezzo, for example, is an independent publisher whose crucial edition is the homonymous monthly street magazine, specializing on issues of migration, social inclusion, and homelessness. Since 1994, Terre di Mezzo has published a guide to responsible tourism (*Guida al Turismo Responsabile*), a catalogue of summer work camps in cooperatives for social inclusion, trips to Fair Trade–sponsored production sites, volunteer work for missionary groups and NGOs in developing countries, antimafia youth camps, and so on. Beginning in 2004, Terre di Mezzo has also promoted the fair of critical consumption and sustainable lifestyles, Fa' la Cosa Giusta (Do the Right Thing). Hosted at Fieramilanocity, Milan's permanent exhibition and fashion district, in 2012 Fa' la Cosa Giusta featured 700 exhibitors on 29,000 square meters specializing in conscious tourism, sustainable nutrition, critical fashion, natural cosmetics, green living, sustainable mobility, Fair Trade, peace and participation, and services for sustainability and was visited by 67,000 paying ticket holders.[22]

Ecotourism is also a growing phenomenon—showing evidence of a need for new ways of relating to the environment and providing an important economic background for the reterritorialization processes discussed above. *Agriturismo* in Italy means on-farm reception and hospitality (including catered meals). It may thus comprise school visits to didactic farms, family animal-watching on farms, tours of on-farm food-manufacturing sites (such as cheese making, grape harvesting and crunching for wine making, or olive gathering and pressing), as well as more mundane lunches and dinners on farm premises.[23] Farmers must have a license to cook and sell their own produce, and agro-tourism outfits are sometimes so popular that they cater for large parties and apply restaurant prices. These phenomena show not only the widespread interest and success for a return to locality through food conviviality but also the ambivalence and sometimes confusion about the ethical nature of this type of reterritorialized consumption.

By contrast, an important voice in the scholarly and activist scenario of critical consumption in Italy is that of Christian missionaries. Among one of the best-known militant global justice priests in Italy is the charismatic figure of Father Alex Zanotelli. A Comboni missionary who worked in the Korogocho slums of Nairobi as well as in the degraded Rione Sanità in Naples, Father Zanotelli is the editor in chief of a politically engaged missionary magazine, *Nigrizia* (roughly translatable as "negritude"). His books are best sellers for EMI, the Editrice Missionaria Italiana in Bologna. A missionary publisher, EMI's topics and interest nevertheless vastly exceed those of missionary practice and certainly those of Catholic orthodox theology. Most of the activist literature that constitutes the primary sources for this analysis—including Davide Biolghini's 2007 *The People of Solidarity Economy*—were published in EMI "New Lifestyles" book series. Nuovi Stili di Vita was inaugurated in the late 1980s by Francesco Gesualdi's *Letter to a Consumer of the North,* with a preface by

Father Alex Zanotelli, entitled *With David's Sling,* and a foreword by Alexander Langer, an influential Italian left-wing pacifist, green activist, and European MP. This keystone in the literature of Italian solidarity economy spoke to Italian consumers as potential owners of a "small power to be taken seriously" (Langer 1996: 1) and proposed boycotts, alternative consumption, and solidarity as the key ways to wield that power. At that time, it was particularly aimed at popularizing the Italian Fair Trade movement and inspiring volunteers to open "shops of the world" (*botteghe del mondo*). By the mid-1990s, in fact, Fair Trade took off, with an increasing number of shops: from 91 in 1993, to 273 in 1998, to 458 in 2004 (Viganò, Glorio, and Villa 2008).[24]

This flourishing of antiglobal campaigns, critical consumerism literature, and pacifist activism happened in Italy at the time of the "Fall of the First Republic," as the early 1990s came to be known in Italian contemporary history. The phrase defines the political demise of the historically popular parliamentary parties, which were revealed as morally bankrupt. The main parties in power, the Christian Democracy and the Socialist Party, suffered catastrophic ballot losses as their main spokesmen were prosecuted for corruption and greeted by angry mobs outside the Courts of Law. At the same time, the then-recent fall of the Berlin Wall forced the Communist Party in a radical rethinking if its mission and agenda, leaving it divided among postcommunists and Democrats, eventually bleeding it with militants and popular support. The two main political parties that rose from the ashes of the First Republic were, surprisingly, the secessionist, xenophobic, and populist Northern League and Silvio Berlusconi's Forza Italia. A sizeable amount of literature has been devoted to this political and anthropological conundrum: how, from a virulent movement of condemnation for the lack of moral integrity of its postwar national government, Italy has progressively sank during the intervening twenty years into a cultural and economic stagnation, for which the entire political caste is blamed. The country's leadership is widely criticized for its incapacity or unwillingness to welcome and interpret widespread grassroots inputs for collective renewal and for subtracting lymph to the social and economic system through a pervasive culture of corruption and connivance.[25]

Back in 1990, the *Letter to a Consumer of the North* must have sounded to enlightened northern Italians with double moral cogence, as twice northerners and doubly privileged: that is, as residents of the richest regions in Italy and as citizens of a country of the so-called global north. It was no coincidence that the *Letter* was followed in 1996 by the first *Handbook for Critical Consumption,* again authored by Francesco Gesualdi—as spokesman of the Centro Nuovo Modello di Sviluppo, a co-housing arrangement uniting three families in voluntary sobriety and research. Its objective is practicing local solutions to inequality and injustice through economic change and communicating them to a wider public. The *Handbook for Critical Consumption* was subsequently republished in various editions and has so far sold 150,000 copies (Centro Nuovo Modello di Sviluppo 1996; Carrera 2009: 94).

The founder of the first solidarity purchase group in the Bergamo area, Mario (a pseudonym) specifically mentioned Gesualdi's book and personal example as his source of inspiration to set up a collective for alternative provisioning. As Mario still recalled in summer 2011, in the mid-1980s Gesualdi gave a seminar presentation in Nembro, at the mouth of the Seriana Valley east of Bergamo, specifically explaining how one could "change humankind's political and economic destiny by changing consumption" and making it clear that "we are all eaters and consumers, rich and poor, left-wing and right-wing."[26] From this lesson, Mario took away the notion that "we do not need a specific political creed to make people reason." This was an important nuance, interpreting the global justice movement and the consequent proposal of a solidarity economy as a universalist and moral mobilization—not as party-political. As we shall see in Chapter 4, these nuances became cumbersome when trying to develop consensus around a Bergamasque GAS network, as people were wary about developing a political agenda lest it be read as a party-political project.

Specifically, Mario was very skeptical of any mechanism of delegation in the supply chain, even though he recalled that at the start, his solidarity purchase group had benefitted from the help of local and established organic cooperatives, which had helped them getting in touch with farmers and agricultural cooperatives in their turn. "Once we start relying on a cooperative shop, we are delegating and this is the beginning of a long slippery slope." Mario was cursorily referring to a banking scandal of 2005/06 popularly known as Bancopoli. Special uproar was stirred by the leakage of telephone conversations from which it appeared that a number of political representatives, bank directors, and the governor of the Bank of Italy—who then resigned—had more than strictly professional conversations about technical decisions over a number of national and international offers for the acquisition of an Italian bank, Antonveneta. The scandal involved several corporate banks and also an insurance company connected to the Cooperative League (widely known as red cooperatives). The reference to the red cooperatives was a shortcut for Mario to point to a well-known aversion within the GAS moment to the conventionalization of the most successful cooperatives into mainstream capitalist practice. According to this criticism, the professionalization of the cooperative movement, by scaling up, delegation, and mimicking corporate capitalism, had resulted in the same moral bankruptcy.

It is then no surprise that ethical banking also took its first steps within the same period of radical rethinking of consumerism and the global corporate economy, with the foundation of the Ethical Bank (Banca Popolare Etica) in Padua in 1999, following the experience of the MAG (Mutue di Autogesione).

These mutual self-managed Funds were organized mainly in the 1970s by nonprofit associations and workers' cooperatives that wished to manage their members' savings through their own projects, instead of seeking funding from conventional banks, which were perceived as politically steered, interest-greedy, and nontransparent in their management of funds.[27] By the end of the 1990s, many of these evolving but fragmented ways of rethinking the contradictions of the dominant economic model came to a head.

The social forums of the turn of the millennium brought together various social movements and actors in the effort of finding sustainable and solidarity-driven counterparts to neoliberal globalization. Davide Biolghini recalls in particular that the roundtable on solidarity economy held in Porto Alegre in the framework of the 2002 World Social Forum was a precious occasion for different national networks of solidarity economies to actually meet (Biolghini 2009: 166). Various types of socially oriented alternative economy networks are in fact active in different countries of the so-called global south. Brazil for instance is home to one of the internationally renowned scholars of solidarity economy, Euclides Mance (2001). A theorist of the network revolution, most influential in the Italian solidarity economy movement, Mance is president of the Instituto de Filosofia da Libertação and has favored the diffusion of liberation theology through community-based research action. Liberation theology originated in South America in the 1950s and 1960s and emphasized practice over doctrine, proposing social pedagogy solutions to the oppression of the poor. Liberation theology was stigmatized in the 1980s by the Vatican hierarchies, particularly by Cardinal Ratzinger, who later became Pope Benedict XVI, as a kind of Christian socialism that would confound "good practice" with Christian orthodoxy. It also inspired the social work of the Italian missionary Father Zanotelli in the slums of Nairobi and Naples.

To this day, a significant number of Italian social workers, volunteers, and educators identify themselves with the mission of social Christianity, though not specifically with Liberation theology. It is a widespread conviction that Christianity is not a question of individual belief but also of practice, an everyday practice that should aim to benefit one's neighbors, namely the poor, the disadvantaged, and the weak. Probably the largest socially oriented organization avowedly inspired to Christianity is the union of the Christian trade unions and after-work associations ACLI—Associazioni Cristiane Lavoratori Italiani. In legal terms, ACLI is an association for social promotion and allegedly counts 997,000 registered members, maintains 7,486 local offices, and offers services to 3.5 million people—ranging from tax return consultancy to professional training courses, to workers' rights defense, support to immigrants, youth, the aged, and women, promotion of cooperatives, and so on.[28] This highly specialized profession of social service is sometimes criticized by alternative provisioners for its degree of conventionalization—just as the red cooperatives counterparts are. In fact, both provide a benchmark and a straw man: admired for their organizational capacity but criticized for having moved too many organizational steps away from their primitive mission of solidarity.

It was also in reaction to this kind of formalized cooperation that the Lilliput Network for an Economy of Justice was born in Verona in 1999, co-founded by Francesco Gesualdi and Father Zanotelli. In the wake of the Seattle mobilization for global justice, Lilliput gathered associations from the realms of environmentalism, pacifism, religious and missionary activism, solidarity economy, and international cooperation. Coordinating over 600 local groups, the mission was "to build a world where every inhabitant of the planet can satisfy their material, social and spiritual fundamental needs, respecting the environment and the future generations' right to inherit a fertile Earth."[29] "Lilliputians [criticized] the choices that concentrate power in few hands, placing the logic of profit, consumption, financial soundness and debt payment before the safeguarding of life, human dignity, and the environment."[30] In the year 2000, the Lilliput language anticipated relevant topics in the current debate about the international financial crisis, the European strategies of austerity, and the critiques of the Indignados and Occupy movements.

Lilliput was conceived of as an intercampaigns table—that is, as a group that would make sure that the many strands of the critics of neoliberalist globalization would be aware of each other and consider acting in unison to guarantee a critical mass. In other words, neoliberal globalization was too big a monster to be tied down by just one campaign or volunteer group, but many of them together could probably work as many Lilliputians. The list of local groups and campaigns that accepted to be represented under the Lilliput umbrella varied from locality to locality, but typically enrolled were missionaries (especially Comboni missionaries), the Christian Boy Scouts, the association Blessed Be the Peace-Makers, and various other missionary groups and associations as well as NGOs, such as Ya Basta!, the Ethical Bank, and Legambiente (the Environment League). As the minutes of the founding assembly of the Padua Lilliput Network declares, for instance, "The aim of the *Rete di Lilliput Padova* is that of giving one voice to the various forms of local resistance against global economic choices that concentrate power in the hands of multinationals and put the logic of profit and consumption before the safeguarding of life, of human dignity, and of environmental health. This is a nonparty, nonprofit network."[31]

The Lilliput Network for an Economy of Justice was especially preparing for the Genoa 2001 Social Forum, a self-summoned forum for an economy of justice that would be held defiantly in Italy, in concomitance with the G8 meeting hosted by the Berlusconi government in the same city (G8 being the formal talks among the self-appointed eight most important national economies in the world, held yearly, to establish the agenda for global development). As I recount in Chapter 5, Genoa 2001 ended in civil unrest and bloodshed, with thousands of peaceful demonstrators caught between block-by-block riots and indiscriminate police retaliation. This bloody mess left a significant mark on Italian strategies for building alternative economies.

After its decennial meeting in 2009, the Lilliput Network decided "to have come to the end of a cycle" and to begin a new one by disseminating its styles of participation and global justice agenda in distributed and thematic working groups. The Lilliput Network website is accessible as an archive but has not been updated since then—which does not mean that Lilliputians are inactive. Specifically, Lilliput has taught and diffused a specific style for nonviolent debating, using simple techniques such as turn-taking, résumé writing, and in-depth discussion in small working groups. The Lilliput networking strategy to bring about an economy of justice through the coordination of existing, local campaigns and groups has born fruits especially in its synergy with the solidarity purchase groups—whose formulas and ideas of local and organic solidarity-driven provisioning formally preceded the establishment of the Lilliput Network. Many of the mailing lists currently active in the GAS movement, for instance those of the working groups that set themselves up at the GAS yearly national assemblies and then continue debating and exchanging information online while physically apart, are hosted by ReteLilliput.org.[32] Nonviolent repertoires for consensus-building have been adopted by the GAS movement and are used during the GAS national assemblies. In other words, gasistas need not be Lilliputians, and in fact, many solidarity purchase groups may have no knowledge of such experience. Nor are Lilliputians by definition members of a GAS. Also, while gasistas are numerous, probably in the tens of thousands, Lilliputians came from the numerically exiguous ranks of motivated and well-informed activists, missionaries, or community leaders—there are a few hundred at most.

But Lilliputians and gasistas—especially GAS founders such as Mario, who were directly inspired by Gesualdi's *Letter to a Consumer of the North*—have in common the idea that to exercise critical discernment in consumption, one needs to set in motion a complex practice, which is about gathering knowledge as much as it is about purchasing. For these food activists, ethical consumption is not about choosing one product over another on a supermarket shelf. It is not about exercising one's consumer's choice on the basis of limited, predigested, and often misleading information. It is to study and exert oneself in order to comprehend the bigger picture in which by bringing cheap food to my table, someone somewhere else in the world starves. It is to come together and get organized in order to limit the environmental and social damage that one otherwise inevitably causes through thoughtless shopping. This type of consumer activism is not about seeking higher-quality products, whether organic or "typical." It is about avoiding large, organized distribution (*grande distribuzione oganizzata*) out of moral, environmental, religious, pacifist, political, existential, or any other kind of motivation that, as Mario would probably put it, "makes one reason."

DISTRICTS AND NETWORKS OF SOLIDARITY ECONOMY

Tavolo RES, the current national working group for an Italian network of solidarity economy, developed out of a Lilliput working group on ecological footprinting. The objective of Tavolo RES is to aid and favor the establishment and proliferation of Districts of Solidarity Economy (DES). According to its self-definition, posted online on February 28, 2004, the Network of Solidarity Economy (RES) is a "work-in-progress experiment to construct another economy based on the experience acquired by the numerous projects of solidarity economy that are already active in Italy."[33] The RES strategy is one of creating networks that link such projects together, in order to "create market spaces that are finalized to the common good."[34] This project was initiated on October 19, 2002, in Verona as a result of a seminar on network strategies for solidarity economy, which defined a charter for the Italian network of solidarity economy publicly presented in Padua on May 4, 2003.[35]

The RES strategy includes the idea to initiate many local districts of solidarity economy, DES, which would work as many nodes in a larger network of networks. The working group Tavolo RES is open to volunteers and moderates an e-mail list. The recipe for district-making is inspired both by the participative political repertoire of the social movements and by the principles of cybernetics: a district of solidarity economy is meant to be the result of a participatory process that achieves recursive, creative, and innovative feedback among actors who would not otherwise act in resonance with each other (Biolghini 2007). Such actors should ideally sit around a table (hence the recurrent image of a Tavolo—that is, a working group but literally a table). Such subjects might be institutional representatives or simply people working in a Fair Trade shop, in an ethical bank, in responsible tourism, in social cooperatives, or in a solidarity purchase group. The imagery (and the practice) of conviviality is not indifferent to the success of this formula, for which sitting around a table is paramount. Several meetings and a process of network formation often precede the milestone step of drafting a charter, a document of intents outlining common objectives, values, and methods. Often the first public events organized by the district are aimed at network-making or network-enhancing: a fair of solidarity economy, a farmers' market, or a public seminar (Biolghini 2009: 168). Nevertheless, this is not enough to have a working DES: real and new economic circuits must be generated for a district to "take off"—an expression also used among gasistas to distinguish between the projects that remain on paper only and the groups that have actually created something new, functioning, and capable of replicating itself. Tavolo RES currently lists twenty-five active DES in Italy.[36] One of them is DES Brianza, whose project Spiga & Madia I commented upon. Another is Milan's DESR in the agricultural park of South Milan (Parco Agricolo Sud di Milano). Here, according to the project coordinators, only a handful of the about 800 registered local farmers practice organic farming. They are being sponsored by a network of Milanese solidarity purchase groups to convert their neighbor farmers to cultivate for local organic provisioning. Three municipalities have offered a distribution point in a public building to aid the collaboration between the park's farmers and the city's GAS. Among its activities, the DESR hosts a market of products of the park (Buon Mercato, or the Good Market) and a swapping-and-storage place for the local GAS networks, so that individual members are relieved of the burden of storing foodstuffs for everyone else. The DESR also hosts social events and book presentations.

Activist literature and projects are reciprocally informative and supportive. In 2010, Tavolo RES published a volume on "how to create and organize solidarity purchase groups and other networks of solidarity economy in fifty exemplary stories," tellingly entitled *Il Capitale delle Relazioni*. A less ambitious pocketbook teaches one how to establish a GAS in one's condo or office, planning a short supply chain with one's neighboring farmers (Ragusa 2010). In March 2009, the Ethical Bank magazine *Valori* provided the first map of the nationwide distribution of GAS networks and DES. Mapping solidarity economy activism went hand in hand with a political rediscovery of the Commons: water, air, soil, energy, and knowledge have to be protected by active citizens—this is the thesis of *La società dei beni comuni (The Society of the Commons;* Cacciari 2011), followed by *La Repubblica dei Beni Comuni (The Republic of the Commons)*, which was authored by the Zero-Mile Democracy Collective, a name that stresses how politics and provisioning are intimately intertwined.[37] However different in scope, style, and size, the common concern of these alternative publishers is to show that it is possible to shift from mall-based provisioning to short supply chains and that this choice can be enabled by local collectives. This campaign de facto brought together GAS and DES in the same picture—which was not banal. In fact, it was only in the 2010 GAS assembly that the agenda of bringing together solidarity purchase groups and districts of solidarity economy under the same rubric was approved. June 2011 saw the first GAS-and-DES national assembly, a self-summoned meeting of interlacing experiences, whose networks crisscrossed and overlapped. An updated map of solidarity economy in Lombardy charts the presence of 451 GAS and 10 DES, plus several GAS networks (sometimes more than one in each province: see Map 2.1).

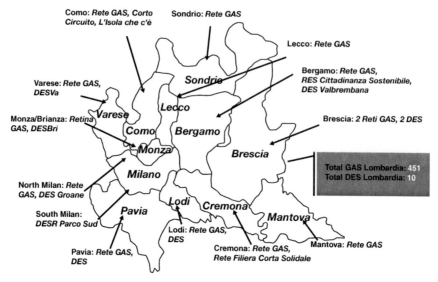

Como: *Rete GAS, Corto Circuito, L'Isola che c'è*

Sondrio: *Rete GAS*

Lecco: *Rete GAS*

Bergamo: *Rete GAS, RES Cittadinanza Sostenibile, DES Valbrembana*

Varese: *Rete GAS, DESVa*

Monza/Brianza: *Retina GAS, DESBri*

Brescia: *2 Reti GAS, 2 DES*

Total GAS Lombardia: 451
Total DES Lombardia: 10

North Milan: *Rete GAS, DES Groane*

South Milan: *DESR Parco Sud*

Lodi: *Rete GAS, DES*

Pavia: *Rete GAS, DES*

Cremona: *Rete GAS, Rete Filiera Corta Solidale*

Mantova: *Rete GAS*

Map 2.1   Distribution of GAS networks and districts of solidarity economy in Lombardy, January 2013. Courtesy of Davide Biolghini; data from Osservatorio CORES, 2013

UNDERSTANDING A COMPLEX SCENARIO

The GAS movement and the DES originate from the same tight circuit of critical consumers and global justice activists. As noted above, it was on October 19, 2002, that a workshop on network strategies for solidarity economy was organized in Verona by Rete Lilliput, resulting in the establishment of a long-standing working group, Tavolo RES, whose objective is to promote a nation-wide network of solidarity economy in Italy. Historically, this is the stepping stone for the enrolment of GAS (the first one having been created in 1994) in a network of solidarity economy with more encompassing objectives.

Initially the GAS movement was not any more successful or well-known than other alternative provisioning networks, and it is not uncommon to find people with previous or additional associative experience among their ranks: from Fair Trade to Slow Food, to the Time Banks, plus a number of environmental, pacifist, and antimafia associations, all of which focus on local consumption as a political act against a naturalized notion of the capitalist market (Saroldi 2001). In fact, as Francesca Forno notes, most GAS groups are to be found in the same regions where Fair Trade has been successful (Forno 2013b). After their beginnings in the 1990s, GAS experienced momentous growth. Registered GAS groups have grown from 153 in 2004 to 394 in 2008, to 1,000 in 2012 (see Figure 0.1).

The activity of the Lilliput Network, which jump-started the districts and networks of solidarity economy with specific methods of leadership, communication, and training, have been influential for the GAS movement. For example the Lombard DES that were mentioned earlier in this chapter were facilitated by start-up projects of Tavolo RES such as EQUAL—Nuovi Sitli di Vita. The Lilliput Network invested in information, communication, and public denunciation as well as in critical consumption, boycott campaigns, and support of alternative economies such as Fair Trade, ethical finance, networks of local economies, collective purchase within a very wide framework of concern about global justice and the north/south divide.

The current Italian solidarity economy scenario has inherited its working method, with a number of tables of coordination and discussion at the national, regional, or local level, and a certain number of referents working on specific projects. Projects and tables often overlap as charismatic referents embody the memory and best practices of past experiences and often participate in more than one working group. Information, opinions, and debates are shared both on e-mail lists and during conferences and seminars but especially at the yearly assembly. DES privilege the idea of the economic district: a small fabric of family-run projects with a capacity for networking toward large scales and volumes. Some DES are consolidating networks of GAS in actual cooperatives, which can generate salaried jobs (as is the case of L'isola che c'è, which runs a yearly fair of solidarity economy in Como). They may collaborate with agricultural parks or lobby local municipalities to obtain public meeting and storage spaces. It is in this variegated and dynamic scenario that the projects to reconstruct local supply chains for bread, as discussed earlier in this chapter, find their natural context.

I have argued that even when projects of heritage-based localized agrifood systems are developed both by territorial development agencies and by grassroots food activists, in the same localities and at the same time, they may not feed into each other and that this happens not because of abstract ideological reasons but because of their different objectives: rethinking the economy in radical terms in one case and doing territorial marketing in the other. Certainly, stressing sustainability through a preference for short food-supply chains has rekindled an attention to local landscapes and territories and a critique of "placeless foods" (Du Puis and Goodman 2005). Nevertheless, the GAS movement displays a networking capacity that goes well beyond the retrenchment to the village farmers' market. Vice versa, geographically distant projects can reverberate together and create fruitful synergies when they are nourished by the same network or when they become nodes in a network of networks. Solidarity purchase groups enable new imaginaries of sociality and exchange at a diffused level within society. As Davide Biolghini notes, GAS, DES, and RES are distinctly Italian experiences that seem to have had particular success in connecting not only consumers on one side and producers on the other but also other social actors who were already present and active but were previously disconnected—such as Catholic and communist workers associations, environmentalist associations, institutions such as conservation parks and agricultural parks (2009: 167). The GAS movement made a leap forward a decade after its initial steps, achieving significant visibility in the media and on the political scene by involving high numbers of consumers and by keeping GAS practice engaged but nonexoteric and accessible to the noninitiated (I commented on not having been initiated in the previous chapter). In the following chapters, I return to these characteristics and networking capacity of solidarity purchase groups, revealing their strengths and shortcomings.

–3–

Reweaving the Economy

On May 25, 2011, our blueberry referent Cinzia reported to our GAS meeting about her visit to the farmer on the neighboring hills. She had gone on foot to see her, as the fields lie hardly half-an-hour away from our suburb, flanking the cobblestone path that leads from the lower suburbs to Bergamo's Venetian walls of the Upper Town (Città Alta), in the vicinity of a long-abandoned eleventh-century monastery. In this idyllic vale, tucked away from the tarmac and traffic of downtown Bergamo, Betty the farmer would sell us raspberries, blueberries, or blackberries, according to the season. One was welcome to come with children to pick them. Late summer sales were publicized by e-mail to collect late berries for homemade jams. Cinzia reported that the price she accepted was 12 Euro per kilo. "Wait a minute," said Gisela, "it was 9 Euro per kilo for our GAS, just last year." Cinzia naively said, "Well, she said, 'This year I can do 11 or 12 Euro.' So I took 12." This sparked some unrest across the table:

"Why 12 when you could have got 11?"

"Well, I thought we were supposed to act in solidarity, right? She was actually suggesting 12."

"Yeah, well solidarity is a great thing, but why should we be the ones that pay her 12 if she is prepared to make others pay 11? She should give us a *discount*, not a higher price!"

After this lively exchange, we accepted the deal that Cinzia had made and promised each other to be less gullible next time. We carried on. It was agreed that people could only buy a maximum of 5 kilos of Parmesan because one car could only take 220 kilos, and we should not buy for relatives and friends—they should join the GAS. The chicken farmer agreed to a price of 9 Euro per kilo but begged us not to all turn up at the parking lot to pick up the chickens: couldn't we organize ourselves and only send one person per GAS? The oranges had arrived—the organic cooperative was storing them for us. Did we want to go and get them at their depot outside town or meet them one early morning at the market?

These notes give a brief insight in the routine of GAS provisioning: meetings, deliberations, preferences, deliveries, orders, quantities, prices. At the micromanagement level, unless some faux pas sparked some resentful remarks about solidarity and why we should be the gullible ones, it did not feel political at all.

Nevertheless, it is by now accepted in the literature of several disciplines that consumption is both perceived and performed as a political act: citizenship and consumerism are not mutually exclusive terms, though obviously they're not perfectly overlapping (Barnett et al. 2005, Johnston et al. 2009). Anthropology's unique insight into the GAS phenomenon consists in the ethnographic understanding that these networks are reinventing value by reweaving relations. In this chapter, I provide ethnographic evidence and quantitative data that show how gasistas are mobilizing skills and exchanging goods and services in ways that can only be understood within a wider anthropological framework, namely as embedded economic practice. Reweaving the economy means reconstituting the relational basis of society. In using these expressions, I refer to what economic anthropology has classically developed as a substantivist approach (Gudeman 2012, Mauss 1966, Polany 1966), according to which economic transactions are embedded in social relationships.

I apply this outlook—usually associated with informal and marginal economies as they encounter capitalist market economy—to solidarity economies in an advanced capitalist society. In using the metaphor of a woven fabric for solidarity economy, my point of reference is also the vast literature on practice, perception, and cognition (see, for instance, Lave 1998, 2011; Ingold 2000) that grants theoretical dignity to the way in which routine practical involvement recursively produces and validates both value and knowledge. Here, I wish to show how GAS practice, as it reorganizes the drudgery of provisioning on a new collective and relational basis, re-embeds values, dispositions, and understandings in economic ties that cannot be formalized in purely profit-driven relationships (Pratt 2007, Graeber 2001).

A GASISTA'S WORLD

What is entailed in being a gasista—as GAS members call themselves? To answer this question, as I said in the introduction, I draw mainly on my personal experience in one GAS group in Bergamo, but I also benefit from data of a recent survey that contacted all the sixty-two GAS groups existing in the Bergamo area in 2011 (Osservatorio CORES 2013). Here is a concrete example of a gasista e-mail exchange:

> Selene from the GAS in Stezzano [a village about 5 miles from the GAS circulating the e-mail list] is about to place a new order for pasta and sauce from the Iris cooperative. If anyone is interested please send me your orders by Tuesday,

November 2nd so that I can collect them and forward them to Sofia as GAS Time
Bank. In any case I'll see you all tonight. Best.

The message usually forwards other messages and attachments (typically
an Excel sheet with instructions on how to fill in an order for one family or one
entire GAS group):

> Hi all! We are organizing orders to the IRIS firm. Here attached is the spreadsheet,
> with costs, for a minimum order of 80 boxes...Last time we ordered about one
> hundred! If we reach this threshold prices are a bit lower—if we don't, they'll be a
> bit higher. But in any case before I send off the order I'll circulate a confirmation
> email with the exact pricing based on the orders collected. As usual we pay for
> delivery, too. Please remember that minimum orders are half a box, but that we
> have to order entire boxes from the firm. So once I have received all the deliveries,
> I'll let you know if we need to 'pair up' to complete the order. Please remember
> that I need to receive these spreadsheets by Friday October 5th. Thanks!

Each gasista bears his or her share of this kind of concrete tasks involving logistics and accounting. In my group, each member had responsibility for
collecting one type of order (for instance, for pasta, or olive oil, or oranges). In
time, through practical involvement and frequent correspondence, camaraderie and solidarity progressively develops beyond the mere provisioning activity.
Gasistas may find themselves carpooling to commute to work or offering reciprocal help on other provisioning tasks outside GAS (typically, offering each
other free shares of crops from their gardens, going chestnut-picking together,
or sharing fruit from their trees). Invitations to public events such as book presentations and debates or opinion exchanges on relevant matters are often
circulated through the group e-mail list (for instance the soft spots in the latest law on energy saving or a comparison among different strategies for waste
management). Sometimes, sociability and reciprocity develop into actual Time
Banks: a token system is devised within a circle of registered members, who
exchange units of time to carry out different types of tasks defined by needs
and offers (for instance, babysitting is exchanged for English lessons, or a
plumbing first intervention for help in the orchard).

The task of coordinating the group is also carried out through meetings and
e-mail, and in general this, too, is considered as a role that should be taken
up in turns. Nevertheless, there are many competences entailed in running a
GAS: from knowledge about organic certification and geographical denominations to managing at least one mailing list and maybe a group's website. Com-
petence in agronomy is particularly welcome in GAS groups, both to promote
local producers' conversions to organic farming and to monitor them. This is
a lengthy and often complex process called *accompagnamento,* or coaching.
The ideas of vicinity and coaching are both implied in the term, as gasistas

are prepared to pay higher prices to producers in exchange for a more socially or environmentally responsible management of their firm.

Much time is devoted to discussing which producer to choose. Sometimes there is a shortage of organic or proximal producers for certain types of provisions (such as oranges), but on other occasions choices are tough if there is more than one producer, each writing letters offering their produce or having been in touch with one gasista or another. Here is an exemplary conundrum:

> I am attaching the spreadsheet for tuna and similar canned food. Prices have gone up a lot since last Spring. I remember that we had opted for this product because it came directly from a small producer in Sicily. If you are still interested I can gather orders for our GAS. This would be our first trial and we have to commit to substantial quantities. So my proposal is to gather as many desiderata as possible amongst ourselves and then to make one single order to be distributed after delivery. Please let me have your desiderata by September 15 so I can then forward the order to Stella.

Similar dilemmas have regarded where to get one's olive oil from. In my group, several meetings in the neighborhood's library were devoted to discussing the choice between two producers: one on Lake Garda and one in Sicily. The former was much closer and buying from there would mean having less impact on the environment because of transportation and logistics. The latter though had proved tastier, the Sicilian oil being described as having more body and being more effective for salad dressing. Others felt that the latter had been delivered out of season, thus consisting of leftovers from the previous season, and had found it rancid. The northern producer, though, applied higher prices. And someone found that their oil was thinner and only acceptable for cooking and deep-frying. It was relevant to me that considerations of taste and price went hand in hand with more idealistic reflections about environmental impact and solidarity with southern producers. The compromise, where possible, was to keep a liaison with both producers and to put in orders for both types of oil, where one could raise enough interest and order enough quantity. The Lake Garda producer was finally dropped because there simply were not enough orders for them.

The practicalities of GAS membership thus regard exchanging information about available providers, procuring and evaluating a sample or a first order of the product, discussing benefits and drawbacks in a meeting, committing to the producer or provider, and sharing the task of managing orders to existing providers. For instance, coordinating apple provisioning means getting in touch with the orchard keeper, getting an estimate of the produce available and at what price for which minimal order, circulating the information, collecting orders, liaising with the producer, collecting the order, and arranging a collective or individual meeting with the other GAS members for them to collect their share and pay their dues. An apple order may include the following information: name and location of the farmer, varieties available, price per crate, instruction on whether crates should be returned, and availability for mixed orders (more than one variety in one crate).

A number of other ideas and information are nevertheless conveyed through meeting attendance and through the groups' e-mail lists, such as announcements of farmers' markets and other ad hoc markets of "green" producers of nonfood products, such as naturally colored or unbleached clothes or shoes. One of the hot items in 2010 was naturally colored shoes, made in Italy from nonchrome-treated skins by an artisanal producer from Mantua. The producer offered a special price list for GAS purchase and made a point of making all the information about the leather providers, modes of treatment, and manufacture process available online to make the production transparent and to justify pricing. The shoes were sold online and tried via a travelling catalogue that was hosted at occasional solidarity economy fairs and at selected Fair Trade shops. Even though the orders were placed individually, eager debates about the quality and resilience of the shoes, the fairness of the pricing, and the efficiency of the distribution regularly took place during the GAS meetings. One firm in particular became famous after its innovative formula of direct sale to GAS groups was reviewed on national television in November 2011, during the primetime journalistic series *Report*. The same popular program of investigative journalism, usually exposing national and international shambles against consumers', workers', and human rights, had dedicated a number of short good news segments about solidarity purchase groups as early as 2006.

The circulation of information on GAS mailing lists did not exclusively regard GAS activity. One of the events regularly advertised, though not directly a GAS event, was an itinerant series of farmers' markets within and around Bergamo, including both suburban and rural locations, organized by the association Market & Citizenship, itself a project of the association Sustainable Citizenship, and conducted in collaboration with the Bergamo Slow Food charter and the district of solidarity economy of Val Brembana. These fortnightly events, involving social cooperatives and local administrations, found their most trusted customers among gasistas. Citizenship markets may be accompanied by seasonal events such as theme sales (for instance, of chestnuts, nutmegs, and hazelnuts in the fall) and convivial events (such as the distribution of roasted chestnuts and mulled wine). Cooperation with the local Slow Food Charter meant, for instance, that one farmers' market was offered during a sponsored theme day dedicated to the local handmade cheese *stracchino:* selling cheese, honey, wine, and jam as well as the usual vegetables and seasonal fruit. It also meant hosting sales stands of wood, textile, and straw arts and crafts or offering a Slow Food tasting lab—that is, a guided tasting session with a Slow Food expert. Other types of events are book presentations and seminars—for instance, on the history of consumers and workers cooperatives in the Bergamo area.

This diverse palimpsest suggests the fluid and dynamic scenario of GAS self-organization. The birth, life, and sometimes death of GAS depend directly from a similar ongoing process of cross-pollination and viral-like contamination with other groups and sometimes across different networks. In the Bergamo area, the first solidarity purchase group was born in April 2002. Its founder, Mario, explained that this was the first GAS with an active agenda of being open to whomever, and to generating other similar initiatives by budding (*gemmazione*) or by grafting (*supporto:* that is, by supporting an initial group through lending them one's list of providers' contacts, sharing orders, or generally holding communal meetings to coordinate strategies). On that date, Mario notes:

> The national GAS census registered the existence of another GAS, which nevertheless had never taken off. Also at that time, there was a collective purchase group, which had been active for quite some time, in Pontida [about ten miles from Bergamo]. This had been set up to serve a group of families affiliated to Bilanci di Giustizia, thus only admitting "budgeting" families.[1] The experience of GAS BassaValSeriana [GAS of the Lower Seriana Valley] was thus instrumental to the birth of other groups, as this practice began to diffuse in the surrounding region, either by budding or through graftings from the initial group.[2]

New solidarity purchase groups can be born of other groups that become exceedingly numerous, though links between them may remain tight. Mario's seminal network of GAS groups grew in a populous and industrialized valley near Bergamo, Val Seriana. A local employee of a comprehensive school and charismatic leader, Mario, in 2009, then led a transition group called Charon toward the establishment of a province-wide network of about sixty GAS groups. I return to this important moment of transition in the next chapter, but what I wish to spell out here is that specific GAS groups have very different capacities to proliferate and reaggregate. The success of some well-established groups counterbalances the short-lived experience of a number of projects that "never take off from paper," in the language of GAS activists. This diversity characterized the GAS scenario in the Bergamo area from the start. Mario's GAS of the Lower Seriana Valley, for instance, grew and evolved into a seminal network called InterGas of the Lower Seriana Valley, which connected and coordinated the many groups that sprung up after its example. In 2009, when I began my ethnography, InterGas included three very large GAS groups (PanGas, Torre-Ranica, and Seriate & Sparsi) each of which budded into other groups.

Gasistas often talk about *budding* (*gemmazione*) to refer to the creation of smaller GAS groups from an original one that is outgrowing itself. The same term is also long-established in the cooperative movement. It refers specifically to the way in which strawberries proliferate: never exceeding an optimal size and, instead, overflowing seedlings in the terrain besides them.[3] In GAS language, new groups can be referred to as *spores, splits,* and *graftings* to figuratively represent these mechanisms of proliferation, diffusion, and contamination among older groups that overflow into new seedlings. These in turn are nourished and supported by the elders' group for some time, until they develop autonomous contacts with enough providers and gain the organizational capacity and the necessary critical mass to place orders for big quantities of individual products collectively. An ongoing capacity for reorganization characterizes GAS as a growing phenomenon. Within very large groups that do not wish to split, the alternative solution of establishing chains is sought. Chains are subgroups within a GAS that organize smaller, faster working groups to facilitate the delivery of fresh produce such as fish. While chains or subgroups can work in a more expedite way through the logistics of order and delivery, a larger GAS can be a desirable venue for identifying and monitoring providers, for debating wider issues—such as a collective stance about water privatization—and for bargaining lower prices in a concerted way.

There is thus no prefixed formula for how a GAS group should be born, grow, and reproduce. Bergamo's first GAS—BVS, for instance—eventually evolved from an initial core of about 8 families into a network of about 100 families. These are organized into a larger group called PanGas, which includes members from the three neighboring villages of Pradalunga, Alzano, and Nese only, and scattered seedling groups that welcomed members from more distant sites of the lower Seriana Valley. Membership is not straightforwardly determined by location or residence either, as groups and networks privilege working partnerships, established friendships, and common sensibilities. For instance, during my fieldwork the large Torre-Ranica group, which included members of the two neighboring villages of Torre Boldone and Ranica, outgrew itself and split into two groups: not into Torre and Ranica (one for each village) but instead into Torre-Ranica 1 and Torre-Ranica 2 (two groups for the twin villages area). Members of the larger group preferred to keep a wider territorial basis while dividing in two more manageable and less numerous collectives. The diversity and creativeness of the solidarity purchase groups were represented even in their names: a group coordinated by a young medical doctor was called GAS-trite (as in gastritis), and another found humor in its small numbers (Quater GAS, which mimics the Bergamasque dialect expression *"Quater Gat,"* literally "four cats," to indicate a nonrepresentatively small number). One called itself Jakob's Well (il Pozzo di Giacobbe). A group in the area of the river Serio was named GAS sul Serio, which can mean both "GAS on the river Serio" and "Seriously GAS."

This fluid scenario represents their largely informal nature and the casual and serendipitous but heartfelt way in which networks of GAS groups are interwoven. Many gasistas in my group practiced what is called in gasista language *self-production (autoproduzione)*: they baked bread, kept a garden patch, or had an orchard. It was not uncommon to turn up at meetings and be greeted with freshly collected honey—wax and all, in a jar that we could freely dip from—to spread on bread baked by another GAS member. Visits to pick up orders would easily result in gifts of excess homegrown apples or persimmons. The organic metaphors that are often used in gasista language (groups being born, cross-pollinating, dying, etc.) may be generated by this self-conscious exercise of proximity to the land but also, as I shall explain in the following section, by the exquisitely gendered relations and subjectivities that are established through solidarity purchase groups.

CROSS-POLLINATING NETWORKS

In January 2010 in the Bergamo area, only fourteen groups were registered with retegas.org (the national GAS network). Nevertheless, the nascent network of solidarity purchase groups in Bergamo, ReteGasBergamo, established in October 2009, had recruited twenty-five groups, and as many as fifty groups were known to the network altogether. Calculating an average of about twenty families per group, this meant that about 1,000 people were practicing gasista provisioning within a province of approximately one million. Only half of them were part of a local network of GAS, and only about one-fifth had made known their existence within the nationwide GAS movement. There were large and long-established groups such as that of Albino in the Seriana Valley, which served more than one hundred families,[4] and small neighborhood groups with no more than eight families. Thirteen GAS kept accounting books, and on the basis of that data, ReteGasBergamo established that gasistas had spent 225,000 Euro on purchases in 2009 (an average of 17,300 Euro per group or 1,600 Euro per provider).

Recent data from the region Lazio in Central Italy ascertains a similar situation: while 58 groups were registered with the regional network, another 100 were informally active inside and around Rome (Fonte et al. 2011). After reviewing e-mail lists and databases, a total of 160 GAS were counted. They indicated disparate origins (a group of mothers that met at their children's primary school, environmental activists, Fair Trade shops, etc.) and their size varied from 10 to 200 members. Out of a sample of the thirteen GAS coordinators who were interviewed, six had founded their group after 2009. Their annual purchases amounted to about 650,000 Euro, for an average of 50,000 Euro per group, and a total impact on the regional economy (mostly food producers) of about 8 million Euro. The typology of providers preferred by GAS are small and local farmers. Each GAS family would spend between 700 and 1,000 Euro a year on food provisioning through GAS. Compared with national statistics, this amounts to 15 to 20 percent of a family's average expenditure on food. GAS provisioning, by eliminating mediators and long-distance distribution, grants families larger quantities of local foods and establishes relationships for direct exchanges between families, thus lowering the overall food expenditure, too.

Most of the exponential growth of GAS economic activity was concentrated in the austerity years of 2010 to 2012, and unsurprisingly so. This had important reverberations on how GAS braced themselves in the face of unprecedented media exposure, popular demand for joining the groups, and offers from self-promoting producers. As I noted, gasistas often use metaphorical terms from the vegetable world to characterize the most important phases of their development: not only *budding* and *grafting* but also *nurturing seedlings, sowing seeds,* and *pruning.* It was at the national assembly of 2010 that I first heard of *fall pruning* to refer to the need of cutting off the *dead branches.* I realized that these phrases referred to people who joined a GAS group in order to secure provisioning of particular items (such as local and organic honey or conveniently delivered recyclable cleaning and toiletry materials). These members were looked down on for not participating in the meetings and not contributing regularly to the collective orders, thus adding to the producers' aggravation of not receiving stable and consistent orders. Furthermore, dead branches join a GAS just to buy (*solo per comprare*). These people may place their orders consistently through the GAS mailing list but try to avoid the burden of managing orders and logistics. The parasitic behavior of "free riders" is particularly annoying for groups that rely completely on volunteer work and do not charge shopping costs, as each member is supposed to do his or her share. This is a key difference between GAS and a consumer cooperative, which can delegate assignments to salaried workers but charges running costs to its membership.

Interviewed about the limits and potentials of the GAS movement, particularly the ways in which they are organized, one of the current coordinators of ReteGasBergamo, Luisa, stressed the difference between their practice-driven strategy and more institutional approaches to sustainability, development, and urban renewal. In her opinion, personal involvement on a practical level reminds one that not anything is possible. As an engineer, she mentioned her training at Milan's Polytechnic and criticized the can-do philosophy that engenders top-down conceptions of logistics, communication, and infrastructure. All these areas are in fact the focus of GAS grassroots practice—rethinking the logistics of provisioning, using the Web to communicate, publicize, and connect initiatives, and bypassing large distribution infrastructures by reinventing and implementing their own distribution chains. Instead of large-scale counter-planning though, Luisa described GAS activity as characterized by curiosity, diversity, and being open to the many and different actors on the territory, "without barricading ourselves into a specific niche."

Expertise plays a paramount role in the practice and reflection of gasistas' provisioning: how to gain the expertise needed, how to monitor someone else's practice, and how to evaluate and circumstantiate experts' advice are extremely relevant abilities when one sets out to rethink supply circuits. GAS network coordinators such as Luisa represent the top-tier provisioning activists who consciously juggle expertise from many quarters to make sense of and bring together data, insights, and solutions from different realms such as information and communication technology (ICT), logistics, and agronomy. Their crosscutting competences across different but collaborating groups constitute a veritable expertise bank. It is with reference to this wealth of practical knowledge that the metaphors of grafting, seeding, and coaching are used within the GAS world, to indicate the sharing, dissemination, and apprenticeship that goes on within and across groups

It is not expected that in any one group of a dozen families one would find viable experience on how to manage a short food chain or how to monitor and assist local farmers in their conversions to organic. Even simple bookkeeping skills regarding how to fill in a spreadsheet and keep the group accounting in order should not be taken for granted. In fact, there was a certain well-deserved self-assurance in the way in which a delegate from one of the earliest GAS, Rodolfo, spoke at a meeting in September 2009: "We are not setting up a network of GAS because we need someone to tell us how to unload a truck full of oranges coming from Sicily. We have already done that, we've been there."

This meeting was called to establish a province-wide GAS network in the area of Bergamo. At the time, we were aware of the existence of about thirty groups. Rodolfo's statement invited a diverse range of responses. Many agreed with him that a network of GAS should meet different and higher needs than those of a single group. A network of GAS, in other words, should answer more fundamental questions than how to perfect one's logistics. Questions such as, Why do we do this? What do we want to achieve? What comes next? But the choral rebuttal from representatives of younger groups was that, before moving on to philosophy and politics, what Rodolfo claimed as a well-digested expertise had to be communicated, shared, and learned across the network. In other words, GAS seedlings did not know how to organize the distribution of a truck-full of oranges to a network of fifteen to twenty families. Preparations had to be made and routinized, such as securing a parking space, coordinating volunteers to download the cargo, having a safe and clean (and possibly free) storage space (a cellar, a garage, or a shop's depository). Not to speak of, how to coordinate orders by typology and quantities, negotiate the price, settle payments, keep track of invoices and receipts, and of course arrange for a clear date, time, and place for the delivery.

This example shows how within gasista experience questions of practice precede, inform, and literally unpack wider political and epistemic strategies. Figuring out how to deliver oranges from a farm in southern Italy to a Bergamasque family a thousand miles away, for instance, is the way through which that particular economic circuit can be liberated from a mafia-ridden distribution chain. This may sound radical, but it finds grounding in the increasing evidence of the economic ramifications of the mafia at all levels and in every region of Italy. Journalists and administrators, for instance, have denounced how the Milan area is ripe with money-laundering activities, to the point that a municipal anti-mafia committee was appointed by Milan's mayor in February 2012.[5] Retail chains and even banks may reintroduce money gained from criminal activities of various types of mafia such as the 'ndrangheta from Calabria in the respectable financial circuit. Since their aim is not to make a profit but rather to launder illegal capital, these enterprises can even afford to run a loss. Specifically, the Sicilian mafia historically grew with agricultural monocultures, and mafia infiltrations in lemon cultivations are documented since the 1870s (Rizzo 2011). Current-day mafia activities span from the importation of illegal immigrants to exploit them in fields and greenhouses, to the disposal of toxic waste in agricultural lands (so that profit is made twice: by the mafia-owned waste disposal agency and by the mafia-owned crops that grow on it). Anthropologist Naor Ben-Yehoyada has identified a seamless connection between the Sicilian fishermen fleet and mafia-sponsored illegal immigration by way of shipwreck-and-rescue at sea. In other words, some of the rescues would be controlled by the mafia in exchange for providing cheap labor for greenhouses and crop fields. This is just one of the informal ways in which borders between northern Africa and southern Italy remain porous (Ben-Yehoyada 2011, 2012).

The Italian Federation of Agricultural Workers (a section of the national trade union CGIL) recently produced the first white book on "agro-mafie" (FLAI 2012). The report analyzes mafia infiltrations in agribusiness all over Italy and estimates that agro-mafia business turns over between 12 and 17 billion Euro (between 5 and 10% of the entire estimated mafia-led economy). Mafia rackets control the entire food supply chain, from workers' recruitment to logistics and distribution; this includes significant sales of fake "Made in Italy" foodstuffs and the recruitment of slave-like labor (an estimated 400,000 workers) through the *caporalato*—that is, local bosses that recruit teams of day workers. Because of this, farming cooperatives that work the lands expropriated from mafia clans struggle to find access to distribution networks (Forno and Gunnarson 2010, Forno 2011a). Gaining direct access to dedicated customers is a condition of survival for these producers. Evidence of the active search for these kinds of direct transactions are the many letters that solidarity purchase groups receive from agricultural cooperatives and family farmers, both at national and at local level. In my own group, we received letters from an inmates' cooperative in Palermo, Dolci Evasioni (Sweet Evasions), from a local, newly established coffee house, from a youth agricultural cooperative in Abruzzo, and so on. The temptation was to say yes to everyone, but some of us reminded the group that "there's an 'S' in GAS, and we should know who we are being solidarious with." Others were more matter of fact and discussed price and quality first.

The networking process of solidarity purchase groups met the need to consolidate more knowledge and concerted strategies about the phenomena I have just explained. Any gasista would know that the group buys oranges from Sicily in solidarity with southern farmers, but knowing exactly how this solidarity can reengineer supply chains and how this may break up the flow of corruption and crime is another thing. Not all gasistas have this militant understanding of their own practice. Districts and networks of solidarity economy aim precisely to enable a reciprocal encounter between critical consumers and virtuous producers to achieve the organization of another economy. One significant example is Sbarchinpiazza—literally "Dropping the anchor in the square," an itinerant sale of Sicilian oranges that was organized in 2012 by RESSUD, the Network of Solidarity Economy of the South, in collaboration with the Sicilian agricultural consortium Arcipelago Siqilyah. This network of orange growers working in partnership with solidarity purchase groups hosted orange fairs in about twenty towns in northern and central Italy. The point of holding a public market instead of just unloading trucks for gasistas was to make these transactions visible and to increase their appeal to a larger public. At the same time, the special liaison between GAS and orange producers was forefronted: only producers already known to local solidarity purchase groups could participate in the fair. This exclusiveness may sound elitist but was in fact predicated on the trusted relationship that ensues between known partners in a shared enterprise.

For the gasistas involved in the orange "landings," co-producing oranges meant enabling the cooperatives working on mafia-confiscated lands to tend their orange groves, knowing in advance that their crops will be sold at an agreed-upon price with trusted buyers. By learning how to organize and manage a short supply chain, GAS thus learn to rethink the fundamentals of economic life through practice, reweaving social aspects into the process. This is a puzzling activity to categorize, since we have learned to equate economy with the market and the laws of the latter with an automatic adjustment to demand and supply. Sbarchinpiazza is one example of how GAS offer a neutral meeting ground to different types of political activism, of economic subjectivities, and of social aspirations that would otherwise not necessarily intersect in fruitful ways. Environmentalists, anti-mafia activists, and defenders of place-based foods come together in GAS on the basis of the shared basic need of provisioning for oneself and one's families on a different footing than a flawed economic orthodoxy. These circuits of alternative provisioning work as second-order networks. For example, Francesca Forno and Karina Gunnarsson (2010, 2011) maintain that, in the case of anti-mafia political consumerism, environmental, political, and social justice activists innovate each other's epistemic and political repertoires, by contextualizing their agenda vis-à-vis the concrete tasks of selling oranges or promoting mafia-free shops. Similarly, Berardino Palumbo notes how the ritual framework of religious festivities in Palermo (such as hanging white sheets outside one's windows on occasion of Corpus Domini processions) was appropriated by a grassroots network of women one month after the assassination of magistrate Giovanni Falcone in 1992 (2009: 407–419). The women shifted and adapted the performative prescriptions of the ritual to a powerful mise-en-scéne of collective anti-mafia dissent.

Both examples demonstrate the flexibility of repertoires in novel but grounded contexts of practice. I will return in detail to the enterprise of the orange landings in the next chapter as one of the significant networking projects of Bergamo's solidarity purchase groups. For the moment, I wish to stress that this learning experience is conducted from the bottom up and that this has important implications on what is learned, how, and by whom, as I will highlight in the next section.

THE GENDER OF GASISTAS

In Chapter 4, I recount in detail the birth of the network ReteGasBergamo: its internal dynamics, successes, and shortcomings. Here, I wish to focus on gasistas' individual commitments and subjectivities, whether through their engagement in solidarity purchase groups or in a network's working group. My thesis is that we may think of GAS as groups of collaborative pedagogy. They are collective laboratories in which GAS members are resocialized into what were common skills for the average Italian family just up to two generations ago: seasonality, cooking from mostly raw or unprocessed foodstuffs, and the manual dexterity and planning capacities that these require. Through family mutualism, alternative provisioning reconnects networks of lower middle-class, but well-educated (mostly) women with smallholders' agriculture, which still employed 42 percent of the Italian population as late as the 1950s.

It is sometimes a visceral reconnection, as younger women in particular have to remember or acquire anew unfamiliar skills, such as how to carve a whole, raw chicken to prepare it for roasting, mimicking what little can be remembered from observing our own mothers. There was a lot of giggling and camaraderie at my GAS meeting after an organic and free-range breeder offered us the opportunity to "plant" chicks which would then be delivered full-grown in three months. We tried out the experiment only to discover that the chickens were delivered free of feathers and entrails but still complete with head and feet—as was common when one bought poultry at a butcher shop or at the market only twenty years ago. Chicken is now usually sold in ready-made cuts in a supermarket. At the following meeting, we discussed the outcome of the experiment. For some, the chicken were "just too big" or "tasty, but hardy." But especially expressed was, "Did you remember how to cut it up?!"

Regaining homesteading expertise was clearly a gendered endeavor, and my further experience with the Mapping Group of the newly born ReteGas-Bergamo made that even clearer. I became a volunteering member of the Mapping Group when ReteGasBergamo was set up in September 2009. Its mission was to map current GAS providers and to recruit new providers among local smallholders. In our first meeting, on November 9, 2009, of the nine people self-designated to work in this group, only two (including me) were women. We made an initial, sketchy list of the most common producers that our respective GAS bought from. When it was the time to discuss detergents, it became clear that most GAS bought from a certified organic firm in Reggio Emilia, some 300 miles away, and that "the women were not happy" with the wash. Alternative forms of detergents were discussed, but on the effectiveness of their washing power I was told to ask them. The only other woman in the group gave me three names of products, stating that they ranged in price between 20 and 60 Euro and would last for up to sixty washes. She could also tell me precisely where to go and buy them. Just to reinforce stereotypes about silently hardworking women, in the following two years I found that the only volunteers to keep minutes, round up e-mails, and convene the group were myself and this other woman, until she gave up when she became heavily pregnant with her third child.

Concerns have been raised about the gender inequalities that the literature on alternative food networks may be glossing over (Parasecoli 2010), as alternative provisioning appears as a kind of activism that denotes in general a middle-class economic status and narrow, individualistic, and localist interests. In fact, in my ethnographic experience, gasistas' renewed focus on short food chains and on a direct connection between consumers and producers did support a turn to the local and to the family as a reference point for constructing meaning and identity. To my knowledge, it does not seem that the GAS movement is taking into consideration as a problematic issue the gendered practices of its membership. Recursively, there are invitations to gender-balance the compositions of steering committees and working groups so that it does not look like a few men are leading a base of women. But the movement is still far from accepting that gender inequality may well be one of the fundamental issues that needs to be focused on, as part of their interest in justice and solidarity.

Interviewed about the current problem areas of alternative provisioning in Bergamo, Luisa, one of the current members of the service group of ReteGasBergamo—which includes volunteer gasistas to coordinate the leadership of the network—underlined communication but also stimulating participation beyond the mere provisioning aspect. She also stressed the fact that most of the female volunteers are working parents who have to balance time-investment in GAS activism with a job, the schooling of the children, and family logistics. In general, the gender balance of the GAS (predominantly female) and of the various steering and ad hoc working groups (predominantly male) seems to suggest a divide between a female base devoted to the provisioning practice—which would be their everyday task anyway—and a predominantly male leadership that theorizes and strategizes about more comprehensive goals and network-enhancement. This is compatible with the kind of "performance" (Butler 1994) that is commonly expected of male and female practitioners at all levels in Italy—where politics, academia, and the economy are largely male-dominated.[6] In particular, providing and preparing food in Italian society is traditionally a female activity that is associated with family ties, practical knowledge, and the power of intimacy (Counihan 1999).

Certainly, prescribed gendered spaces and skills, such as the kitchen and cooking, also reserve for female practitioners what Donna Haraway has called "the privilege of partial perspectives" (1991). In the average Italian family, it is ultimately up to women *how* to weave the networks and to manage the time-scape of food provisioning—which is why it is women who mostly attend GAS meetings. It was again mostly women who self-appointed themselves as household heads and filled in the online questionnaire about GAS membership that CORES carried out in 2011 and 2012 at Bergamo University. In 70 percent of the cases, in fact, it was women who "carried out most of GAS-related activities." As requested in the survey, they were therefore required to respond to it, as they had the necessary information. At the base of GAS provisioning, we find female foraging, neighbors' relationality, and the "gift of reciprocity" (Hahn 2006). Within the female base of the GAS movement, pragmatic solutions are found to a general shortage of time. Time banks appear as a formalized version of a widespread informal practice that I would call "looking after your neighbor while you look after yourself." Many a time, in my two years of active GAS participation, I forgot to place my own orders, and there was another woman who either bothered to give me a call ("I wonder if you were interested in the Parmesan we are going to get in two weeks") or simply placed the order on my behalf and called me afterward to say that the stuff was there, if I cared to go and collect it; otherwise, they would keep it and pay for it or find someone else interested. The same kind of informal but solicitous care would take the form of other impromptu offers: this is a phone call I received from an elder member of the GAS, Diana:

> I have just been to see the breeder to collect the butchered meat. He says he has a lot of unwanted cuts leftover that no one has claimed. He gave me a whole cow liver for free. Do you like liver? If you do I'll have it ready sliced for when your husband comes to pick up your steaks...I am keeping the tongue for myself because I know that you young chicks don't know what to do with cow's tongue.

My fellow gasista was making a number of assumptions based on memory, taste, and motherhood. Diana's perception of my age, marital situation, and professional engagements allowed her to guess a number of (right) intuitions: that I had forgotten to order my Parmesan; that I had eaten liver in the past and would like to eat it again; that, considering its disappearance from the ready-made cuts that large distribution chains now make available to hurried customers, I had not bought liver in a long time. These were highly gendered guesses: the assumption that I would be the one who cared about providing high-quality, if slightly exotic cow liver to the family table, for instance. Yet her sensibility did not accommodate the opportunity of giving a call to my husband about it. After all, I was the one she met at the GAS meetings, but, unlike other families, my husband was the one who often went to collect the orders. Modernity (or postmodernity) and the commodification of provisioning had resulted in a complex balance of senses and sensibilities, in which Diana—a mother of two and a grandmother, a retired housewife, and an activist in the local Time Bank—would be best placed to do the guesswork, the relational weaving, and the repairing. I remember how we used to eat cow liver and tongue regularly as a child, with radish. "Liver is good for you; it's full of iron," said my father. Lost skills and cherished memories mixed in the spongy sweetness of that liver.[7]

Lidia Marte (2007) has proposed "foodmaps [as a] tool to trace gendered boundaries" of private/public spaces among working-class immigrant communities in the United States, showing how migrant women negotiate familiar sense-scapes in alien spaces. Likewise, the ethnography of provisioning activism exposes the nitty-gritty of alternative networks as inevitably rooted in the webs of relations and the contradictions of the society that expresses them. This is especially because provisioning regards food as well as other everyday items of reproductive and care work that have never ceased to be the task of women in Italian society, despite the fast transition to an indus-trial, and then a postindustrial, economy (Counihan 1999). In this case, very local cultures of taste work as mediators of meaning, helping women to make sense of what they wish to be a transformative experience while abiding by their prescribed roles of providers for the family. Chandra Mohanty (1997) has focused on women's real opportunities for reciprocal and cross-class solidar-ity in grassroots activities. According to Mohanty and Biddy Martin's seminal essay "Feminist Politics: What's Home Got to Do With It?," the importance of the politics of solidarity lies in women's capacity to reappropriate the no-tions of home and communities in ways that do not hand them over to con-servative political appropriation, especially considering the way in which their identities are societally molded around the concept and experience of home. They thus insist on "our responsibility for remapping boundaries and renego-tiating connections" (Martin and Mohanty 1986: 197). The gasista guess-work amounted to female solidarity and reciprocal assistance, bridging e-mail blackouts and lapses in provisioning plans. It foregrounded shared sensorial landscapes (including the sweetness of liver and the rancidness of old olive oil). It also projected a common, often female, sensorium onto a political di-mension, in which sharing sensibilities meant enabling each other to experi-ment new provisioning circuits.

These experimentations included creative economic formulas for solidar-ity. These became particularly apparent after the Tomasoni case mentioned in Chapter 2 (the dairy firm that was salvaged from bankruptcy by a network of solidarity purchase groups). In particular, they proliferated following the two earthquakes that shook L'Aquila in 2009 and Modena in 2012. In these cases, solidarity took the pragmatic form of buying damaged produce for the quaked Parmesan dairies and Christmas packages from Abruzzese farmers. With limited local knowledge of the US experience of CSA or of the French AMAP, these formulas were largely improvised. They were tried out case by case on the spur of an individual's proposal, contacts, or previous experience. For instance, the idea of acquiring Christmas gift packages from Abruzzese farmers came to ReteGasBergamo from Luisa—the engineer who complained about having to adjust her children's timetable to the demands of GAS activism and vice versa. After a summer holiday spent in an ecotour-ist farm in Abruzzo—which had been affected by the 2009 earthquake—in 2010 she circulated and promoted a list of Christmas items (such as cheese, salami, and preserves) that could be acquired from a network of Abruzzese farms. The Christmas gift list was not a project of her own invention but was sponsored by the local Catholic association and the agricultural park. It would have never made it to the GAS network e-mail list in Bergamo without her per-sonal coordination, though. The project raised a total of 11,000 Euro and was one of the first and most significant collective actions of ReteGasBergamo.

It then became part of the Bergamasque GAS standard purchases in 2011. Ideas and projects on how to assist the post-quake areas continued to flow through the network mailing list. In June 2012, for example, summer camps were being advertised for volunteer labor to rebuild a school in Emilia-Romagna. The school, gravely damaged the previous May, was an agricultural training college. The initiative was coordinated by an NGO based in Bologna, but the call was travelling across Italy through solidarity economy networks' mailing lists.

The extent and variety of gasistas' initiatives of this kind illuminate how GAS activism is more than the collective purchase of high-quality foods at a competitive price that is also rewarding for the producers. In fact, the latter would be a reductive description of what actually goes on. At least in the gasistas' intentions, economic motivation co-exists with social and cultural practice. In fact, the GAS groups I interacted with put every effort into avoiding collective purchase becoming a functional and perfunctory act. There would be many ways in which GAS activity could be streamlined, the most obvious of all being collecting orders online through a website, but the preferences expressed at the monthly meetings of my own GAS, for instance, were outspokenly in favor of maintaining face-to-face contact, first of all among members of the same group and ideally with all the producers, too. ICT solutions do exist.[8] In my research experience in the Bergamo area, ICT tools were used to carry out surveys across the network, to check if there was enough demand for first-time orders to new providers. Also, questionnaires for self-evaluation were drafted by ReteGasBergamo and put online so that new producers could propose their services to the network by filling them out and answer a first few crucial questions about what they produced (crops and quantities), how (organic or not), where (location), and when (seasonality). For all the rest, ICT tools were not preferred. In my own GAS meetings, the reasons given were that "one does not want to spend the day online" and that, precisely, the point about adhering to a GAS was to link producers and consumers as much as possible directly and that meant face-to-face.

The CORES report on GAS activity in the Bergamo area confirmed such tempered use of the Internet. Almost 98 percent of the Bergamo solidarity purchase groups interviewed in the Bergamo area hold regular meetings and have internal mailing lists. Facebook is not used by any GAS group, which reminds us of the average age of Bergamo's gasistas: less than 7 percent are aged below 29, another 7 percent is older than 56, and about 38 percent are over 45. The fact that GAS sociality and decision-making continues to be grounded in face-to-face meetings and in e-mail messages shows how ICT tools are instrumental to the run of the mill activities (no one uses the telephone as a means of communication within the group), but they definitely have an ancillary role to actual meetings (Osservatorio CORES 2013). This clearly demarcates GAS practice as different from a digital social network. It also clearly distinguishes GAS from commercial networks that exist for the promotion and distribution of organic produce or of zero-mile foods. In sum, if the idea of GAS as a social movement evokes young students demonstrating and the stereotype of GAS as an alternative food network conjures up middle-class foodies, we should keep in mind that the average portrait of the gasista is that of a middle-aged woman with children, going to meetings.

While face-to-face interaction is preferred, it is not always festive or leisurely. Deliberation is lengthy and time-consuming. From the point of view of gasistas, in fact, liaising directly and collectively with all the producers is burdensome. While in general every GAS member has the task of liaising with one particular producer, many take more as the list of products bought by a GAS is potentially infinite—and it is the ambition of the most radical gasistas that the list should cover all of the purchase needs of the members, thus shifting all of their economic transactions away from the anonymous capitalist market. On average, a gasista's shopping list includes weekly delivered vegetables and fruit from one or more local farmers or farming cooperatives and seasonal crops such as berries or oranges, and their naturally processed outcomes such as juices, jams, and purée, as well as wine, dairy products, meat, olive oil, rice, and pasta. It can also include Fair Trade products bought collectively at a discount (especially coffee, cocoa, chocolate, tea, and spices), ornamental plants, seedlings and garden seeds, fresh fish, environmentally friendly cleaning products and toiletries, non–animal tested cosmetics, recyclable diapers and sanitary pads, toilet paper made of recycled paper, clothes made of unbleached, natural fabric, handmade shoes, handcrafted, plastic-free items such as kitchen utensils and pottery, and so on.

First-time providers are visited and monitored and feedback is given to them on the products. The group may sometimes have specific requests, such as assorting vegetables and fruit in ready-made family baskets, or preferences for specific cuts of meat. Certain providers become particularly cherished because they are available to put in the extra time to prepare personalized baskets or crates with different orders for each family. Other producers are less keen to do this and impose a sample delivery of identical crates, containing a balanced sample of the produce available from the fields that week. Some farmers balance out fresh produce from their own fields with ad hoc orders from other providers, typically organic farming cooperatives that may have a wider palette of produce on offer. Lack of diversity and quality of fresh produce is an issue, especially in the winter. For all the product referents, liaising with the producers means gathering orders and product feedback, managing payments and deliveries, negotiating prices and amendments. The group coordinator is a point of reference for all other members: she calls the assembly, monitors that each member has a task and fulfills it, and manages the e-mail list. It is a delicate task, requiring precision and sensibility.

Unsurprisingly then, gasistas' self-training focuses not only on technical expertise (such as cooking fresh and seasonal foods or agronomic knowledge) but also on relational expertise.

Food activists' capacity for self- and peer-help parallels their eagerness for independent scientific expertise and for practical training, for instance, in organic farming, recycling, or even network analysis: to better learn about their own network dynamics. One learns a lot as a gasista, not only about seasonality but also about pricing and issues of quality certification. While concern about food quality is mentioned as one of the primary motivations for joining a GAS group in the CORES survey of Bergamo's gasistas, about 40 percent of them maintain that in time, as a result of their GAS membership, they introduced much more comprehensive changes than just a quality improvement in the foods they buy: these include new practices such as bread baking, keeping a garden patch, or avoiding the supermarket (Osservatorio CORES 2013).

In turn, these changes called for further exchanges of information and collaboration within the group (through the exchange of recipes, of readings, or of tips about trustworthy providers). An apt example regards organic and Fair Trade certification. According to the CORES questionnaire, only about 19 percent of gasistas trust organic food certification, while 41 percent trust Fair Trade certification (Table 3.1). Gasistas have a fairly good knowledge of certification logos. The organic certification logo was identified correctly by 65 percent, the Fair Trade logo by 53 percent, and the Forest Stewardship Council logo by 57 percent of interviewees (Osservatorio CORES 2013) (see Table 3.2).

As a benchmark, in a survey on the styles of consumption of the average Bergamasque family (Forno and Salvi 2012: 21), about 60 percent of

Table 3.1   Trust in Certifications amongst Bergamo gasistas. Credit: Osservatorio CORES 2013.

		A lot	Enough	Little or None	Missing	Total
Organic Products	N	56	192	42	9	299
	%	19,3	66,2	14,4		100
Fair Trade Products	N	120	155	15	9	299
	%	41,4	53,4	5,2		100

Table 3.2   Logo Recognition amongst Bergamo gasistas. Credit: Osservatorio CORES 2013.

		Correct	Wrong	Don't know	Missing	Total
Organic Certification	N	189	39	63	8	299
	%	64,9	13,4	21,6		100
Fair Trade CTM	N	153	1	135	10	299
	%	52,9	0,3	46,7		100
Forest Stewardship Council	N	166	14	110	9	299
	%	57,2	4,8	37,9		100

interviewees claimed that they did not know the Fair Trade logo (and a further 25% got it wrong when asked to recognize it) nor the organic certification logo (and a further 10% got it wrong). Nevertheless, 77 percent of interviewees claimed that they had a high degree of trust in organic certification. Their trust, therefore, did not seem to be grounded in actual knowledge, not even of the logos that signal organic certification on the product package. On the other hand, GAS prefer direct knowledge of the producers to certification systems, even though they seem to be better informed about them. In general, having organic certification is not a prerequisite for a farm to provide GAS. When asked what are the most essential GAS requirements, the statements most adhered to were: "GAS should buy only from producers who respect workers' rights" (80%) and "GAS should only buy from producers who present regular tax documentation" (69%); meanwhile, the response "GAS should only buy certified organic products" scored last (12%).

Possible alternatives to the institutionalization of trust through certification of standards were discussed in the 2010 GAS assembly in Osnago under the rubric of "food sovereignty," whose working group I took part in. After a long incubation period, three districts of solidarity economy in Lombardy have begun supporting self-certification among small farmers providing GAS. In lieu of institutional certification, participatory guarantee systems that involve both farmers and representatives of the consumer networks are being negotiated, identifying a viable protocol for converting to organic or for keeping pesticides at a minimum in every particular case.[9] The toxicity of postindustrial grounds, the loss of fertility of fields that have been intensively farmed for decades, the lack of phosphorus and potassium in organic products that have been grown on insufficiently prepared soil, and landgrabbing by large-scale certified organic agribusinesses are all concerns of these actors. The idea of a participatory guarantee system should take into account viable and local solutions to usually compromised starting points, such as nitrogen pollution in the soil and water from excessively fed cattle grazing the land or infiltrations of industrial toxins in water collection points. Rather than applying an abstract evaluation grid in the name of audit-like accountabilities, GAS activists prefer to invite transparency from the producers about their actual hurdles so that a protocol and a roadmap can be agreed upon collaboratively. From the point of view of the producers, though, GAS customers can be a real headache, as I wish to illustrate in the next section.

THE PRODUCER'S POINT OF VIEW

As he turned down an invitation to a GAS-organized workshop on short supply chains in Milan, a well-known provider from the model farm Pond Farmstead (a pseudonym) noted, in a very elegant prose, "Unfortunately I have to decline participating in your round table, as I am tied down to my ecotourist activities here on the farm at weekends, and I am in no position to delegate my specific expertise to others. I apologize for the late response, due to the sudden crowding of my September engagements."[10]

He added:

I would have very much liked to participate in the meeting, especially because over the last months I had many occasions to reflect with other producers on the complexity of our valuable relationship with the Solidarity Purchase Groups: I have the impression that we still have a long path ahead of us if we wish to build a solidarity economy that really is mutual and reciprocal, with equal accountability on both sides on each other's engagement. In other words it seems to me that often a relationship that is still in the making is declared winning and all problems solved. A lot is written about our successes and little about the difficulties.[11]

This successful solidarity economy entrepreneur was voicing his caveats while turning down the organizers' invitation to one of the best-known public events of the so-called other economy, a grassroots conference on sustainability, practice and politics, where he would have been highly profiled as a speaker. His farm in fact had a long-standing relationship with the network of Milan's solidarity purchase groups, south Milan's agricultural park, and the concomitant project of a rural district of solidarity economy.

What kind of complexity was he hinting at in the GAS-producers relationships? The relationship between producers and gasistas is, at least in the gasistas' intentions, straightforward. The GAS practice of visiting the provider's farm plays a key role in selecting producers and in orienting the group's decisions on what is acceptable as solidarity-based food (maybe not organic but local, or maybe not local but mafia-free and obtained with respect of animal welfare, workers' rights, etc.). Every gasista liaises with a producer. Occasionally GAS groups have to actively look for providers that are close enough and virtuous enough. This is the main function of networks of GAS groups, which share information about their trusted producers, their previous experiences, and any complaints about specific providers. First-time providers are contacted (or, increasingly, since the GAS phenomenon has gained exposure in the media, propose themselves via e-mail, letters, etc.). Then they receive one or more visits, and finally a brief report is circulated about them with facts about crops availability, price, and quantities. After a trial order, the group discusses how expectations were met, if there were any logistic glitches, and so on. Decision-making in the meetings is of paramount importance: each group is sovereign, and after debating, deliberation is collective. After passing the group evaluation, the relationship with the provider becomes a standing transaction—though continuously monitored, and occasionally renegotiated.

The relationship with providers is considered as one of ongoing support. For instance, at GAS meetings one would hear that the cow breeder who butchers the group's meat has just opened an ecotourist restaurant serving meat, dairy, and vegetables from the farm—and maybe organize a dinner there. Or, gasistas would be warmly invited by the wine-provider to participate in the grape-harvesting season in the vineyard of a local cooperative, which employs recovering addicts. Or one would encounter one's provider at farmers' markets and recommend his or her products to friends and family. There is so doubt that, especially at a time of environmental and financial crisis, when the crop delivery is often endangered by frequently extreme weather (drought followed by flooding for instance), and when large distribution buying prices are increasingly compressed, having a trusted networks of customers in one or more solidarity purchase groups is a viable strategy for farmers. This is why GAS coordinators, especially when their name is publicly disclosed through the GAS websites, increasingly receive commercial propositions both from local and more distant farmers, agricultural cooperatives, or artisanal food producers: during the last six months of my fieldwork in Bergamo, we received and discussed at least a couple of them at every monthly meeting.

Nevertheless, as the opening testimony from the Milanese farmer brings to the fore, the relationship between providers and purchasers (however solidarity-driven) is open to ambivalences, and an ethnographic insight into peasant entrepreneurship, as well as an understanding of the gasistas' viewpoints, adds complexity to an otherwise feel-good scenario. Alternative provisioning networks have been critiqued for falling short of the expectation of developing into a full-fledged "civic agriculture" (DeLind 1999, 2002) that promotes citizenship and environmentalism, superseding market-based models of economic behavior. Instead, they have developed an "economy of affect" that nurtures common ties to place and locality, both in rural and urban settings. For Lucy Jarosz (2008), alternative provisioning networks are typical of a new type of merger between city and country—a metropolitan phenomenon, in fact, that would set new social expectations on farmers, beyond their commitment to sustainable food production. One of these requests would be precisely that of a new type of spatial and relational proximity to their customers, through participative retail venues such as farmers' markets. This would be a novel aspect of a rural restructuring that is part of urbanization and gentrification, resulting in an uneven power balance within the network, privileging some producers and further marginalizing others.

This producer's point of view and my ethnographic experience confirms that alternative provisioning may and does introduce elements of further stress to producers. An increased demand for seasonal and organic produce is difficult to meet. Requests can be particular: we do expect to bring to the table a wider palette of produce than what is in fact available in the fields at any one time. When butchering a cow, everyone would have wanted steaks, not ribs, stew, or mince. Consumers, too, though have to deal with sometimes overwhelming numbers of applications from self-proposed providers, which in turn need to be approached with a clear and competent assessment. How to choose between more than one possible producer is often a thorny issue for gasistas: shall we privilege the local over the organic; the self-certified over the certified; fresh conversions to established organic farmers? Trying to answer these dilemmas, GAS activists do helps farmers identify a variety of critical points and collaboratively seek solutions—for instance, by setting up especially rewarding protected markets and by participating in the entrepreneurial risks by guaranteeing to buy out crops. In the Bergamo area, in fact, there are many difficulties among small-scale producers in adopting more sustainable farming strategies—such as low-impact environmental management, organic farming, the introduction of energy-saving technologies, the reduction of transport and packaging, or the use of alternative energy sources.

Despite the effort put in to connecting and co-producing, consumer–producer communication is an issue. First, the quality of the crops, and virtuousness of the management, prove difficult to discern at first sight, even during an on-site visit. Second, both the solidarity of the purchasers and the virtuousness of the producers are open to a certain degree of performativity. To elaborate on the first point, one should keep in mind that each individual solidarity purchase group frequently lacks the expertise or the training to be able to see with its own eyes what's actually going on in the fields or in the shed of the providers it works with. In some of the outings I participated in, the visitors had to be told which cultivation was which. Choice of nonorganic fodder or recourse to the occasional use of pesticide was always motivated on technical grounds that the GAS members could not dispute. The gasistas' blindness in the face of actual agricultural and food-manufacturing practice was apparent and should not be surprising. I refer to my own notion of skilled vision (Grasseni 2011a, 2012b; see also Faeta 2011) to recall how knowing what to see in what one is looking at is a learned ability, often the result of a long apprenticeship. Skilled vision characterizes communities of practitioners that share common tools, techniques, processes, and the corresponding aesthetic and moral imaginaries. Thus, when gasistas visit farms, the fields' position and exposure, the crop varieties, the quality of plant growth, soil aridity, and so on were largely lost on our untrained eye and had to be patiently explained to us (Figure 3.1).

The difficulty and vagaries of co-production became apparent to me as I became more engaged with a working group established by ReteGasBergamo,

Figure 3.1   A farmer shows us a fruit orchard suffering from lack of water after an arid winter season. Photo by Cristina Grasseni.

in the fall of 2009, as I recount in the previous section. The working group on mapping and liaising with the producers (known as the Mapping Group) was put in charge of mapping who exactly were the producers providing each GAS in the network and successively establishing new contacts with local farmers and breeders to widen the scope of our provisioning network. This was a felt necessity, and in fact our working group was one of the most numerous. Solidarity purchase groups, as they grew exponentially in number, simply could not find enough trusted producers and would sometimes discover that another GAS had beat them to securing, for instance, oranges from the same Sicilian farmer. There was talk of shady businesses—the possibility that trusted orange growers might begin selling intensively grown produce as their own, for instance. Also, the concept of food sovereignty was beginning to be interpreted in terms of preferring the closest producers, as this would solve two problems at once: transparency and sustainability.

The irony of the situation dawned on me on an early February morning in 2011 when a farmer, who had probably got up around 5 a.m. to milk his cows, found the time to meet us at 7 a.m. in his fields in order to deliver us the last remaining potatoes from his first almost-organic crop, which had only received one pesticide treatment against the parasitic insect *Leptinotarsa decemlineata,* and to make negotiations for the next round. We agreed to buy out the remaining yellow and red potatoes at 80 cents per kilogram (roughly the equivalent of Peapod's retail price for red potatoes in 2012[12]). We agreed to send out a call to other GAS to join in and make a collective order for higher quantities for the end of summer 2012. We negotiated a higher price (1 Euro per kg) to convince Gabriele, the farmer, to hold back as much as possible from using pesticides and to make it such that the crop could be delivered to the GAS families in 10-kilo installments between the end of the summer and over fall and winter, keeping the potatoes stored in a cellar on the farm's premises.

Then, to our surprise and delight, he asked us if we were interested in selecting a plot that he would seed in March for untreated maize in order to deliver us corn flour the following winter. He knew that Slow Food activists were engaged in reviving the use of flour from a local variety of red maize, which an elderly peasant farmer had preserved without crossbreeding in a Bergamasque valley. Slow Food restaurants in the area were offering maize-based dishes using this exotic *mais rostrato rosso.* The local press had praised this successful reconstruction of an organic and short supply chain food. In fact, already in 2010 the farmer who had been growing the maize had become a provider of the GAS network, with an experimental first collective order of organically grown potatoes (which he rotated with his red maize). Now Gabriele volunteered the information that he too regularly rotates potatoes and maize crops and offered to plant the much-sought-after typical red maize, *rostrato rosso* (roughly translatable as "red hooked" maize). In his good will, he misspelled the name as *nostrano rosso* (literally "our own red" maize). It was a moment of understated clarification, for all of us present, about the reciprocal work of performance and repositioning that was going on among us.

First, the same producers were being scouted by Slow Food activists and gasistas. This was no surprise, and in fact I participated in the end-of-year meeting in early 2010 of the *condotta* Slow Food Valli Orobiche that rediscovered red maize in the Seriana Valley, specifically in Rovetta (hence the same *mais di Rovetta* for *rostrato rosso*). The group's collaboration with the National Institute for Cereal Farming, the ageing farmer, and a network of Slow Food restaurants guaranteed that red maize flour would become a fixture in local menus and would gain notoriety as a typical food. This recuperation of a local cultivar for a zero-mile market was celebrated by Slow Food and was a personal success of the head of the Charter, a motivated school teacher and an inspired leader who then moved on to become governor of Slow Food for Lombardy. Second, this convergence enacted a certain degree of social performance on the part of this particular GAS provider. Rachel Black discusses the meaning of the term *nostrano* in her ethnography of the fresh-food market of Porta Palazzo in Turin. Quoting also Melissa Caldwell's (2002) analysis of similar terms and their appropriation in local discourse in Russian, she stresses its ethnic undertones as a place-based food (Black 2012: 151). By probably inadvertently pronouncing a botanical variety's name (*rostrato rosso*) as "our own," the farmer was implicitly paying homage to his own interpretation of the GAS agenda as one of relocalizing food provisioning—which he probably equated with that of Slow Food—but adding a localist twist of his own. After we all scuttled out to begin our own day jobs, we did in fact send out a call to the GAS network to join in and ordered Gabriele's organic maize flour, which was ground at an organic mill, for 2.50 Euro a kilo (Figure 3.2). On that same evening, some of our gasista equivalents would likely meet the same breeder/farmer-turned-host at his ecotourism restaurant, where his wife cooks and his daughter helps serving tables. Rather than convivial co-production, this seemed like a twenty-hour, round-the-clock job for Gabriele.

The forms of co-production that GAS encourage between responsible consumers and local producers proved to be exacting for both parties and

Figure 3.2 An activist with a corn cob produced at an ecotourist farm and restaurant. Photo by Cristina Grasseni.

sometimes invited the performance of mutually expected stereotypes. However, as shown in this chapter, the high prices exacted for an often not pristine quality provision were topics of soul-searching debates. Were we gullible prey of cunning peasants—well-rehearsed in the prescribed performance of the underdog? During our on-site visits to farmers, breeders, and gardeners, the attitude was sometimes of simplification: their work was presented as simple, natural, and straightforward—when it obviously was not to us. Chemical treatments, compost balancing, time-lapses between seeding and cropping, composition of the fodder, provenance of the fattening animals were all presented as matter-of-fact ready-made processes, when we were expecting to unpack each and every one of them, though obviously lacking both the expertise and the experience to pronounce a final word on them.

A symptom of the disproportionate expectations that GAS activism elicited was also noticeable in the remarks of the director of the agricultural park who was accompanying us on our farm visit: "The Parco dei Colli covers about 150 kilometers of paths, 20 percent of which are on private land, and I have no waged laborer to deploy to their maintenance...Everything is soft money. We have a project to monitor the crows and make a census of them but not to tend the woods." As I listened, I considered the implicit hope to find in us gasistas a pool of volunteer wood-keepers, but I knew that we were strung up for time, exhausted by evening meetings (of the GAS proper, of the GAS network, of the Time Bank, of the GAS working group on mapping the producers, etc.) and that we would not be the best candidates for the job.

The potentially disastrous effects of GAS conversions were felt in the winter of 2009/10 when, after the on-site visit to three farmers at the close-by agricultural park, one of them accepted to cultivate a field organically for potatoes. The field had been previously grazed or left fallow. Since the soil was not prepared with manure, when planted with potatoes without fertilizers and pesticides, it produced nothing. A generous price had already been negotiated (1 Euro per kg) and orders had been collected through the network, but the net result of this experiment was that the producer got nothing, at least this time round. Building on this infelicitous experience, the following experiments were followed by the park's agronomist, as part of a project to launch the park's palette of branded local products (mainly potatoes, cheese, and wine), having already worked on another experimental conversion to organic maize and potatoes, which had been adopted as one of the first networked projects of the nascent ReteGasBergamo.

All things considered, by laborious and painstaking trial and error, gasistas were succeeding in making themselves known and available to local producers to co-produce quasi-organic produce, skipping both distributors and certifiers and acknowledging the need for an extra amount of expertise on the ground. This strategy paid off, particularly thanks to the convergence of a radical project—that of reweaving the economy on premises of solidarity and reciprocity—and the pragmatic way in which gasistas and producers went about performing prescribed roles in the market, as buyers and sellers, as well as aligning with a number of other prevalent discourses about locality, identity, and place-based foods. The key phrases used in the project proposal that was sent around to the GAS network were *prodotto di vicinanza* (proximate produce), *rapporto condiviso con i produttori da costruire* (a shared relationship with the producers that has to be built), *prodotto quasi bio* (quasi-organic produce), and *condividere un percorso di qualità* (embarking upon a collaborative path toward higher quality).

As Heather Paxson (2013) shows in the case of the recent renaissance of artisanal cheese-making in the United States, both material "ecologies of production" and motivating "economies of sentiment" are at work here. Paxson details how "some producers frame artisanal food-making not merely as an 'alternative' to industrial production but as a means of 'reterritorializing' the food system by drawing legible, meaningful connections between the taste of a food and its place—and method—of production" (2013). Similarly, gasistas cultivate an aspect of what I have called the reinvention of food—that is, the contemporary revival of traditional foodstuffs at the foot of the Alps (Grasseni 2011a, 2012b). Co-production goes hand in hand, in other words, with relocalization. As the solidarity purchase groups strive to enable local farmers to withstand the many challenges that global agribusiness poses to the sustainability of regional economies, they use co-production to find a language that defines an emergent economic relationship between food producers and consumers locally; a relationship that entails negotiating prices for crops in advance of reaping them, self-certifying conversions to organic farming, and monitoring animal welfare and the farm governance on its own premises.

It was clear to us, as gasistas on a mission to map the producers, that in our meetings with the farmers we were concretely weaving new relationships, enabling them to produce in a safer and nonexploitative way. During the course of two winters, the nascent network ReteGasBergamo divided itself geographically to manage producers on two fronts: the eastern half of GAS continued to support the first and successful experiment in the Seriana Valley, with the organic potatoes, the organic mill, and the autochthonous variety of red maize; the western groups committed to the Parco dei Colli and its recently converted producers, sustaining their projects to progressively convert salad, blueberries, apples, cheese, and salami—starting with Gabriele, the potato farmer and restaurant keeper. A third front toward Lake Lecco and Lake Como was not even opened, as the farmers we contacted were already selling everything to their own GAS! It was encouraging to see that smallholders, breeders, and gardeners did find the time to see us, talked to us, and accept our evocative language. The immediate validation of our action came from rewarding a twelve-cow local breeder with payments of 9 Euro a kilogram for twenty-five kilograms of mixed cuts, rather than having her sell her calves to the butcher for 6 Euro a kilogram of cut meat. In exchange, we asked her to substitute soy-based fodder—which my gasistas friends simply dismissed, "It's all transgenic, don't you know?"—with peas and organic maize, bran, and carob beans.

To the producers we visited, it was explained that GAS aim to be networks of producers and consumers. It was illustrated how GAS members buy as much as they can of their food collectively and directly from farmers, privileging organic and local foods, and how their main motivation in selecting their providers was solidarity, to be understood as respect for the environment, as well as solidarity with one's providers. We soon realized, in our interactions with farmers, breeders, gardeners—but also directors of agricultural and conservation parks, agronomists, restaurant owners, and managers of agricultural cooperatives—that solidarity purchase groups and the agents of food heritagization shared numerous presumptions and lent themselves to common agendas (Grasseni 2011a, see Chapter 2) as they focused on food as a shared need, a pivot for change, and a cultural resource. Distinct social milieus were involved in this reinvention: the educated but not affluent gasistas, the discriminating Slow Foodies, and the entrepreneurial smallholders. They all shared, though, a discourse of sustainability as a measurable value, in terms of short supply chains, natural farming, and minimal processing. In other words, both solidarity economy activists and food-heritage actuators appropriated a discourse of "econo-sociality" (Roelvink 2010). Their common declared goal was to thrive on the relocalization of supply, on face-to-face relationships, and on self-education as an important aspect of provisioning.

Sometimes, though, the overlapping of the heritage discourse and the solidarity agenda was cunningly appropriated, and we felt that we were treading a fine line. When visiting a producer on the terraced gardens of Bergamo's Upper Town, renowned for his "white" salad (a local variety reaped early and matured in a dark cellar so that it loses its pigment), we were told that he bought his seedlings from elsewhere, using selected seed prepared with a comprehensive treatment that he could not specifically name. Doubtful about the idea of planting 30,000 preprepared cubes of treated soil and seedlings a year to obtain five tons of salad production, we decided not to pursue this any further. A few months later, we learned that this farm had also been considered for nomination as a Slow Food presidium for its heritage cultivation technique of the Bergamasque white salad. Against this empirical check, the convergence between reterritorialization and solidarity economy proved an interesting potential but sometimes difficult to achieve.

With the increasing popularity of heritage branding, solidarity purchase groups could be seen as convenient ports of call for local farmers. Still, GAS activists went producer-mapping not to discover hidden gems of artisanal production or to bargain on the quality/price ratio. The added value they gained was a better insight, knowledge, and control of the local food system. By farm-visiting and through a convivial approach (which exposed gasistas to multiple ways of preparing and serving the food they bought), in the long run they gained both technical knowledge (seasonality, types of grounds, types of natural and toxic pesticides, soil productivity and capacities, traditional crops, new crops, etc.) and status (by getting to know about the distinction and identity of certain cultivars and *cru,* of certain mature cheese or typical foods, etc.). Their contribution to co-production consisted of trying to enable small producers to be less enslaved by the market vagaries, by the environmental challenges, and by the diktats of the seeds and fodder distribution chains. It was meant to be transformative of the economy through the transformation of the gasistas' own lifestyles, and—at least as far as the latter is concerned—it was.

SOLIDARITY PURCHASE GROUPS AS LABORATORIES FOR COLLECTIVE LEARNING AND ACTION

Gasistas, because of their increasing numbers and their fragmented organization into self-standing groups, are difficult to cast in terms of a social movement exercising collective action. But they did prove to have an impact on Italian society in a Lilliputian way, consistent with their origins in the global justice movement (see Chapter 2). On the occasion of the 2011 administrative elections, solidarity economy advocates played a vocal role. Their support was sought by candidates with participative and environmentalist agendas and vice versa: they succeeded in injecting local electoral campaigns with concrete debating issues—about the governance of the territory vis-à-vis landgrabbing or about consumer supported agriculture.[13] Solidarity economy topics made a difference, for instance, regarding the election of left wing administrations in Milan, Turin, and Genoa. In the controversial political elections of 2013, the newly established "5 star movement," founded by former comedian Beppe Grillo and openly accused of populism by both right- and left-wing parties, reaped about 25 percent of the votes nationwide and included solidarity economy themes in its Lombardy regional program, explicitly mentioning GAS and DES, though without any endorsement by them (Movimento 5 Stelle 2013: 7).

One particular example of gasistas' capacity to make a difference was their mobilization on occasion of the referendum against the privatization of water that was held in Italy in June 2011. The referendum called to abolish a government decree[14] that, in the opinion of the referendum organizers, had effectively privatized water provisioning by making it available to private entrepreneurship and by establishing that profit was a legitimate criterion for establishing service fees (currently it is not so, as water delivery is supposed to be a public service, and water provision is administered by public companies or public/private partnerships). Another important question regarded the reintroduction of nuclear energy production in Italy—banned after a post-Chernobyl referendum—which the Berlusconi government wished to reintroduce as a form of greener energy. The fact that the Fukushima nuclear disaster occurred less than three months before the Italian referendum obviously played a major factor in orienting the public opinion. Nevertheless, it was still a victory that the referendum reached its quorum, although the voting day had been scheduled at the beginning of the summer holidays. In other words, more than 50 percent of the entitled voters actually went to vote and voted in favor of the referendum—so that it passed. In my local experience, this was probably also thanks to the dedicated campaign of public information to which the GAS movement contributed with a liberal use of their mailing lists and websites. The mobilization repertoire was low-key but inventive: for example, on the referendum day, the public fountain close to the schools where the polls were being held was wrapped by anonymous hands in red and white tape, with a radioactivity sign saying "Private and Radioactive Water." On a hot and sunny June day, it made a creative and convincing electoral message.

The kind of activist literature I have described in the previous chapter is a constant source of information, inspiration, and instigation for gasistas. Solidarity purchase groups are reminded to coalesce into GAS networks or to develop local collaborations (with Fair Trade, social cooperatives or like-minded public administrations) with a view to setting up districts of solidarity economy. GAS-supported initiatives may include the promotion of dedicated farmers' markets or the financial backing of a local producer in difficulty. Nevertheless, GAS do not have a capillary organization and a clear internal hierarchy, as does—for example—Slow Food, nor one strategic transformative ambition such as Transition Towns. As my work in the Mapping Group showed, they are not as advanced as the French AMAPs in establishing protocols of collaboration with local farmers (through advance payment or direct participation in fieldwork). In this respect, for instance, the DES project Spiga and Madia mentioned in Chapter 2 is a model, not the norm. GAS do not always transition smoothly toward a geometry of networks of networks, as I show in the next chapter. But they are numerically successful, they reach deep into the fabric of Italian society, and they generally take the revitalization of local rural economies seriously, pushing it beyond territorial marketing.

In GAS meetings, lowering the carbon footprint or increasing green entrepreneurship are not so much discussed as general strategies in the abstract but rather in terms of decisions about helping out this producer, encouraging that short chain experiment, or participating to one particular initiative. Socialization into a GAS also exposes one to concrete practices of sustainability—for example, carpooling to pick up products or getting to know social cooperatives that employ disadvantaged workers. Individual consumers would probably not be faced with these choices through anonymous daily shopping. Nevertheless, in order to make these choices conscientiously, gasistas have to micromanage supply chains and take sustainability in their own hands, so to speak. When their own demand grew unsustainably (as enough organic eggs, meat, dairy, fruit, and vegetables were not to be found locally), gasistas began to scout and contact local farmers to find out about their availability to convert to organic. Their missionary zeal in converting producers was responding to a real need of exercising food sovereignty.

I point out throughout this chapter and the next that the gasistas use an evocative language of birth, renewal, and conversion. Nevertheless, unlike other alternative provisioning circles such as *Bilanci di Giustizia*[15] that are inspired by religious charismatic leaders, GAS is an entirely lay practice. I do not recall one single reference to religion or even to religiously driven morality in my conversations, meetings, or e-mails with my fellow gasistas. Their efforts, however, require dedication and sometimes veritable self-immolation. It is about changing the world—with the humility and modesty of the humble and the unassuming. Nevertheless, individual gasistas may be more or less motivated, more or less active, and more or less strict in their practices of ethical consumption. However flexible, tolerant, and piecemeal, GAS practice was measured by gasistas themselves as being transformative: in the CORES survey of Bergamo's gasistas, concluded in June 2012, about 83 percent found that they had increased their intake of organic produce, and almost 80 percent found that they were consuming more local foodstuffs since they joined a GAS. About 28 percent had introduced environmentally friendly detergents, more that 40 percent had begun avoiding supermarket shopping altogether, and just as many had begun producing certain foods, such as bread, by themselves. Almost 24 percent had begun to get more involved in issues regarding their municipality, and more than 40 percent found that they were behaving in a more cooperative way. More than 27 percent found that they were more capable of influencing politics (Osservatorio CORES 2013).

This data suggests that participating in a solidarity purchase group changes gasistas' lifestyles over time. In turn, this corroborates my own ethnographic experience of a relational solidarity developing through practical engagement and reciprocal frequentation. Moreover, in the gasistas' own perception, the changes induced by their participation in GAS activity affect not only their consumption patterns but their lifestyles more comprehensively, including their capacity and motivation for civic participation and their collaborative styles of thinking and acting. This quantitative data also suggests that the type of people one meets in a GAS is rather homogeneous from a socioeconomic point of view (high education, middle-income, middle-age, married with a young family). Nevertheless, my own ethnographic observation also indicates that GAS is a common ground for people with diverse associative and political experiences. People with as diverging creeds and associative experiences as social Catholicism and communism cross paths quite regularly in solidarity purchase groups, meeting on the apparently neutral grounds of food provisioning and collaboratively learning new patterns of consumption.[16] Their lifestyles change not as a result of specific theories that are disseminated within GAS, nor through particular political action that is organized by GAS, but as a result of an ongoing practical and relational engagement with the nitty-gritty of provisioning, conviviality, and communication. This explains why it is not only styles of provisioning that change (where to buy, which products, and when) but also of consumption more generally (how much to consume, what kind of products, and how to dispose of waste and packaging). Ultimately, specific styles of participation are developed within GAS, as meeting after meeting is devoted to deciding together what to consume and whom to buy from. How to make this decision is up to each group, and solidarity (with the environment, with the producers, and with each other) has to be worked out collectively. The potential economic, environmental, and political impact of this grassroots reappropriation of consumption is apparent in the common reference to the principle of co-production.

To unpack what is actually entailed by it, I use Francesca Forno's analysis of social networks as facilitators of redundant but fruitful overlapping across groups (Forno 2011b). We have seen that, through working groups and shared projects across networks, constructive repertoires are successfully learned and scaled up. Meetings are regularly held, decisions are made, groups proliferate, and local farmers are recruited, even among many difficulties and sometimes ironic misunderstandings. On the basis of the obvious pressure of the financial downturn and building upon a pervasive societal network of kinship and mutuality, many share an interest in the practice of solidarity. Gasistas are motivated to disseminate and share information about quality foods and to facilitate alliances with other associative movements such as Slow Food but also with local administrations and with farmers' unions. In the next chapter, I dwell on the workings of the GAS network in the Bergamo area, ReteGasBergamo, and on national level. Because of their nonpartisan overlaps and thanks to a capillary presence in local communities, GAS can successfully amplify and propagate specific messages, such as one of food sovereignty.

Food thus functions for gasistas as a social aggregator through a routine of practical involvement and of reciprocal exchange that, over time, constitutes a veritable co-production of both political and epistemic practices. Politically, GAS support the collective learning of active citizenship. Epistemically, GAS are creative laboratories that reinvent provisioning. I mentioned in Chapters 1 and 2 how food activists have inherited and appropriated specific meanings for co-production from the writings of rural sociologists, especially Jan Douwe van der Ploeg. I am now contaminating this notion with that of co-production as it was coined by the Science and Technology Studies scholar Sheila Jasanoff in her seminal work, *States of Knowledge* (Jasanoff 2006). In this sense, co-production denotes the simultaneous and reciprocal definition and co-creation of *nature* and *culture* as terms of normative practice and discourse. According to Jasanoff, *nature* and *culture* are co-constituted as oppositional terms within normative frameworks whose sociocultural a prioris are not subject to political deliberation and scrutiny. Within such taken-for-granted boundaries, collective imagination and political practice are constrained, and it is through cross-cultural comparison that the specificities of their historically grounded premises can be brought to the surface. The GAS interlocutors I spoke with were more aware of the rural sociology scholarship on co-production than of the Science and Technology Studies (STS) notion of co-production. Nevertheless, I argue that in their use of co-production as a collective political and epistemic practice, they are closer to the latter body of literature than the former. GAS members envisage themselves as social networks involving both producers and consumers in practices of co-production (Biolghini 2007, Saroldi 2003) with a further-reaching engagement than that of consuming ethically. They practice an active contamination of different roles and bodies of expertise, trying to contribute problem-solving capacities and the ability to self-train on issues of technical knowledge such as organic certification, geographical indications, and logistics. This kind of involvement requires the capacity to rethink the political framework of one's practice. The language of co-production thus creates a discourse through which GAS members describe themselves as activists with a constitutional mission: rethinking the economy on their own terms.

The efficacy of GAS, as solidarity-driven purchase groups ultimately depends on their local rooting. As I have described in this chapter, weaving new circuits of value is a highly situated practice, which involves knowledge of the territory, of its local economic actors, and of various other local networks with overlapping agendas and specific cultures of participation. As we saw in Chapter 2, solidarity purchase groups benefit from the legacy of decade-long grassroots practices that aim to be transformative of political participation and collective deliberation. Since at least the aftermath of the 2001 Genoa's Social Forum, the Lilliput Network and other pacifist associations have disseminated nonviolent styles of assembling, debating, and decision-making. While individual gasistas may or may not be aware of this legacy, it certainly transpires in the national assembly yearly meetings, in the nationwide working groups, and in the materials available online to the readers of retegas.org. Certainly, the cultural and regional specificities of Italy's different political sub-cultures continue to play an important part, especially with regard to the propensity of organizing themselves in cooperatives and registered associations (especially in the "red regions") vis-à-vis the preference for informal associative activities based on voluntary work and networks of friendship (typically, in the "white regions"; see Baccetti and Messina 2009, Trigilia 1986).

In the run-of-the-mill activities of GAS groups, food provisioning becomes the pivot around which to refound social and economic relationships, thus re-weaving the fabric of the entire society. The ambition of solidarity purchase groups to move beyond just food nevertheless spurs them to build more comprehensive networks for alternative provisioning of energy, insurance, telephone utilities: in the years 2009 to 2011 a number of initiatives were launched, aiming to build second-order networks that would circulate information about specific topics and coalesce around network-wide projects. I shall talk about these in the next chapter. As the nascent network of Bergamasque GAS, ReteGasBergamo, was making its first steps with the Mapping Group—whose workings and visits I discussed here—each GAS remained nevertheless the focus of the never-ending labor of food provisioning. Second-order networking proved to be extra labor, and the organizational solutions and conceptual capacities that were generated in the process maintained their potentials and limitations in the pragmatic task-keeping and the relational involvement of gasistas. Certainly the relational training and distributed leadership that the GAS movement wanted to instill were put to the test.

–4–

Networks in Labor

When I began to take part in a solidarity purchase group in 2009, the oldest-established groups were already planning to coordinate all the local GAS into a network that would be representative of the province of Bergamo. Caronte (Charon) was the telling name chosen by this seminal working group. Charon is the infernal boatman who, in Dante's *Divine Comedy,* shepherds the souls of the dead across the river to Hades. It was clear from this ambivalently self-appointed name that what could ensue from this networking effort might well be hell—and that such a result was expected. As they tried to interpret and communicate their mission to ferry the existing uncoordinated GAS cloud into a network that would be conscious of itself, it became evident that GAS numbers, membership, and goals were still largely in the making in the Bergamo area. The network was charting its own boundaries and creating them by this very act.

I participated in the inaugural meeting of ReteGasBergamo on Sunday October 11, 2009, at the Cascina Terra Buona (Good Land Farm) in Nembro, a restored co-housing farmstead, seat of one of the three groups represented in a network of GAS called PanGas. About 100 people gathered: families with children, bringing food in potluck style, playing in the courtyard and in the playground. On this occasion, I began to experience the distinctive quality of GAS conviviality, by which one assumed each other to be friends and would be friendly, without necessarily having ever met before. Striking up a conversation, it would become clear which connections could be drawn and assuming them was safe: "Oh, you are in the Time Bank GAS. I am the husband of the woman who buys Parmesan for you." Or, "We met at the Sustainable Citizenship seminar, but I am not in your GAS—I am in the neighboring one." The GAS delegates (a fluid crowd of forty to fifty people) took part in the works inside the auditorium. I was one of the two delegates from my GAS. The atmosphere was optimistic and relaxed. The same mood carried over to the afternoon assembly. We all felt that this was more of a celebration of a result achieved than the moment to put hurdles on a path ahead.

The tentative structure of the network was only briefly discussed and decided based upon the models of other functioning GAS networks such as the Retina dei GAS della Brianza (a network of solidarity purchase groups supporting DES Brianza, between Lake Lecco and Milan). Every GAS could participate in the network simply by nominating two representatives and paying 1 Euro per GAS member toward basic expenses for the network (such as setting up a website or renting a meeting space). Crucially, each representative would be required to participate in a working group of his or her choice. Eight groups were proposed, with functional names about their missions but no further instruction: starting up new GAS, communication, training, mapping and liaising with producers, network projects, relationships with administrations and institutions, GAS census and economic impact, and logistics. I joined the Mapping Group.

Four network coordinators were elected, with a view that two would step down after a year, and two new coordinators would join the initial two, thus setting in motion a yearly renewal of the leadership without losing continuity and expertise. The elected coordinators were four men, and the understanding was that they would also act as spokespersons of the network. Later on, these simple rules and decisions gave grounds for criticisms that, with hindsight, bore weight on the following developments of the network. First, the request of money upfront was seen by some as a tax or an entry toll that had no right to exist. Second, GAS groups are already very busy provisioning and liaising with producers and did not like the idea of overburdening two of their members with network duties. Finally, it was soon clear that communication between the eight working groups and between the working groups and the coordinators was not perfectly functional. Often, one group did not know what the other groups were doing or felt that the network was being directed in a distant and messy way.

The fact that the coordination group was entirely male did not reflect the GAS population and membership (70% female, according to the CORES questionnaire) and confirmed the stereotype that females would do the domestic, relational, and reproductive work quietly in the background, while men would provide a front for the movement, the media, and the institutional contacts. This added to the perception of a distant directorate, as it increasingly came to be called, and gave the perception of a dictatorial style, though totally unintended. Also, it became clearer in the following assembly that the question of representation was not at all to be taken for granted. Crucially, many GAS felt that they did not want to delegate their choice of providers to the network: they wished to retain their own right to contact, liaise with, and monitor their own producers. Moreover, an increasingly vocal fringe felt that they did not want to be represented in any way that might seem political, neither to the media nor to local institutions. If anything, opinions should be surveyed among the GAS groups, and they could be voiced by the network representatives if and only if there was a unanimous consensus.

These, in brief, are the nodes that slowly and laboriously emerged over the two years that followed that limpid and optimistic Sunday. In the intention of Bergamo's GAS coordinators, networking meant establishing robust and extensive alliances, engaging in more complex organizational tasks, and moving beyond the day-to-day provisioning practices of each individual GAS. In the previous chapter, I began to describe my own involvement in one of the network working groups: the *gruppo mappatura* or Mapping Group. I continue this ethnography in this chapter, while in the next one I focus on the several network-wide meetings that were called to remedy what became tellingly known as the crisis of representation. Telling the story of the Mapping Group and how it struggled to position itself within the workings of the wider ReteGas-Bergamo will allow me to uncoil the many sticky points that, with hindsight, were already in full view on that sunny day—but only came to unfold through the impact of specific personalities, serendipitous procedural outcomes, and decisional fuzziness.

While I was personally involved in the Mapping Group, I also gained information about other networking activities by attending meetings, by being registered in mailing lists, and as a result of interacting with several volunteers who were involved in more than one project at the same time. In the previous chapter, I recount how since the October 2009 assembly, my participation in the GAS movement continues to this day, mainly through mailings and Web discussion groups. Thus a prolonged firsthand ethnographic insight was later nuanced and complemented with news and debates from longer-distance groups and networks.

MAPPING CHICKEN AND POTATOES

The complex toolkit of GAS expertise and the wide range of practices associated with GAS provisioning became more apparent to me as I joined the Mapping Group of ReteGasBergamo. With GAS numbers quickly rising from the thirty-two that had been charted in 2009 to the sixty-two finally pinned down in 2011, the shortage of local producers vis-à-vis demand was becoming a problem. Our task was mapping producers that were available to provide the Bergamo GAS network. Seeking a direct relationship to new producers meant crossing a recently created rural/urban interface. Each GAS group was experimenting creatively with bottom-up, light-weight logistical solutions to food distribution and transportation. Some GAS members took their own cars to the farm and collected for everyone (but rice or Parmesan for twenty to forty families was a heavy load for a private vehicle). Renting vans did not seem to be a good option, so chains of transportation were being devised to deliver fresh product from one family to another, and further on to the next, the goal being to mobilize as few vehicles as possible while keeping the produce fresh. We met the fish provider from Venice at the motorway junction at 7 a.m.

on a Saturday to initiate such quick-and-fresh chains. I was always hoping to be last in the chain in order to squeeze in a 9 a.m. slot. Collecting freshly butchered meat meant taking the car to the abattoir and collecting a twenty-five-kilogram assortment of cuts (everyone wanted steak, and they would only get some). I gained lifelong gratitude by giving up my steak share to the buying partner with whom I shared my twenty-five kilograms of meat. Roast and boiled cuts and minced meat had to be arranged in the freezer with some careful planning ahead.

Some burgeoning GAS with nearly 100 families that did not want to shoot or bud because they wished to keep their good collective bargains with trusted producers were organizing themselves in chains of manageable numbers, subdividing the collective orders. It was the job of the Mapping Group not only to find new producers but somehow to harmonize the distribution networks and the creative circuits that had sprung up around GAS.

In the first meeting of the Mapping Group in December 2009, we discussed how to interpret our mandate, and we agreed that it meant to enable local food production through reciprocal knowledge and collaboration with the existing agricultural and natural parks (such as the Parco dei Colli) and with established certified organic producers. We analyzed the existing state of affairs of organic agriculture in the Bergamo area and concluded that certified organic farming was not representative of the average smallholder. On the whole, smallholders represented a marginal and residual category, underrepresented by farmers' unions and using outdated and conventional techniques that had been adopted from intensive agriculture without seriously rethinking them for small and environmentally specific contexts, such as hill farming or mountain breeding.[1] Among gasistas, as noted in Chapter 3, skepticism about certified organic products was rampant, conscious as we were that organic certification does not rule out problems of scale, context, or the shortcomings of corporate agribusiness (Guthman 2004, Getz 2006, Johnston et al. 2009, Raynolds 2004). One of the Mapping Group members, who also served on the board of administration of a local consumers' cooperative specializing in organic products, turned up with an Excel sheet listing 137 certified organic providers in the Bergamo province alone and proceeded to point out how the majority of them were food manufacturers that transformed raw materials coming from elsewhere so that they in fact did not have the local dimension that we were looking for. We should instead try to support and maintain a proximal and sustainable agriculture, he convinced us.

Only fifty-seven of the listed producers were 100 percent devoted to organic farming, as mixed farmers maintained only one line of production as certified organic. The list included both smallholders and agricultural cooperatives. Also listed were some well-known workers' cooperatives for social inclusion that employed both rehabilitating addicts and patients with psychiatric issues in activities in the fields or in food preparation. These cooperatives neverthe-less also included artisanal workshops and small-scale manufacturing, so their agricultural output was relatively small. About 20 percent of the certified producers were in conversion—that is, in the process of adopting organic pro-duction protocols and leaving the fields fallow while introducing new organic cultivation. By listing all existing GAS providers, we soon became aware that most of the already converted small-scale producers were well-known to the local GAS and already at capacity. We discussed whether to contact the more distant organic producers that supply local food manufacturers, but instead we agreed to devise ways in which we could map, contact, and convert further small-scale farmers in the surrounding territory, offering our support as a net-work of trusted and solidarity-driven customers.

We envisaged possible areas in which we could make our presence imme-diately felt and took into consideration the offer of a poultry breeder to take orders from the network. The letter that the farm had sent out to its "most valued customers" stated that in the latest four years it had committed it-self to organic farming and humane animal treatment, never breeding free-range chicks for less than four months. Because of the conversion costs and the added costs of maintaining a certified on-site butchering facility, though, the farm had had to suspend chicken production and had scaled down to ex-clusively eggs and Christmas capons, adding instead an organic vegetable garden. The farm was proposing to start chicken breeding again in exchange for a guaranteed order of 500 items per breeding cycle. The price was not en-ticing (9 Euro per kg for the entire animal, which weighs around 2.5 kg, proba-bly twice as the price of ready-made cuts in supermarket chains). Our referent had already underscored the initiative with its cooperative order (not exceed-ing 10% of the quantities discussed) and acted as a guarantor, knowing the enterprise owner and swearing by the quality. Only a network order could sus-tain this quantity, so, aside of the potatoes and maize discussed in the pre-vious chapter, one of the first networked activities concerning provisioning in Bergamo dealt with chicken.

In fact, an ad hoc coordination between different GAS groups had suc-ceeded in the previous months, as a large quantity of potatoes had become available from a local farmer who recently converted in the Seriana Valley. On that occasion, one particular gasista, who was also involved in charting the emerging map of Bergamo's GAS, had simply launched an e-mail to all the known GAS groups and invited them to participate in an on-line survey to co-ordinate orders for this one farmer. By March 2010, as I and four other mem-bers of the Mapping Group were figuring out how many new potato producers had become available, about 100 families had responded to the e-mail sur-vey, and 80 were interested in buying in the Seriana Valley. The Songavazzo producer was thus reassured that he had buyers and planned to double his organic production from ten tons to twenty tons. He would thus supply GAS groups with potatoes, onions, and heritage red maize (*mais di Rovetta*). As I mentioned also in the previous chapter, this autochthonous grain invited the simultaneous interest of gasistas and Slow Food. It was treated and ground at the neighboring organic mill of Cerete—all within five miles within each other. In fact, the success of this first short chain effort in the Bergamo area encouraged an open and free public seminar on potato farming and orchard keeping, sponsored by the municipality of Songavazzo in April 2010, in the hope of capitalizing the combined interest of Slow Food and GAS in local agriculture and of supporting young entrepreneurship in a valley of dwindling demography (Songavazzo counts about six hundred inhabitants).[2]

This first collective purchase was also a test for the network website, entirely managed by volunteer gasistas working in the IT sector. At this point, our efforts included Web design, strategic planning, and logistics. It also involved the burden of political representation. To the practical and matter-of-fact management of spreadsheets and potato-counting, we added the diplomatic task of liaising with new producers (Figure 4.1). We bore responsibility for guaranteeing that the network members would be behind us and would, indeed, order and pay for potatoes and chickens. In doing so, we were "adding our

Figure 4.1   A potato farmer with a group of gasistas chatting by the loaded car. Photo by Cristina Grasseni.

own face" to the mantra of co-production and putting our own personal re-spectability in jeopardy, should promises be betrayed.

We began working on the chicken project in fall 2009. Considering the mo-tivation of supporting a known farm that already supplied items to GAS (es-pecially eggs) and encouraged by the potato and maize success, we launched a network-wide online survey. Nevertheless, it took three breeding cycles and three delivery dates to devise the apt logistics for the order distribution: the first time delivery was arranged in front of the local organic cooperative, but the farmer did not know how many chicken should go to which GAS nor who would pick up on behalf of which GAS. Some gasistas walked into the cooper-ative to ask about the delivery, and the cooperative workers were annoyed at being involved in a logistic task that had not been arranged with them. There were also problems with finding a parking space, so people turned up late, and the breeder ended up spending two hours handing out chickens in plastic bags in the street. The second delivery date was arranged in the parking lot of a big supermarket. This time we could not even find the breeder amidst the crowd. Awkwardness was the name of the game for a long time. A member of our Mapping Group, a policeman, Antonio, gracefully took it upon himself to sort out the mess of the chicken deliveries. It felt strange at first to receive phone calls from a policeman on my mobile phone (could I tell him that I had to cut this short because I was driving?). His job required no less than calling up each GAS coordinator to make sure that he or she would have a product referent. Thanks to Antonio, who also paid in advance for the entire order dur-ing the first rounds, by the third delivery date we had an Excel sheet with a referent for each GAS. Each GAS referent knew how many chicken to pick up and had to pay for them. Orders could be double checked with the breeder, and if there was produce left over, it could be traced down to the order. We had finally ironed out a normal gasista run-of-the-mill activity but on network scale.

The somewhat laughable complications of grassroots chicken deliveries going astray amidst the shopping craze of supermarket parking lots should remind us of the giggly reactions of the women in my GAS when they discov-ered that they had to cut the legs and heads off their whole chicken once de-livered (see Chapter 3). Just as each of us had to remember or learn anew how to cook and prepare food in ways that we had probably witnessed or done until not long ago, so the basics of logistics and distribution, even on a small scale, had to be worked out in practice by trial and error. On the potato front, our new orders with Gabriele, the farmer who offered us organic potatoes and local corn (see Chapter 3), were not going according to expectations either: only one order came through for the winter 2010/11, while the GAS located east of Bergamo had initiated the conversions of potato farmers in their own valleys. They were consistently sticking with their farm (opportunely renamed Happy Garden). In other words, we really had an aptly delocalized situation, based on personal knowledge of the farmer, as we wanted. But the aggravations came from the fact that no real internal communication pattern was yet established within the network. So, for instance, the Mapping Group had to ask Gabriele how many orders he had received from how many GAS—alas, we did not know.

The Mapping Group meetings took place monthly, in a scarcely heated and barren room adjacent to the smelly changing rooms of the local soccer team, on the sports grounds of the municipality of Mozzo, near Bergamo. The twelve members, of as many GAS groups, that had been delegated to participate in the meetings were hardly ever all present, and minute-taking was invariably down to myself and another woman. The most experienced member of the group had to abandon it soon after the first couple of meetings to subject himself to cancer treatment. His knowledge of organic farming and certification, as well as his personal contacts with many cooperatives and smallholders in the province, was lost for a long while, until he returned after more than a year later. Disorientation was palpable. Luckily, new resources were sent in, eight new people altogether, from other working groups and even from the directorate itself. Some of them excused themselves straightaway, but others lingered, and after about a year we found that a hardheaded core of about half-a-dozen people had managed to stay afloat. In the meantime, the changing rooms next door had become smellier and smellier as the season warmed, and we began meeting in private houses or in bars.

Still, coordination with the other working groups was surprisingly difficult: we found a new potatoes provider and drafted a presentation document to propose him to the network, but the info sheet was never uploaded on the network's website because of the procedural entanglements of the communication working group. One of us sent the document to a mailing list of all known GAS coordinators in the province of Bergamo, whether they had adhered to the network of not. This raised criticisms. Some GAS actually did not want to be bothered with offers of collective orders, as these distracted them from their run-of-the mill liaisons with their own trusted producers. As one member of my own GAS put it, "If we buy potatoes from this new guy, the farmer that provides us regularly with assorted vegetables will see his own potato sales plummet, and he won't be happy."

Lack of communication and of clarity about the reciprocal expectations between the GAS adhering to the network and the working groups became increasingly hot issues. E-mail exchanges over the summer of 2010 signaled confusion and a lack of information on what the network was actually doing, after 374 people from 22 GAS had officially adhered to the network the previous fall by contributing 1 Euro each. There was a palpable disenchantment about the fact that no one knew what the network was doing or that this information was not on the website. The proposals to send more frequent general e-mails to all the GAS collective mailing lists was dreaded as an increase of spam. The network coordinators for their part complained that each GAS was carrying on as usual, some having their own websites on which they were promoting regional or national initiatives without even bothering to inform the province network.

The logistic mayhem of a first ambitious year, trying to coordinate nine working groups, eventually settled into a tested routine. As I write, retegasbergamo.it dutifully records all the current providers in the network and, on a separate page, all the projects initiated by the Mapping Group, including the ones I was involved in. Subsequent additions were organic berries from three local producers, which we had visited in February 2010, salad gardeners, and apple growers. Overall, the Mapping Group achieved small-scale but rooted success, drawing about a dozen new local providers into the GAS network in its first two years of life. It scouted and enrolled small producers, mostly without organic certification but with negotiable protocols of productions that could be supported through a dedicated relationship with a sustainable number of guaranteed customers. The gasistas of the Mapping Group were not scouting for pristine rural communities but were making recourse to their own kin, contacts, and neighbors to regain proximity with marginalized subsistence farmers, smallholders, and retired farmers.

This proximity was geographical, relational, and temporal. Agriculture became a marginal activity only within the last three generations and employed half the Italian population well into the 1950s. It is not uncommon to have relatives who bred cattle or pigs. I personally remember my visits to Uncle Vincenzo, a peasant renting farm and fields. He made a treat of showing us kids his horse's foals. Every winter brought a share of sausage and salami. After pig-slaughtering, the winter chill filled with rising damp from the hot water used to wash away the blood from the patio. My father reciprocated with dinner invitations to rustic mountain inns that served *polènta* and pig entrails in a soup (*trippa,* or in Bergamasque, *buzèca*). The fields my uncle worked were sold in the late 1980s and disappeared first under the tarmac of a towering road interchange (which incidentally interred the local stream and wiped out the wood, where sharecroppers used to go fishing in the shade), and in 2012 they became the car park of Bergamo's new hospital development (which incidentally was years late on the building schedule, running millions in losses, because of problems with unexpected spring water infiltrations; the developers should have asked the local peasants about it).

In short, the Mapping Group members could capitalize on a widespread farming experience that was still close at hand or fresh in our memories, however brutalized during the roaring years of Italy's race to surpass no less than the UK gross domestic product and become acknowledged as the world's fifth economic power (after the United States, the USSR, Germany, and France).

Just last year, while visiting my tax preparer in his lofty office, we were commenting on the sorry state of the nation's finances, crippled by the unsustainable interest on moneys spent in Craxi's 1980s and Berlusconi's 1990s, when the tax preparer's father turned up unexpected, bringing a bag of fresh eggs—of course, he offered me some, too. With some embarrassment, this forty-odd-year-old tax consultant, wearing an impeccable white shirt and suit over immaculately polished leather shoes, confessed that his parents still kept chicken and rabbits for self-consumption.

Gasistas hoped that guaranteeing a pool of faithful customers might stimulate rural entrepreneurship, if only to convince a local youth to carry on with her parent's farm—and it sometimes did. This way, our efforts had a direct though limited impact on the economy of the territory. The Mapping Group also did the precious job of ground preparation for the census of the GAS, liaising with each group and listing them: at one given point as many as seventy-seven GAS groups were mapped, though their level of activity varied (for instance, one group only functioned to make collective orders of oranges and apples), and the final census settled to sixty-two. We discussed the possibility of more ambitious projects, similar to the organic bread-making short chain Spiga & Madia but concluded that it was not a priority for us to follow the model of DES Brianza: it would be overambitious to reconstruct an entire food chain, convincing local bakers to be part of the supply network. Our priorities were to quantify and map how much produce was being acquired and to make sure that more and more would be provisioned locally, so that a stronger relationship with the producers could ensue and potentially lead us to play a role in transforming regional agriculture into a more sustainable enterprise altogether. In doing so, we would collaborate with the other network working groups: the logistics group, the census group, and the economic impact group.

One of the problems discussed was the reliance of a high number of GAS on the very same producers: the Tomasoni dairy, located fifty miles away in the province of Brescia, was quoted as "being always on tour all over Lombardy" to supply all the affiliated GAS with milk and organic Grana Padano cheese (as well as fresh eggs from the chicken farm mentioned above). Given that, the group felt that it was recommendable to find a local dairy or to rely on proximal dairy breeders, possibly making cheese directly from their own cows' milk. Encouraged by the farmers' trade union, cheese-making had become a regular activity for many small-scale dairy farmers. This was by no means a traditional pedigreed cheese production but rather an artisanal innovation to make the most of excess milk production,[3] so that dairy farmers could directly sell a more valuable product than just conferring milk at a fixed price to large dairies. As late as September 2012, the Mapping Group (which continued working without my personal presence, of course) proposed to support a local family of dairy farmers by sponsoring their *alpage* cheese. Produced during the summer grazing season in the high pastures of the Bergamasque Alps, the cheese would be supported by ordering in advance, for delivery after three months of ageing in cellars. Thus the focus on locality and on proximal producers found a compromise between higher quality (mountain cheese is usually deemed superior to lowland cheese) and the strictures of certifications and geographical indications (the cheese of this project is not a geographical indication or a protected denomination, just mountain cheese).

In conclusion, through the work of the Mapping Group the GAS network transactions began to involve more immediately the surrounding territory and its regional economy. Nevertheless, when we discussed the results of our first experimental network-wide orders of chicken and potatoes, we found ourselves divided over them. For some—typically those who had experience of management or were involved in other forms of alternative provisioning circuits such as consumers' cooperatives—the future of GAS provisioning entailed collective orders and more online coordination. Some even envisaged our work as a mapping group as one of drafting legal documents for partnership packages that would be offered to each and every provider, independent of their trade (potatoes, chicken, or other), on behalf of the entire GAS network. For others, collective orders were justifiable on an ad hoc basis—for instance, to help a specific farmer sell an exceptionally good potato crop or to make a new provider known to all the GAS in the network—and in general for any situation, that needs to obtain a sizeable result in a short reaction time. But once the contact was established and the emergency dealt with, the baseline was that each GAS should be left free and responsible for maintaining its own liaison with each producer. Several GAS had apparently vented their opposition to the systematic use of online surveys and collective orders. To buy collectively as a norm would generate orders for large quantities, which would not match the capacity of the small-scale, local producers we were supposed to show solidarity to! On the contrary, large collective orders would probably put our customary providers under pressure, inducing the temptation of selling us third-hand produce that they would gather from other producers.

A compromise was reached by avoiding the idea of collective purchase in abstract terms and applying it in an ad hoc way to specific projects and opportunities. While third-party dealings were felt as a concrete danger, especially for longer-distance providers that could not be monitored on the ground, some hoped that GAS networks would encourage a mirror-image self-organization among producers. Producers could and should network, too, and coordinate among themselves in order to reap the most of the partnership with GAS. This process would become tangible within a couple of years, with the first "orange landings" in the market squares of northern Italy.

ORANGE LANDINGS

In Sicily, faced with increasing requests for his organic oranges, the activist and agricultural entrepreneur Roberto Li Calzi became well-known in the GAS circuit because of his capacity to scale up his organic farm, Le Galline Felici (the Happy Hens), to a cooperative of producers capable of matching the request for "virtuous oranges" from northern Italian GAS. "Virtuous" implied that oranges should not only be organic but produced without labor exploitation (which is especially widespread; illegal immigrants from the nearby African coasts are often coerced into such positions). In early January 2010, the inhuman labor conditions of illegal immigrants exploited in the agricultural sector in Southern Italy came to the fore, making national headlines on TV and in the press. Several hundred African day-workers organized a violent demonstration in Rosarno, in the fertile plains of Gioia Tauro in Calabria, after two of them were wounded with shotguns by *mafiosi* who were competing with local circuits of cheap labor providers.[4] The scenario consisted of about 1,500 exploited illegal workers faced by policemen in riot-gear and a few hundred local youths. The municipal government in the area had recently been disbanded by the court because of ascertained mafia infiltrations in the public administration.

Two years later, the situation did not seem to be much different; however, it was no longer profiled on national television. At the end of November 2012, six Romanian day-pickers in mandarin groves were killed in Rossano Calabro, on the opposite coast of Calabria some 200 miles away from Rosarno. The press quoted a witness maintaining that the Romanians had been hired and imported across the border by a mafia broker, following a widespread pattern of sponsored immigration at the price of indentured labor service on agricultural sites (Rivera 2012). On December 3, 2012, an "SOS for Rosarno" message circulated on a GAS network mailing list, pointing out that about three thousand immigrants were concentrated again in the plains of Rosarno, crowding the tents that the government had made available following the revolt of 2010, having run out of any external oversight or means of sustenance. With the current economic crisis, most of them remained jobless in the bid for a day's work picking oranges or mandarins in the surrounding plain. The suggestion to the solidarity economy networks of the north was to somehow organize expeditions of means of immediate material relief, using the same trucks that travel up north full of oranges for GAS customers.

In this context marked by economic, political, and humanitarian crisis, a solidarity economy network of the south was born. A consortium of Sicilian producers, Arcipelago Siqillyah, and a network of growers' consortia, RES-SUD, began to specialize in "anti-mafia organic oranges" and were particularly active in organizing further opportunities for Sicilian farmers and gasistas to liaise, coordinate, and actually meet. In one of the rare English versions currently available on the websites and forums of solidarity economy networks in Italy, Arcipelago Siqillyah defines itself as a "communication platform" for Sicilian alternative producers, which was "born with the purpose of creating an economic, social and cultural circuit among local production realities" to "allow them to answer the requests of exigent consumers that ask for services and products made in the respect of the people and the environment."[5] The Archipelago sees itself as enabling the "encounter between the economic and the trade realities from the north and south Italy": "This is a project where each will participate as the direct actor as well as the beneficiary and the person responsible for his own success."

In Spring 2012, Arcipelago Siqillyah and RESSUD organized a number of *sbarchi* (landings) in the town squares of sixteen cities in northern and central Italy. In Bergamo, the landing was supported by ReteGasBergamo in one of its first and most significant public events, in partnership with the municipality of Bergamo and with Bergamo University. The fair sold about fifteen tons of organic oranges, some at the market stands, the bulk being preordered through the GAS network. This public event was also the occasion to launch a so-called citizenship market, namely a GAS version of a farmers' market, organized by the association Market & Citizenship in three different locations in Bergamo and around.[6] The landings also happened during the university outreach week Unibergamorete (Bergamo University Network). As a result, a forty-five-minute ethnographic documentary on the orange landings, *L'Altra Faccia dell'Arancia* (*The Other Side of the Orange*), was produced by an anthropology graduate student, Federico De Musso, who also followed the other landings in various Italian towns and documented them as they "dropped the anchor" in squares, market places, and parking lots.[7] The initiative was so successful that, as I write, ReteGasBergamo is already organizing the second landing in Bergamo and Milan for April 2013.

Sbarchinpiazza allowed several aspects of the same phenomenon (buying and selling oranges) to come to the surface in a public space. The economic transaction was obviously key, but the surrounding seminars, speeches, and entertainment informed and sensitized both gasistas and the general public to the fact that environmentally concerned consumers should also be socially and politically concerned. For instance, the public presentation of Marco Rizzo's journalistic report, *Supermarket Mafia,* at Bergamo University made the orange buyers conscious of the fact that the mafia-ridden economic circuits selling tangerines at low prices can do so because they exploit paperless immigrant workers and monopolize distribution circuits through laundered cash, extortions, and intimidations. Certified organic or not, these citrus fruits are obviously not sustainable.

As part of this process, a solidarity economy network of the south (RES-SUD) developed, coordinating consortia, associations, agricultural coopera-tives, and GAS of the Abruzzi, Basilicata, Apulia, Campania, Calabria, and Sicily. The network's manifesto declares that their mission is to create an economic and social system that is nonviolent and solidarity driven, ecologi-cally oriented and aiming for the common good, as well as bottom-up and based on relations rather than on capital. It acknowledges the need for an equitable distribution of resources and prioritizes respect for the environment and for the community. In doing so, it adheres to the "Ten Columns of Soli-darity Economy," a manifesto underwritten by the GAS/DES movement at the national assembly of L'Aquila in June 2010 to define solidarity economy.[8] The recurrent image used in the document is that of the network as a woven fabric that emerges from local activities and relationships. According to the RESSUD manifesto, following the Brazilian social network theorist Euclides Mance, a solidarity economy network is an organization that integrates self-governed production with informed consumers and solidarity-driven finance, in such a way that all actors involved contribute to build ecologically sustainable and solidarity-driven supply chains.[9] While underlining that the network has no ju-ridical identity, RESSUD stresses the "economy of the *we*" (*economia del noi*) (Carlini 2011), through a reappropriation of the means of production and of consumption.

The postcapitalist tones and the liberation theology references borrowed from the Brazilian theorist transpire clearly from this manifesto, through the frequent underlining of the conscious, collective, and participatory dimension of solidarity economy. The revolutionary tones nevertheless co-exist with a relentless networking practice that sells, informs, and advocates a better livelihood for both orange growers and agricultural workers. The main revolu-tionary traits of this practice are, on the one hand, to try and educate while selling and, on the other side, to cultivate legality together with fruit. Finding innovative ways of placing higher-than-average priced products on the popular market is key to the endeavor, precisely because its objectives and scope are intentionally radical and far-reaching, speaking to the solidarity of workers and families and certainly not wishing to be niche or radical chic. Once again the manifesto stresses the need to meet face to face, to gather and share the stories of small-holders and day-workers.

The Internet is celebrated and enacted by these agricultural activists as a tool for empowerment, a channel for better communication, and a means of reaching further than one's immediate contacts, but as we saw in the previous chapter, virtualization and digitalization are not foregrounded as a modus operandi of GAS communication. Conviviality and collective deliberation play an important role in solidarity economy, well beyond the objective of securing specific types of products in the quickest and most efficient way. In other words, purchase is a means, not an end in itself. The preference for embedding economic transactions in a local dimension sets solidarity purchase groups apart from other social movements, which did gain much digital momentum after the 1990s, both to diffuse alternative information and to coordinate events and initiatives. In fact, some of the most spectacular boycott campaigns, against Nike and then Shell for instance, were mainly conducted and disseminated online (Forno 2013a and Rosenkrands 2004).

In the case of Sbarchinpiazza, conviviality co-exists with the peaceful invasion of the market squares, linking together reflections and discussion on food sovereignty, democratic participation, and environmental sustainability. The performance of sociality and the guarantee of trust both play an important part in reclaiming the economy, making it violence-free, direct, and transparent. Only producers previously known to the GAS network bring in oranges for Sbarchinpiazza, so that the landing event is a true occasion to meet a long-distance provider and not an act of blind philanthropy. Through the mentoring and networking mechanisms that are in place within each existing GAS and GAS network, these contacts are strengthened and expanded but never left to the blind mechanisms of supply and demand. A pact of solidarity is requested of the producers as well as a protocol of production and distribution that makes the produce traceable at every stage of the supply chain. Furthermore, the producers are requested to make their price transparent—that is, to share the accounting costs that amount to the unit price. This obviously entails transparency with one's peers and with one's customers about production costs, labor conditions, and margins made. It should be clear at this point how alternative these networks of solidarity economy aim to be.

Through the mafia-free orange landings in the squares and markets of the north, GAS networks and their mirror networks of Sicilian producers were consciously testing innovative scenarios of accountability, both in economic and in political terms. They reacted to the tacit governance of the market's invisible hand to make the many types of "hidden hands" involved in the market visible, from those of exploited immigrants to those of mafia rackets, and offered their own hands as an accountable alternative (see de Neve et al. 2008). The GAS volunteers hosting the event in fact helped to unload the trucks, negotiated spaces with the local traffic police, and set up and publicized the accompanying events (Figures 4.2 and 4.3).

Sbarchinpiazza exemplifies the GAS ambition to "think globally and act locally" (Carrier 2008), specifically by highlighting the ethically problematic aspects of the political economic framework in which basic, day-to-day provisioning transactions are immersed. Furthermore, the innovative framework of conviviality and spatiality that the landings inaugurated aimed to be foundational for a citizenship market, a market of citizens and not just consumers.

Figures 4.2 and 4.3   Two moments of the orange landings (Sbarchinpiazza) in Bergamo, April 2012. Courtesy of Cinzia Terruzzi.

In the previous chapter, I dwelled upon the notion of co-production as one way of framing the ambition of the Italian solidarity purchase groups to move beyond a consumer/producer division. This chapter further illustrates how gasistas' alternative practices of provisioning also aim to bridge the consumer/citizen divide, by showing the intimate connection between the economy and society as *res publica* (public thing or public good). How much it actually succeeds in building new economic circuits and democratic scenarios is a matter for debate and deserves a case-by-case analysis. After having focused on the practical hurdles that characterized collective purchase in ReteGasBergamo, in the following paragraphs I focus on the debates and doubts that accompanied its birth as a network that would be representative of GAS in the Bergamo area.

THE BIRTH PAINS OF CO-PRODUCTION

On April 3, 2010, the Bergamo section of the national newspaper *Il Giorno* devoted its color front page to Bergamo's GAS, featuring two smiling female gasistas holding milk bottles and packages from the Tomasoni dairy under the title "Bye-Bye Crisis." The paper announced that, in the Bergamo area, 800 families carried out their everyday provisioning through solidarity purchase groups. The article underlined how quality food could be bought at low prices if consumers organize themselves collectively and explained that "GAS are free associations of citizens who say no to mass consumption in shopping malls and to compulsive spending, saying yes instead to saving and to genuine products of straightforward traceability." The article stressed that about 2,500 people were already enrolled province-wide and mentioned the first attempts at aggregating GAS groups, with Inter-GAS Valle Seriana serving about 90 families and the burgeoning GAS Torre Boldone-Ranica serving 41 families for a total of 1,230 people. The journalist celebrated the recent establishment of a Bergamo GAS network, ReteGasBergamo, in October 2009. The article enthusiastically identified solidarity purchase groups as "happy degrowth," summing up their objectives as "freedom and self-production [*autoproduzione*]" (Purcaro 2010).

This is just one example of how, on the whole, press coverage of GAS is very positive, sometimes overenthusiastic, and often slightly misleading (the objective of solidarity purchase groups is not self-subsistence but rather solidarity economy). On the whole though, GAS media exposure pictures a fair portrait of the range and diversity of actions pursued: the proliferation of small groups as well as the aggregation in inter-groups and networks; the support to local enterprises and the economic convenience for both parties;

the public initiatives (such as markets and fairs) and the search for a new dimension of conviviality. It was no coincidence that the first public assembly of ReteGasBergamo in September 2010 took place within the framework of an ambitious public event, CiboVicino (Close-by Food), a "fair of conscious consumption" organized by the hosting GAS group (GAS Nembro) and sponsored by three farmers' unions as well as local enterprises (a winery, a green energy provider, a solar panel installer, and a building company, among others) and endorsed by Bergamo province. The two-day event hosted pioneer organic farmers, representatives of agricultural cooperatives, and spokespersons from the farmers' trade unions. The chairperson was Andrea di Stefano, a business journalist directing the magazine *Valori* (see Chapter 2) who later ran as a candidate for the primaries of the Democratic Party in the Region Lombardy in 2012. CiboVicino also hosted a citizens' market on a splendid fall weekend. Nembro (12,000 inhabitants) boasted its modernist square dotted with white gazebos against the red bricks façade and the marble relief of the Auditorium Modernissimo, which had been erected under the Fascist regime, in autarchic conditions, in the 1930s (Figure 4.4).

As in the case of Bergamo orange landings, in the square of Nembro, at the mouth of the Seriana Valley, providers sold on previously negotiated terms

Figure 4.4 Nembro Auditorium and square, hosting a citizenship market on the occasion of the ReteGasBergamo first assembly, September 2010. Photo by Cristina Grasseni.

and not on the apparently neutral grounds of demand and supply. All the invited providers had a preexisting liaison with a GAS group and had committed to answer specific surveys about their quantities and methods of production. Formal certification was not the issue—disclosure, reciprocal knowledge, and trust gained through a continuous relationship were the main criteria of selection. It was not, therefore, any farmers' market. It was a market by invitation only, orchestrated and controlled by gasistas. It was also a public display of the capacity to liaise with public institutions: from the municipality, to the farmers' unions, to the provincial government.

The main event of CiboVicino was the first public assembly of ReteGasBergamo, after its foundational but closed-doors meeting of a year before, which I recounted in Chapter 3. The event was organized in such a way that the market, the entertainment for children and visitors, the bread-making workshop, the tastings, and the aperitif would provide a suitably convivial framework for friends and family. A popularly priced Sunday lunch would be served at 13 Euro per person on open-air tables and benches in the nearby public park by the students of the College of Food Studies and Tourism of the town. The menu featured local products selected by GAS Nembro, and the food was prepared by the student-chefs. The screening of the renowned film by Ermanno Olmi, *Terra Madre* (*Mother Earth*), sponsored by Slow Food, closed the two-day event.

In the shadows of the auditorium's vast arcade, a cross-network meeting was already building a network of networks, gathering representatives of a Bergamo University study group on Sustainable Citizenship, its spin-off Market & Citizenship, and the committee for the promotion of a district of solidarity economy in Val Brembana, together with representatives of ReteGasBergamo (Figure 4.5). Market & Citizenship (Mercato & Cittadinanza) had formally registered as an association in March 2010. Since June 2010, it was the successful promoter of the so-called citizenship markets, which had taken foot in Albino in Val Seriana—not far from where we were—thanks to a tight collaboration with members of a very numerous and well-organized GAS of the area (which had not adhered to ReteGasBergamo, incidentally). The citizenship markets were a steady and growing success over the following years. After Albino, the citizenship market set foot in Corna Imagna with the support of DES Valle Brembana, and after a couple of years, the orange landing of spring 2012 inaugurated citizenship markets in the Bergamo city center. "Farmers' markets and beyond," as they eventually called themselves, are currently offered once a month in three different locations in the center, the west, and east of Bergamo on staggered dates.

The agenda for the cross-network meeting included the proposal of underwriting a common charter of principles of solidarity economy, which DES Val Brembana had drafted. The charter underlined a number of fundamental

Figure 4.5   Joint meeting of Sustainable Citizenship, Market & Citizenship, DES Val Brembana, and ReteGasBergamo; Nembro, September 2010.

values: participation and relationship, solidarity and cooperation, legality, respect for persons and environment, promotion of critical consumption and culture.[10] The project identified both social and environmental aspects of sustainability: organic farming and minimal ecological footprinting, on the one side, and legality and support of the local communities, on the other.

On its part, Sustainable Citizenship was proposing no less than drafting a map of solidarity economy in and around Bergamo. Sustainable Citizenship would be a network for solidarity economy (called RES Cittadinanza Sostenibile), promoting the nascent DES in Val Seriana and feeding ideas, training, and research in the activities of Market & Citizenship. The GAS movement had de facto inspired and supported all these associations and projects even though it was not formally part of them. Many people were having the same idea: mapping the producers, setting up farmers' markets, spreading best practices. The network of networks would avoid repetitions, conflicts, and wasting resources by creating coordination among the GAS network and these other projects. Most of the people involved in DES and RES were, after all, gasistas themselves. Nevertheless, we were reminded by two of the current coordinators of the GAS network that each GAS has its own history and that viewing the GAS network as a homogeneous movement would be overly optimistic. We could think of it as a vast and still largely amorphous base, while Sustainable Citizenship, Market & Citizenship, the DES, the RES were ambitious and focused projects driven by a handful of enthusiastic activists—students, scholars, unionists—who were maybe too confident in using acronyms and flaunting charters that sounded too abstract to the average gasista.

Such cautionary concerns would be confirmed too soon. Only a few hours later, inside the auditorium, the GAS assembly of September 19, 2010—the very base network that should have supported this intricate architecture of second-order networks—caved in. Once we entered the fresh and musky spaces of the ample auditorium, the debacle of the Bergamo GAS network became palpable. While the market outside was a crowded success, the assembly proper was scarcely attended. We were sitting in a vast theater, formerly employed as a cinema; there were scarcely seventy of us. We first listened to the reports of each surviving working group, which had been dutifully formatted on PowerPoint: training and education, starting new gas, mapping and liaising with producers, liaisons with public administrations and institutions, logistics. We approved of the network logo that had been designed by Bergamo College of Arts as part of a school competition launched by the network. Trouble started when one member of the assembly asked to adhere as ReteGasBergamo to the anti-mafia demonstration that was being organized by specific associations in a nearby town, in support of clean finance and clean trade. After much debate, it was decided that only initiatives proposed by a GAS group (not an individual) and regarding GAS activity specifically would be endorsed by the GAS network. It was a conservative move, which was in keeping with the apolitical feelings of important players in the GAS movement—specifically the largest groups. They were already busy trying to find a common ground among people of diverse political allegiances in order to coordinate practical choices and activities and felt that politics would have introduced too many elements of division, making the group unstable and difficult to govern.

Within my own GAS, the same draconian division of spheres between GAS practice and political practice were to be upheld—against all the media interpretation of GAS as a coherent movement and as straightforward political activism. My own GAS referent, Gisela, noted how difficult it was to gain consensus, even within a single group, for initiatives that are felt as political and not directly instrumental to GAS activity. For instance, she and other members of my GAS organized a very successful fundraising Sunday lunch the previous November, 2010, in support of a left-wing newspaper, *Il Manifesto*. Run by a workers' cooperative and operating on the verge of bankruptcy for several years, this reader-funded radical paper is defiantly subtitled as a "Communist Newspaper." Though successfully attended by about ninety people, raising more than 2,000 Euro, and voluntarily run by about ten gasistas who cooked products from GAS providers, the fundraising lunch was not endorsed by ReteGasBergamo, nor by the association Market & Citizenship, nor by my own GAS. The group did not wish to endorse an openly political event.

Back to the infamous September assembly of Nembro, events unfolded quickly. The coordination working group, jokingly called the directorate, gave its end-of-year report and two of the four coordinators stepped down. But the assembly was unable to elect two new coordinators. First, there were no candidates. Second, and more importantly, the discussion stalled over a much more substantial question: who was supposed to elect them? We were reminded that with 22 GAS currently enrolled in the network, ReteGas Bergamo should be representative of about 1,200 people, only about 70 of which were present. Someone noted that, while the previous assembly had been carefully orchestrated by a number of e-mails which spelled out that each GAS should send two representatives as their envoy, this time communication had only revolved around the publicity of the event. No representation mechanism had been agreed upon. How could the gasistas that just happened to be present presume to be delegated to vote on behalf of their entire group? Some felt that they had not been clearly mandated to do so and that they had come to the assembly out of personal interest and initiative. They would not risk casting a vote for one rather than another candidate in the name of their fellow gasistas because they had not discussed the issue with them. They did not have a mandate for deciding based on their own opinions only. No candidature had been advanced in time to debate it in each and every GAS. This, however, had been a deliberate choice, as it would have transformed GAS meetings into a kind of primary in a run up to a presidential election. A year before, two GAS delegates per group had been clearly mandated to represent their GAS groups in the assembly and to participate in the working groups. This year, this rule had not been spelled out. Should the members of the working groups be considered delegates, since they had obviously taken active part in the network development on behalf of their GAS groups? Someone challenged the whole idea of having a coordination group and advocated a spontaneous coordination from below, maintaining a clearer sense of relationship. The assembly closed with no clear answers and a sense that everything was back to square one.

After this disaster, a lot of soul searching went on, and a number follow-up meetings took place to transition toward a new equilibrium that would gain a larger consensus. Yet, the Nembro assembly and the events had been meticulously prepared—a pre-meeting dry run of the PowerPoint presentations by each working group had engaged us in discussion until 2 a.m. just two weeks before. We needed further debate and a clearer document, a charter (a constitution?), which would give representational powers to the assembly, lest all this work be lost on good will and wishful thinking. These reflections began to take place even during the failed assembly itself, under the telling charismatic presence of the founder of the first GAS in the Bergamo area (actually not far from Nembro in the lower Seriana Valley), whom I have referred to previously as Mario. He had not been part of the initial four-person directorate but had been a driving force behind the initial Charon networking project and was now steering the repair meetings as a newly self-appointed Charon. I attended the first follow-up assembly, which was called three months after the failed September assembly and preceded by a number of e-mails on the network listserv. Some of them explicitly mentioned the need to pick up the pieces and work for a fresh start.

The first follow-up meeting took place on a freezing night of December, under the neon lights of a community center in Ponte San Pietro, west of Bergamo, in an ample though bare room with school chairs that we arranged in a wide circle—attendance at the beginning was below thirty. I participated together with my GAS referent, Gisela. The meeting was officially called by the two network coordinators who had not stepped down. They opened the debate by proposing to restructure and strengthen the network, so that it would continue thriving as GAS groups continued to bud. Their offer was to change the terms of adhesion to the network into a simple registration to a mailing list, without the obligation for GAS to send delegates into workings groups or pay a quota. This, it turned out, was not an issue, since GAS are entirely based on volunteer work. Expenses paid over the previous years amounted to 8 Euro, and the overall budget of the network averaged about 300 Euro. Each participant to the meeting was called to talk, and Mario spelled out the proposal: to lighten the burden of the meanings associated with the word *network*. To be in a network of GAS would simply mean to be connected so that information can be circulated. There would be no adhesion, integration, or coordination.

We were also aware, by then, that a year before we were working under the assumption that there were about thirty solidarity purchase groups in the province. In the meantime though, sixty-two had been identified. Besides its internal discussions, then, there was the fact that only about twenty GAS were represented in the network. A paramount distinction was made between serving and coordinating the network. Serving meant enabling the circulation of information about training events, mobilization opportunities, and new producers. Coordinating meant representing a number of groups as one single entity and wielding that power—for instance, the power of deciding to endorse an event or not and especially of selecting producers. A network-wide working group should propose new producers to the network, but each GAS should be free to choose to pick up the offer, or not. The fact that the network mailing list reached each individual gasistas, bypassing their GAS referent, was not welcome, especially in the case of collective orders. Once again, network-wide orders were criticized—though they were in fact used only two or three times and only in cases where there was a need for an urgent response to farmers with excess crops. It was decided that network-wide orders should be avoided altogether. It was finally spelled out that the Mapping Group should circulate information about new available producers, not select them.

Nevertheless, some of us (my own GAS referent, for instance) were not satisfied with an entirely nonrepresentational position. As Gisela aptly put it, the problem was media exposure and the inevitable liaison with institutions and administrations. Whom did our network represent, then? And whom should be delegated to represent the network? If we wanted to initiate a project in collaboration with a municipality, for instance, we would need to be registered as an association, with a statute, a president, registered members, and a secretary. There was a basic chasm between those who thought that having representatives and coordinators was inevitable and those who considered a radical rethinking of representation in terms of sharing: sharing information, resources, and attendance. To the issue of how to give GAS endorsement to this or the other event or project, someone retorted that what solidarity purchase groups actually deal with is not culture or politics but how to decide which pasta to buy: from this producer or from another? But then, choosing producers is strategic: in a territory such as Bergamo, encased between sprawling metropolitan areas and depopulating mountain valleys, with a surviving fabric of marginalized smallholders lacking in organic expertise, should the network follow the example of some of the earlier groups, which strictly bought organic only, or adopt the strategy of converting local farmers to obtain higher quality produce and try to impact the local economy?

It was also noted that working in a network had always been a GAS prerogative that never really constituted a political issue. The first solidarity purchase group, in Alzano, progressively incubated other GAS, said Mario.

Nevertheless, once born, these other groups did not maintain a hierarchical umbilical cord with the their forefather, PanGas. On the contrary, proliferation was allowed by the loose relationship and the substantive autonomy of the budding new GAS: Albino, Nembro, lower Seriana Valley, Clusone, and so on. When they felt that they needed to get together to share information or make collective decisions, they got together in a network called Inter-GAS of the Seriana Valley. Might a limited number of such territorial chains work just as well as a province-wide network? The problem with the latter was that relationships were not as tight, not all GAS knew each other, and therefore a number of tacit assumptions about what a GAS is or should do could not be taken for granted. A kinship metaphor was explicitly used, together with floral ones of the buds and seedlings. Let each GAS flourish and contact each other by proximity, kinship, and preexisting budding ties. Each GAS is different and holds its autonomy dear. In this soul-searching, free-floating debate, of which no minute survives on the ReteGasBergamo website, all participants were profoundly recharting the grounds and the coordinates not only of their future but of the past and the present. Foundational histories, territorial ties, and budding genealogies were being put on the plate to counterbalance the felt need to create a critical mass vis-à-vis the media and local and national politics. A further issue was how to live up to the expectations of smaller but more ambitious associations, networks, and projects such as Market & Citizenship, DES Val Brembana, or Sustainable Citizenship. The latter was poised to build no less than a network for solidarity economy in the Bergamo area, a RES. What role did the GAS network wish to play vis-à-vis this agenda? Would we adhere to it? Would we sign its charter of principles? Or would we duplicate and triplicate existing experiences, reinventing the wheel each time?

The crisis of representation was not an abstract issue. Specifically, there were pressing local questions to be answered, agendas to be drafted, and decisions to be made, now. Could we formally support a newly born cooperative, which was asking for our endorsement and was collaborating with Market & Citizenship to set up a citizenship market west of Bergamo in collaboration with farmers and orchard keepers in Valle Imagna? Would we want to be formally represented in the working group on the postindustrial redevelopment of the Seriana Valley and in particular of Albino's textile complex? Could we leave it to the local GAS group to liaise with environmentalist associations, with Sustainable Citizenship, and with Market & Citizenship? The latter was already organizing a public meeting with the municipality's mayor and the owner of the disbanded factory. They wanted to force a public debate about the future destinations of the area and fend off potential mafia infiltrations from the commercial malls that were already being planned on the site. Some felt viscerally against it: "We are solidarity-driven *purchase* groups: our only sphere of action should be ethical *purchase*! Not politics!" Others responded:

"We vote every time we spend a penny!—go and read the national GAS charter on line!"

However divided, the assembly's baseline was that there was a fundamental difference between the base of GAS, which should be represented and served by its network, and a number of more focused and well-organized associations and groups, such as Sustainable Citizenship, Market & Citizenship, and the DES projects. We were not there yet and should not feel pressured to hop on the train of solidarity economy, if that meant anything more than reciprocal respect in our diversity, while sharing one simple common objective. Defining that common objective was our goal for the following meetings. We had to come to share a common framework or, as someone put it, a value framework. We would devise it, subject it to discussion, and sign it. Those who accepted it would be represented by our logo. But for other participants, all we needed was a lighter solution, a mailing list. The network would be nothing more than a bundle of one-to-all communications. In the face of such dichotomous proposals, we did not cast a vote. It was felt that the right path should be found by building consensus. Little did we know that we would travel this path for fifteen months.

In the second meeting, called in February 2011, the discussion was moderated by Mario, who took notes of the main concepts on big paper posters that he had previously arranged on one wall. The meeting was publicized and well-attended: by the end of the evening, we had sixty people present, both from adhering GAS and from new or nonadhering groups. A volunteer service group was appointed with the new mission of supervising the transition period until the next assembly. The parallel with the Charon group, which had ferried the pre-network GAS groups to ReteGasBergamo, was explicit. Upon request by a gasista and member of Sustainable Citizenship to join the service group, it was explained that there was no conflict of interest with being at the same time in Sustainable Citizenship and the service group but that maybe the specificity of viewpoints would be lost. Someone else from the same GAS thus joined the service group. The *gruppo di servizio* was larger than the initial four-person directorate: it included four men and three women from different GAS groups, and anyone could volunteer to become part of it at any point. The service group did not aim at directing—not even at coordinating—and certainly not at speaking on behalf of anyone. Its mission was serving the network—that is, aiding and enabling its refoundation. In the meantime, the working groups would continue to pursue their more pragmatic tasks, and they were reorganized around a more limited number of core functions: the Mapping Group (including census and logistics), the new groups (including training and liaising with other entities and institutions), and the communication/website group. There would be a common mailing list, to which only practicing gasistas could enroll, giving one's name and the name of one's GAS and group referent. A further meeting would be called, inviting the solidarity purchase groups that had not adhered to the network in the first place to join the network under new assumptions.

For its first closed-door meeting, March 2011, of which minutes were made available, the service group had many hot issues on the plate: managing the communication within the network, on the one hand, and with the producers, on the other. It was the beginning of a slow process, which led first of all to a halt in public meetings organized in the network's name. The concerns about representation were yet unsolved and this meant that, for the time being, the service group would simply circulate information to each GAS about campaigns and projects, without presuming to represent them. Thus, for instance, there would be no formal representation of the Bergamo network at the National GAS Assembly at L'Aquila, in June 2011. On the important political campaign for the referendum against the privatization of water—also scheduled for June 2011—the network did not take a formal position but publicized all useful information to mobilize the individual GAS. The service group was thus inaugurating a new style keeping a low profile: linking and facilitating communication among GAS groups but not steering, representing, or coordinating them. The staggering realization, which also emerged in subsequent conversations that I had with members of the service group, was that while GAS quickly proliferated, the network's capacity to define itself was painfully slow.

In the last meeting I personally attended, in May 2011, in the same community center of Ponte San Pietro, thirty-two GAS were represented, both previously adhering and new or previously nonadhering to the network. The unsettling hurdle this time was the resignation of the webmaster and his two helpers, which reduced the communication group to two people. While they directly joined the service group, it was agreed that there could be no website with a clear workload without a clearly structured network. In the passionate ensuing debate, which ran late into the night, we then tried to disambiguate the issue of representation: did we mean delegation to make decisions in the name of many, or did we mean a function of public visibility (the representative would be the spokesperson of the network)? Some said, "We should leave militancy to the associations." Others believed, "To shop ethically, one only needs to join the right consumers' cooperative." What was different then about our own collective action as solidarity purchase groups? According to one of us, "Our specificity was to work *through* consumption and according to *consensus*." Others offered, "We are *purchase* groups, but we respond to a *relational* need." Along the same line, it was noted that we had a working group on training that offered seminars to the wider public about why someone would want to be a gasista and what that identification means. "We should also have training for ourselves," it was commented, to reach a consensus about what we are. Inspired by the national charter of the solidarity purchase groups, it was decided that a charter for ReteGasBergamo would be drafted. Six people—not already belonging to the service group—formed the working group that would provide a value framework to specify the identity of the network and thus to disambiguate the question of representation.

In the following meetings, the value framework was drafted and presented in nine open meetings over the 2011/12 winter. The four-page document, available online, is really a statute of the network and a call to the more than seventy GAS that had, in the meantime, sprung up. Its objectives are spelled out as networking, coordinating, and promoting projects of individual groups or of the network as a whole, while providing training and supporting the proliferation of solidarity purchase groups in the province. The charter spelled out the nonconfessional and nonparty nature of the network, while offering its clear identification with the national charter of Italy's solidarity purchase groups, *Another Way of Shopping,* as well as with wider principles such as "respect for humankind and the environment; health, solidarity, sustainability, taste and the realignment with natural rhythms."[11] As for its openly political nature, ReteGasBergamo would "work to build a sustainable and solidarity-driven economy, as a concrete alternative to the current economic system." The statute also spelled out which of the principles of GAS culture this particular network was focusing on: reciprocity and cooperation with small producers, respect for labor, social justice, and social inclusion; respect for the environment and for health, with particular attention to local and organic farming; defense of the commons and of democratic practice. In its ambitious organizational section, the value framework spelled out that the network could and would request spaces, endorsements, and economic support, promote collective initiatives, tutor new groups, and promote collective purchases.

The charter was publicly presented in nine zonal meetings in October, November, December 2011 and March 2012, with the specific objective of encouraging discussion and feedback in small groups. According to conversations I had with members of the value framework group, attendance was around twenty gasistas per meeting. One of the criticisms publicly raised was that the network, already born thanks to the enthusiasm and dedication of a small group of people (initially five, then fifty), would represent a passive mass twenty times more numerous. About the political or apolitical nature of the network, one comment posted on the forum was, "I have a dream: going in all the school canteens and eliminate the use of plastic water bottles, to have jars of tap water instead. This is politics." Other comments made a comparison with advanced districts of solidarity economy in Lombardy, which promote participated certification so that they can certify their own producers. Among the good points about the network, there was the transparency of the new rules and the capacity to finally make decisions. Among the bad points were the fear that representation would mean delegation and the possibility that the network logo would be interpreted as just another type of quality certification but also the idea of hierarchy, distance, difficulty, and size: "The network scares me. It's too big and abstract" was one of the comments posted online.

The assembly of June 2012 brought new coordinators, and as I write, this new model is being tested. By February 2013, ReteGasBergamo comprised twenty solidarity purchase groups out of the sixty-six then charted in the province of Bergamo. According to one of the current members of the coordination committee, Antonio (a pseudonym), over two years lessons were learned. In other words, the steering committee had to abandon the ambitious goal of building consensus with everyone—which includes both those who see GAS as an apolitical activity of provisioning and those who see themselves as a prime form of political engagement, starting from the economics of everyday life. Being prepared to lose some of the membership on the way seemed to pay off, as the most well-populated GAS, those counting more than one hundred families, finally joined the network after many initial reservations and criticisms.

ReteGasBergamo emerged from this trying process as a confederation of staunchly autonomous and self-directed groups that did not like too much hierarchy or coordination but were instead capable of self-organizing around issues that were felt as crucial at the time. It is telling that while the Bergamo network was incapable of calling its own assembly, in June 2011 the national referendum against the privatization of water experienced a huge success, seeing a flourishing of mobilization also among local GAS groups. While campaigning for the referendum was largely an ad hoc contribution of motivated individuals acting within and across GAS groups, building a shared platform of principles and procedures required a much more sustained effort. It was also largely a stop-and-go process, heavily influenced by the personalities that would actually attend one meeting rather than another and by the succession of events. Certainly the failure of the first network fueled ingrained oppositions to having any kind of structure at all. But particularly, in full view came the schism between gasistas who just wanted to provision and gasistas who wanted to interpret politically their way of provisioning.

In particular, the basis of the GAS movement proved to be less homogeneous and less motivated than other associations that had nevertheless been inspired by GAS activism in the first place and that recruited their membership from GAS groups: the Bergamo network of solidarity economy Sustainable Citizenship (RES Cittadinanza Sostenibile), the association Market & Citizenship, and the district of solidarity economy (DES) Val Brembana. I devote more space to Sustainable Citizenship in the next chapter, where I also explain the connected mission of Market & Citizenship, as both were the key outcomes of the co-research collaboration between social movement scholars at Bergamo University and the GAS movement in Bergamo and nationwide. Neither Sustainable Citizenship nor Market & Citizenship should be taken to represent the GAS movement in its entirety. These networks and associations enroll a much more restricted number of activists who volunteer their time and resources to study the solidarity economy phenomenon as a worldwide social movement with economically and politically relevant effects. Sustainable Citizenship offered several public activities including training and research. Its spin-off, the association Market & Citizenship, became the successful promoter of the so-called citizenship markets in Albino, Corna Imagna, and Bergamo (respectively east, west, and in Bergamo) and, through its collaboration with DES Val Brembana, aimed to enable and support solidarity economies in the Bergamo area. As we have seen in the case of the Nembro assembly or of Sbarchinpiazza, citizenship markets were GAS-monitored farmers' markets that invited GAS providers to offer their produce within the framework of GAS-organized public events. The meaning of free market was redefined in this circle as "liberated from the violence of capitalism and globalization"—that is, from the violence of indentured and illegal labor, of high-yield and genetically modified (GM) crops, and of ignorant consumption. Because they were at once more ambitious and more focused in their actions, these circles did not display the animosity and disorientation that the GAS basis had to face when confronted with the realization that the movement had to be charted, governed, and represented.

SOLIDARITY AT THE RIGHT SCALE

Almost exactly two years after the infamous Nembro assembly, on September 12, 2012, *L'Eco di Bergamo,* Bergamo's local newspaper, published an article entitled "Solidarity Purchase Groups: there are more than 1,600 in Italy, they involve 40,000 families and turn over 80 million Euro a year."[12] This latest estimate was based verbatim on the GAS national self-census, registering by then 900 groups, and on the confident estimate of the nationwide working group for solidarity economy, Tavolo RES, that at least as many unregistered groups probably existed, without being charted.[13] Following Retegas. org, then, about 180,000 Italians would be involved in solidarity purchase groups—that is, about 45,000 families. As the average annual expenditure of one family per GAS averages 2,000 Euro, the estimate of 80 million Euro would even be conservative and matched with our local calculations. According to the CORES Report on GAS activity in the Bergamo area in 2011, in fact, thirty-five solidarity purchase groups spent collectively almost 80,000

Euro per year—on average more than 2,200 Euro per group (Osservatorio CORES 2013).

When the article was issued, the census of the GAS groups in the Bergamo area had already risen from the sixty-two known to me the year before, to "more than seventy," as my friends in the service group told me. Among the most apparent successes of GAS activism in the Bergamo area was thus its proliferation. Why was it so significant? As I said, solidarity purchase groups work well in peri-urban contexts in Italy because they capitalize on its social and geographical proximity to farming contexts. Our work as the Mapping Group was greatly aided by the fact that the traces of residual smallholders' agriculture were all around us—on a couple of occasions, I actually walked to the farm we were going to visit—they were lying within the boundaries of Bergamo's municipality. In 2012, a map of the green and solidarity economy of Bergamo was produced, thanks to a funded project led by Market & Citizenship in collaboration with Bergamo University, charting ninety-one farmers and enterprises that supply solidarity purchase groups. A triumphant picture, which seemed to contradict the "birth-pains" of three years before.

Though uncoordinated by the GAS network, the events promoted by Bergamo's RES and DES, combined with media attention, progressively connoted in specific local ways the public practice of an otherwise underdetermined expression: solidarity economy. Events and meetings spelled out that for these social actors, solidarity economy is not philanthropy or radical chic spending, nor ascetic living, but rather a collective practice: first with an economic objective (provisioning for one's domestic unit and, further, impacting proximal economies) and second, a civic vocation (to transform lifestyles through educational and informative actions). The co-existence of these diverse objectives is mirrored on the ReteGasBergamo website, where network projects include not only the Mapping Group's invitations to make collective orders with new providers but also to participate in specific public events and market fairs or to participate in training workshops and study seminars. Thus, GAS public events restage economic transactions at the center of public life: the market square.

The most important realization of the laborious transition from the first, informal, and optimistic network to the second, more formal and chartered ReteGasBergamo was that networking was by now a necessary stage to avoid duplications, chart resources, and generally be on the same page. As Luisa, currently a member of the network coordination, noted in her wrap-up of online discussions on the draft charter, a stronger network would not impinge on the single GAS autonomy but rather enable it. A network, she explained, would be able to impact the regional economy and exercise pressure on economic and political contexts—two areas of influence already implicit in the GAS ambition to create new economic circuits by contacting local farmers and persuading them to convert to organic and socially responsible production practices. The network was ready to go public. It participated in the prestigious international science festival, BergamoScienza, in October 2012, in a section on economic ecology.

Despite the positive media exposure, why did so many issues have to be drawn out and discussed one by one in ReteGasBergamo? It should be kept in mind that GAS usually do not take the shape of formal associations: each GAS is an informal group, rather than a cooperative. Therefore it has no specific internal hierarchy: one of the participants in the brainstorming meetings defined solidarity purchase groups as a "rigorously organized anarchic collective." In GAS, strategies are usually decided on a strictly parliamentary and ad hoc basis during the group's meetings. This modus operandi, based on direct democracy, has also been maintained at the national level. At the national assembly of the GAS network, for instance, a number of working tables discussed specific topics in small groups and then reported back to the assembly. Delegation and hierarchical representation were avoided as much as possible. Only when voting for the new charter did ReteGasBergamo call an assembly with a clear representational mechanism (two voting delegates per GAS), but this formal moment was preceded by e-mail exchanges, brainstorming collective meetings, and the presentation of drafts to zonal meetings. It was clear at this point that these alternative food networks were not just reinventing foodways but democracy itself. This required finding relational styles that were not only inclusive but also conducive to decision-making within the network.

Why was coordination so laborious? The main issue at stake was the fact that GAS were exploring constraints and possibilities of scale: they were not building a network of people but a network of networks (each solidarity purchase group already being a network of people). Naturally, even second-order networks are made of people. But while gasistas debated logistics, providers, and orders in their own solidarity purchase groups, the same gasistas in networks of GAS found themselves debating representation, democracy, and power. According to Larch Maxey (2007), referring to alternative provisioning includes "processes and contestations [that] take place at every temporal and spatial scale; indeed, part of the attraction, complexity and challenge of food is its potential to simultaneously collapse and distil various scales and categories through which we may seek to make sense of it" (2007: 55). As Sallie Marston, John Paul Jones, and Keith Woodward (2005) propose, though, to engage with a definition of scale means redrawing ontologies that one would take for granted. Within the GAS network, each node (working groups, individual gasista, coordinator, service group) had its own identity and perceived mission—even though a handful of people may transition from one role to another or act in both roles at the same time. But within a yet undefined and unchartered nexus, each node was also a key enabler—whether consciously or not—to another proximal sphere of influence. Each group was affected by the push-and-pull forces of the other groups. Each working group resented of the success or failing of other working groups. Resistance to scaling up was reasonable for those GAS that felt well adjusted to their local status quo. ReteGasBergamo was now a candidate to represent them, was proposing new routines, and was exacting time and dedication. Fears were justified, as there would be no return, indeed.

In a void of everyday exercise of political practice, GAS were discovering their own political nature through the effort of devising rules and missions of their own network. Contemporary Italians feel strongly about the distinction between party-political and political practice in its nobler sense—that is, the collective deliberation of the goals of a polity. Both in terms of practices and of beliefs, this is a very different scenario from that described by David Kertzer in *Christians and Comrades* (1990) or by Chris Shore (1990) based on fieldwork research conducted in the 1980s, when active participation in party politics, starting from the base associations of party sections, trade unions, after-work circles (or vice versa parish churches, Christian associations, and unions) subsumed belonging, ideology, and everyday sociality, whether red or white. It is widely felt that political parties have betrayed their mission to organize and channel civic practice and active citizenship, and this has found an evident confirmation in the political elections of February 2013, where one in four Italians voted for a movement (*Movimento 5 Stelle*) that denounced Italy's parties as corrupt across the political spectrum. It is fair to state that the average citizen is disenchanted with politics in so far as it is managed by political parties. ReteGasBergamo's headstrong, laborious, and ambitious search for agency in the economic and political realms is the best evidence of a renaissance of political needs through economic practice.

The example of ReteGasBergamo shows, in other words, how it is at this grassroots level of participation and through novel forms of mutual help and association that the rules and styles of civic participation are being rediscovered and reinvented, unsurprisingly, at a time of economic pressure and of political disorientation. This might be the reason why, as the CORES report shows, gasistas display more faith in a sense of efficacy regarding participation in the community, while they are extremely critical of traditional democratic institutions such as the parliament and government. However labor-intensive and sometimes extremely slow, the networking capacity of GAS groups supports the hypothesis that grassroots solidarity economy can develop integrated and deep-reaching projects of economic and social transformation—although the scale at which this should happen is continuously debated and negotiated.

This critical trait nevertheless sets solidarity purchase groups unmistakably apart from commercial initiatives simply aiming to promote and distribute quality foods, through online purchase, on-farm sales, or farmers' markets. GAS are not a means to obtain quality and healthy foods. They are a social experiment to achieve a common good through the collective pursuit of those goods. As such, they not only purchase but construct new economic circuits, instill models and practices of sustainable farming, and find creative low-impact solutions to logistics and distribution. Their intervention is at once cultural and pragmatic, political and economic. Graziano and Forno (2012) have categorized them as social aggregations with a tolerant identity—that is, at once strong and inclusive rather than strong and exclusive (as in political parties or social movements, where one's strong adherence to one prevents one from adhering to others) or inclusive but weak (as in coalitions or ad hoc mobilizations, where adhering to one cause does not exclude adhering to another too, but there is no defined identity core). Certainly the economic crisis that began to be felt in earnest in Italy in 2009 has favored new forms of mutuality and a change in scale for various types of solidarity economy. New spontaneous forms of mutual help sprang up among proximal social actors (such as the collective purchase groups of factory workers or condominium neighbors), while the overall interest in so-called critical consumption increased, according to some gross indicators such as participation in alternative economy fairs like Fa La Cosa Giusta (Do the Right Thing; see Chapter 2). The most difficult but successful effort of ReteGasBergamo was that of identifying, in the midst of this burgeoning growth, a number of principles, or framework values, as a point of no return. They were thus moving beyond critical consumption and exercising collective social responsibility (McFarland and Micheletti 2010).

–5–

Seeds of Trust

The previous two chapters were based on participation in one solidarity purchase group, in the meetings leading to the setting up of ReteGasBergamo,
and in the workings of the Mapping Group of ReteGasBergamo. In this chapter,
I take stock of these ethnographies to propose an overall reflection on trust,
networks, and engaged anthropology. I shall propose that food activism can be
seen as building trust in times of societal crisis, that it does so in various ways,
bringing an eclectic convergence of activists from different paths of life and political repertoires onto the common ground of family provisioning, and that the
apt anthropological stance to research about this type of activism in the making
is engaged anthropology (Aiello 2010, Low and Merry 2010, Herzfeld 2010).

First, I explore the idea of trust as social capital, in the light of a review
of significant notions in the recent history of the anthropology of Italy (such
as familism and corruption). I test these notions in light of my own ethnography and of quantitative data about gasistas' perception of politics. I then
argue that gasistas seek a practical response to a crisis of trust in contemporary Italy, and based on my participation in the GAS national assemblies
of 2010 and 2011, I review some of the most ambitious models of solidarity
economy in Italy: the districts of solidarity economy (DES). I show how, in my
ethnographic experience, an overlapping geometry of networks of networks
developed fruitful synergies across a widening spectrum of competences and
experiences, which I call crosscutting counter-epistemologies, through which
proactive practice and discourse fed back into everyday GAS routines. Vice
versa, GAS practice acts as a constant reality check to ground activism in concrete action and feasible objectives. As I comment on the networks' mapping
projects, I discuss my own positioning as, at the end of my fieldwork, I engaged
in co-research with some of the very protagonists of the movement I was
studying.

IN WHOM WE TRUST? SOCIAL CAPITAL, FAMILISM,
AND MORAL BANKRUPTCY

Chapters 3 and 4 have shown ethnographically how GAS carry out a patient
and painstaking reconstruction of both an economic and a political fabric,

stressing collaboration (co-production) and mutual trust. The active search for an inclusive and effective style of participation yielded, as we can see in the case of ReteGasBergamo, a political result—that is, the constitution of a polity that claims representation and responsibility for advancing the governance of its own territory, according to specific solidarity principles. From this point of view, GAS collectively reconstitute a relational resource—trust—that, in Italy, has been squandered by countless political misdemeanors and administrative abuses.

In 2002, Dame Onora O'Neill, a Cambridge philosopher in charge of devising a more reliable normative framework for bioethics, asked, "Can a revolution in accountability remedy our crisis of trust?" (O'Neill 2002: 4). At the time, the UK government was decidedly going down the path of bio-banking. Mortgages thrived, well before the financial crisis struck—starting with the bankruptcy of the Lehman Brothers Bank in the United States and the concomitant unearthing of one of the furthest-reaching financial deceptions in world history. Dame O'Neill pursued the answer by asking the following questions: "What does it take for us to place trust in others? What evidence do we need to place it well? Does the revolution in accountability support or undermine trust?" (O'Neill 2002: 5). Anthropologists were asking the same questions, with Marilyn Strathern (2000) comprehensively critiquing the idea of "audit cultures" while at the same time denouncing the fact that auditing had become a widespread instrument for assessing and enforcing accountability—especially in schooling and research, and in every other sector claiming evidence-based knowledge and results. One of the questions was whether the affective quality of trust in societal relationships was necessary to engender cooperative behavior. Diego Gambetta had offered the definition that

> trusting a person means believing that when offered the chance, he or she is not likely to behave in a way that is damaging to us, and trust will *typically* be relevant when at least one party is free to disappoint the other, free enough to avoid a risky relationship, *and* constrained enough to consider that relationship an attractive option. (1990: 219)

Based on this definition, Gambetta claimed that "there is a degree of rational cooperation that should but does not exist" and that "cooperation can come about independently of trust"—ultimately, that "trust can be seen as a result rather than a precondition of cooperation" (1990: 213).

Ethnography does the work of unpacking trust, instead of taking it as "a sociological given" (Corsìn-Jimenez, 2005). The idea that trust is a valuable social capital but that it is very difficult to define, if not for the negative consequences of its absence, had been anticipated by Robert Putnam's much debated work, *Making Democracy Work* (1993). Putnam famously based his theory of social capital on the comparative analysis of Italian regional

governments, introduced in the 1970s though prescribed by the 1946 constitution. Their styles of governance varied widely, not only because of the
imprint that the regional governments received from as many "charismatic
crusaders—such as Piero Bassetti, president of Lombardy's Christian Democracy; Guido Fanti, Emilia-Romagna president of the Communist Party; and
Lelio Lagorio, president of Tuscany's Socialist Party" (Putnam 1993: 24)—but
especially because of their rooted territorial political subcultures. The plurality
of civic traditions in Italy depended on the diversity of associative models and
the flexibility of peer-to-peer bonding that build social capital. Political science
literature has stressed the difference between the facility of formalized cooperation in "red" territorial subcultures (for instance in Emilia-Romagna) and
the proliferation of informal, volunteer associations of mutual help in "white"
subcultures (for instance in Lombardy and Veneto) (see, for instance, Bagnasco 1977). According to Putnam, the trust effect would be engendered by
the closeness of decision-making and by the civic engagement and participation of citizens, whereas too many passages of delegation created hierarchy
and disaffection.

Breach of trust has especially damaging effects. As Donatella della Porta
shows in her analysis of political corruption in Italy as a system of exchange
that remains hidden from public view (*scambio occulto,* Della Porta 1992),
corruption undermines the robustness of the system of democratic representation. It is now well twenty years after the fall of the so-called First Republic
in the early 1990s, with the downfall of the Craxi government in popular furor
over issues of corruption at the highest institutional levels as well as in local
administrations. While the state is on the verge of defaulting and imposes
austerity measures on civil servants and tax-paying employees, tax evasion
is pandemic in entrepreneurship and was even hailed as a right—that was by
a too-well-known entrepreneur who, as prime minister, said that it is a right
of citizens hassled by more than 50 percent tax-rates to evade them. According to scholars of Italian geopolitics John Agnew and Michael Shin, "apparently it was Craxi who, in April 1993, 'seeing that his own days in power were
numbered' (Stille 2006: 132), first suggested to Berlusconi that he become
actively involved in national politics" (Shin and Agnew 2008: 71) Yet Italy's
moral bankruptcy cannot be pinned down to prime ministers only. The Italian
democracy is the most expensive in Europe: not only do members of parliament receive the highest salaries, but they continue to enjoy lifelong benefits
and pensions. As of yet, senators and deputies (945 in total) have not had
the decency of substantially cutting their own salaries and benefits, in solidarity with the citizens whose wages are being eroded.[1]

Slow, underfunded, and exceedingly bureaucratic, courts of law cannot
guarantee that justice is done in reasonable time, even for penal crimes,
while repair and reimbursement remains a mirage for the common citizen who
finds himself or herself wronged over administrative matters. In this situation,

many types of mafias thrive—that is, organizations historically born to offer private protection in lieu of the state's failing governance (Gambetta 1993). It is equally clear why third-party guarantors—such as organic certifiers, but also insurers or investment funds—cannot inspire trust, as the recursive delegation of authority is known by all to stand on a moral vacuum. No promise cannot be broken; no pact cannot be called void. The code of honor is, paradoxically, seriously binding only within mafia clans, where it stands for a feudal tie to one's master, at the ransom of one's, and one's kin's, life or death.

As an Italian citizen, student, patient, voter, tax-payer, university professor, mother, and post office goer, I am mindful of Dieter Haller and Chris Shore's comparative study of corruption in Italy, the United States, the Balkans, Russia and postcommunist states, India, Portugal, and Bolivia, as well as the European Commission, and corporate America (Enron). I agree with their conclusion that an anthropological approach to corruption should eschew from adopting puritan tones and appreciate it ethnographically as a form of exchange: "a polysemous and multistranded relationship and part of the way in which individuals connect with the state" (2005: 7). In her own work on the Italian practice of nepotism, Dorothy Zinn (2001) proposes reading the "poetics of clientelism" into the ubiquitous system of *raccomandazione*. This is an often unsolicited recommendation, mostly verbal, that is made not on the basis of an honest appreciation of the candidate's merit but of his or her personal links to oneself. A *raccomandazione* is usually made by a person of power, as part of an ongoing exchange of favors with the functionary or notable who receives it. In his ethnography of Rome, *Evicted from Eternity*, Michael Herzfeld (2009) has captured the ambivalent co-existence of lights and shadows in Italy's capital city. Herzfeld introduces an original distinction between the civic and the civil, the first denoting idealized civic-ness—that is, the virtues of accountable citizens and of the trustworthy institutions that civic citizens should place their trust in. The second describes the actual practice of being civil to each other in an ever-failing institutional context, where it is only by personal appeal to the functionary, the traffic warden, or the tax collector that things can get done (possibly to one's advantage).

Civic and civil, of course, do not exclude each other. But a realistic ethnography of civility includes the thick description of the many ways of dealing with the expectation of human and institutional failure that, on the one hand, could be categorized as turning a blind eye or, on the other hand, connivance. The specific socioeconomic contexts, framework values, and concrete tactics in which solidarity and reciprocity are privately perceived, publicly performed, and socially negotiated in Italy suggest many shortcomings of the civic. Only fools would trust the government, the corporations, or the Church at face value as sources of truth, efficiency, and righteousness. There is nevertheless ample space for active civility in close-knit relationships. GAS practice straddles, in this respect, the gaping margins between failing institutions and an intense and pervasive practice of reciprocity that, nevertheless, is hardly a guarantee of equity and inclusiveness. It is, in this sense, an attempt at reconciling civic values with the civility of face-to-face relationships.

Decades of anthropological fieldwork in southern Europe warrant a special attention on the ethnographic analysis of affective versus instrumental relations within communities. Solidarity purchase groups are at once communities of practice and community-based in specific localities. Anthropological studies of the Mediterranean in the 1950s used community both as an analytical concept and as a methodological device: one would study close-knit small communities that would be representative of wider cultures. According to Julian Pitt-Rivers, "A conception of community based upon locality runs through the cultural idiom of Southern Europe" (Pitt-Rivers 1954: 30). This explained at once widespread attachment to one's place and a number of antagonisms, belligerence, and superiority complexes directed toward neighboring villages (known in Italy as *campanilismo*). Classic edited volumes such as Pitt-Rivers's *Mediterranean Countrymen* (1963) and Peristiany's *Honour and Shame* (1965) were important turning points, focusing on relationships in contemporary communities and their political and economic nature. While Eric Wolf pointed out the distinctiveness of the European Mediterranean (1969) by contrasting the cultural complexes of bilateral kinship plus nuclear family plus dowry system in the Latin countries vis-à-vis agnation plus segmentary organization and bride wealth in the Maghreb, the community studies trend in sociology and anthropology in the 1950s, 1960s, and 1970s associated certain Italian regions with correspondent cultural traits. Southern Italy was the place to look for the honor and shame complex and for patron-client relations; central Italy would display the roots of a city-centric idiom of civilization in a rural/urban divide; the Alpine ridge would provide diverse and competing ecological models of smallholders' subsistence agriculture (see Filippucci 1996).

Southern Italian community studies focused on the limited separation of affective vis-à-vis instrumental relations in political, economic, and social life. Southern Italy was seen—as the rest of Southern Europe—as being half-way along the path of modernization. The honor-and-shame cultural complex, campanilistic identities, and personal forms of political allegiance were underlined as cultural hurdles preventing Italians from becoming rational capitalists. The analyses of sociologists F. G. Friedman and Edward Banfield in particular set milestones for the following scholarly debate. Poverty (*la miseria*) was defined as a cultural attitude (akin to Oscar Lewis's 1969 definition of a "culture of poverty" as endemic among Mexican peasants). Banfield predicated *miseria* of peasants alone, as a cultural factor explaining a noncollaborative spirit and an ad hoc, pro tempore individualism that defies any civic, associative enterprise, due to the certainty that one's efforts to improve oneself are hopeless because of everyone else's untrustworthiness: a public officer will take bribes every time he can, and in any case it will be assumed by society that he does, regardless of his actual behavior (Banfield 1958: 92). Banfield also observed a pervasive culture of noncollaboration among peers—whether cultural or social, political or economic in nature: from the paucity of cultural associations, to the lack of workers' associations, to the absence of civic spending by benefactors, to the unimaginability of constructive strategies for local development beyond political nepotism. Following de Tocqueville, according to Banfield, the very same mechanisms that contribute to an economic form of association are the ones that contribute to a political form of association, so the lack of culture of cooperation was crucial to explain both the fragility of the democratic system and the minimal hopes for self-sustained economic development in the south.

For Banfield, *la miseria* results in amoral familism: the widest possible sphere of reference to elaborate one's interests and economic strategies is the mere nuclear family (husband and wife plus dependent children). This is both a cultural model and a social syndrome that becomes engrained in an ethos. The idea was famously accepted by Italian sociologist Carlo Tullio-Altan (1974, 1995), according to whom the Italian youths of the 1970s generally upheld traditional values and favored authoritarian arrangements in politics and society. He blamed this "syndrome of socio-cultural backwardness" on the lack of a "civil religion" of the nation-state. This line of reasoning was critiqued among others by feminist anthropologist Amalia Signorelli (1990), who showed how the culture of familism is first and foremost a "guarantee system"—that is, a form of insurance against risk, which is based on the most proximal and trustworthy guarantor, the next of kin. Furthermore, nepotism cannot be explained away as a cultural complex, as it is embedded in objective economic, political, and social relations of domination, so that patterns of personal advancement (either through migration or by resorting to kin's and friends' favors, or even criminal activities) often perpetuate the general contexts of economic inequity and social injustice. Finally, gender plays a fundamental role in familism as it is the women's role to ensure the reproduction of the nuclear family as well as, traditionally, its welfare and well-being. The inventiveness and creativeness of rural entrepreneurial women, who not only produced crops and children but also commodities and skills for the local markets, is celebrated by Signorelli (1990).

A long debate on kinship, land-property, inheritance patterns and labor organization thus exposed a much more diverse historical and juridical landscape than a blanket amoral familism. If landless peasants in Banfield's Chiaromonte found their point of reference in nuclear families, the nuclear family itself proved to succumb to the pressure of individual survival strategies in Naples' slums. In other regions, or even in neighboring localities to

Banfield's Chiaromonte, in Lucania, smallholders tended to build extended families rather than nuclear families (as shown by John Davis [1973] in Pisticci and Tony Galt [1991] in Apulia). In sum, there were many types of peasants in Italy, and a simplistic division between landowners and landless peasants does not portray the complexity of the socioeconomic scenario: central Italy's sharecroppers for instance organized themselves in descent groups precisely because "where there are many working hands under the same roof, there is abundance of bread," as Cristina Papa documented in Valnerina near Perugia (1985). The gender and age imbalance within such lineages has been painstakingly documented by a rich and thorough anthropological scholarship in Italian (see for instance Solinas 1993). Moreover, kinship patterns, which guarantee the availability of human resources for family rural entrepreneurship, can change and adapt over generations, according to changing economic circumstances—as Donald Pitkin (1992) found, studying the story of a family of landless peasants from Calabria who managed to establish themselves as smallholders in Abruzzo. Add to this the ethnic diversity and the associated land-inheritance patterns found in Alpine valleys and one has a suitably fragmented and complex scenario for the rural society that Italy was well into the 1960s, hardly warranting a generalized theory of amoral familism, let alone of trust.[2]

From smallholders to small entrepreneurs, equally and diversely rooted in the family as a unit for social and economic reproduction, Italy transitioned fast to one of the G8—the club representing eight of the world's largest economies. The impoverished middle classes of Italy's second millennium have direct lineages in the smallholder agriculture, which employed 42 percent of Italians as late as 1951 and now barely 3 percent. As noticed in the previous chapter, solidarity purchase groups restore lost social webs creatively, tapping with alternative forms of provisioning into a proximal rural context. Even the metaphor of district of solidarity economy, currently adopted by gasistas to conceptualize a model of alternative development, employs an analogy with Italy's diffused and family-driven industrial districts, which characterized Italy's "third way" to globalization in the 1980s and 1990s (Becattini 2000, Trigilia 2005). Unsurprisingly, Italian solidarity economy activists do not use the langue of community economies, which reproduces a naturalized notion of community fiercely critiqued in Italy by Gramscian anthropology (Clemente et al. 1985).

How distant is the societal canvass portrayed in 2002 by Dame Onora O'Neill who—one should be reminded—was writing in the United Kingdom:

> We constantly place trust in others, in members of the professions and in institutions. Nearly all of us drink water provided by water companies and eat food sold in supermarkets and produced by ordinary farming practices. Nearly all of us use the roads (and even more traditionally, the trains!). Nearly all of us listen to the

news and buy newspapers. Even if we have some misgivings, we go on placing trust in medicines produced by the pharmaceutical industry, in operations performed in NHS hospitals, in the delivery of letters by the Post Office, and in roads shared with many notably imperfect drivers. We constantly place active trust in many others. Do actions speak louder than words? (O'Neill 2002: 11–12)

They do, and I suggest that grounded ethnography speaks louder than philosophy. The subjects of the former British Empire may be confident that if they go to the post office, their parcel will arrive. They do not need to gain the solidarity of the post officer to make sure that he or she will do as good a job as possible to ensure that the parcel will arrive (for instance, checking that all the customs regulations are abided by or that no signature is lacking in any part of the cumbersome form that is handed out to the customer). Italians know that the parcel may arrive or not and that this depends on the good will and professionalism, or lack of, of a number of unknown people along the way. They may decide to be confident. They may well have no other alternative. O'Neill's description, if we take Gambetta's definition of trust, seems to correspond to confidence, rather than to trust: "Confidence, in the sense defined by Luhmann [1990], might be described as a kind of blind trust where, given the constraints of the situation, the relationships we engage in depend or are seen to depend very little on our actions and decisions" (1990: 224).

Gasistas try to change precisely the contexts of provisioning that situate them in a state of affairs that they could only accept with confidence. As individual customers, they can only try to appropriate commodities as end users—however relevant this may still be in anthropological terms.[3] As gasistas, though, it is precisely the fundamentals of service, of provisioning, and logistics that they engage with and try to control collectively. Individual GAS notably focus on food provisioning and try to renegotiate the conditions that make the food available: cultivation, working practices, distribution, price-setting, and logistics. But as members of networks of GAS, gasistas try to move beyond food to question the privatization of water, to manage short supply chains, and to locate perspicuous information about available tools and strategies to advance their mission.

The CORES report on GAS activism in Bergamo in 2011 portrays a distinctively political profile: of the 273 people who responded on the issue of political interest in the Bergamo area alone, about 43 percent declared to be sufficiently interested in politics, almost 31 percent very interested, 22 percent a little, and only about 4 percent not at all interested (Osservatorio CORES 2013: 7–16). Gasistas cultivate diverse sources of information: Internet and e-mail (87%), radio and television (86%), and discussion with friends and colleagues (86%) (Facebook came last with 22%)—which is indicative of how they socialize information in face-to-face relationships.

Despite their political interest and in-depth information, though, their trust in various types of institutions is low. They mainly trust social entrepreneurship (defined as providing goods and services for the public good; 86%); the magistrates (80%); and consumers' associations (79%). The police also score highly (70%). Among institutions for political representation, tellingly, the European Union attracts by far the highest degree of trust (52%), whereas the Italian government, political parties, the parliament, banks, and the industrial confederation score well below 15 percent. Somewhere in between we find municipal administrations (46%), the Catholic Church (36%), the trade unions (36%), and individual entrepreneurs (21%). Political parties are perceived to be interested exclusively in being voted, not in people's opinion (73% of interviewees agreed to this statement).

Only 24 out of 299 people had taken active roles in local administrations or had been elected as politically representatives, whereas the majority of them had taken part at least once in the last two years in grassroots political action (such as signing a petition or supporting a referendum): 95 percent had signed a referendum proposal, 70 percent a petition, 64 percent had boycotted specific products, 42 percent had participated in authorized demonstrations and 34 percent in strikes, while only 7 percent had taken part in a party-led political campaign, and 8 percent were registered with a political party. While about 39 percent of the interviewees visited Fair Trade shops, participation in other groups of alternative provisioning such as the Time Banks or Tavolo RES was limited, under 10 percent. Less than 5 percent had personal experience with the global justice associations that initiated the solidarity economy movement in the first place (such as the Lilliput Network, the Social Forum, or the de-growth movement). This clearly shows how GAS practice grew well beyond the network boundaries of the activists who initiated it, to the point that there is almost no memory of its historical rooting in the global justice movement. Again, this sets gasistas' styles of participation clearly aside from social movements such as Occupy, both in terms of discourse and of political practice. Gasistas seem to prefer individual actions with a collective critical mass, such as petitions and boycotts or the occasional authorized demonstration. Of various public causes that the Bergamo gasistas had supported, 83 percent were for the referendum against the privatization of water, and 75 percent were not only for the referendum against the reintroduction of nuclear power stations but also the defense of public schooling (56%), anti-mafia mobilizations (44%), the defense of pensions and social security (34%), and the rights of immigrants (35%).

Nevertheless this does not result in an apolitical attitude: almost 65 percent of Bergamo gasistas believe that one's actions do have an impact on government (although 41% agree that a right-wing government is the same as a left-wing government, and 46% agree that politics is so complicated that one does not understand what is going on). Political action is therefore distinct from satisfaction with the current system of political representation and with its actual representatives. The idea that amoral familism is a natural outcome of a failing state is also tempered by these results, as 44 percent would agree that one's prime responsibility is to one's family (and 29% would accept the statement that "one is never cautious enough dealing with strangers"), but, despite this, 70 percent of gasistas believe that one can trust people in general and only 0.3 percent would accept that immigration is a danger to our cultural identity. These survey questions spoke specifically to the issue of amoral familism and social capital, two key sociological concepts that, as I have argued above, have obscured the ethnographic analysis of how trust may actually be working in grounded contexts.

A first interesting symptom of GAS heterogeneity is the fact that gasistas are evenly split about religious practice: about one-third never goes to temples of any type, one-third regularly visits places of religious devotion, and one-third does so occasionally. As for political allegiances, about 20 percent did not wish to declare any position, while 74 percent described themselves as center-left (and only 5% as center-right). But when it comes to associative experience, it turns out that all but 7 percent of gasistas are members or have been part of at least one association. The diversity and range of associations is staggering, varying from recreational and sportive (57%) to cultural (51%), to NGOs and third world cooperation (43%), religious (41%), environmentalist (36%), care and health oriented (33%), student and youth (31%), civil and human rights (25%), trade unions (237%), pacifist (22%), consumers' rights (17%), professional (16%), Scout (15%), women's (14%), political parties (13%), and social movements (9%). We specifically asked to list any type of association that we might have overlooked and the list is long: Christian Association against Torture, Parents Association, Catholic Action, Time Bank, Animal Welfare, Interculture, Ecovillage, In Defense of Public Schooling, the People's School, Amnesty International, World Wildlife Fund, the Red Cross, Mothers in the World, Legambiente, Libera, Auser (popular housing association), and many others. Bergamo has one of the highest densities of associations in Italy, nevertheless, these data are still surprising not only for the number of associative circles and experiences listed but also the fact that 93 percent of scarcely 300 people represent them all. The diversity of their missions and political connotations confirms the fact that alternative provisioning acts as a neutral meeting ground for diverse types of activism which, in GAS, learns to share best practices and elaborate a specific discourse of solidarity economy and presumably disseminates them across preexisting networks.

It is in the solidarity purchase groups, and not elsewhere, that resourceful and motivated people meet and learn to share a common ground through food provisioning. Asked about the peculiarities of solidarity purchase groups, gasistas mentioned concreteness, sustainability, and solidarity in everyday practice. This was an open question on the survey, and someone also mentioned that GAS are not paternalistic or proselytizing. Others underlined the tolerant and welcoming atmosphere and the nonhierarchical relationships within the group. The coincidence of personal interest and common good was also underlined, as well as the fact that GAS usually involve whole families and are therefore educational spaces for the children. This enables a transformation of lifestyles for the whole family in provisioning choices. It was also stressed that GAS practice requires dedication, time, and a change in everyday life. But also the fact that GAS allow each to give one's time and resources according to one's capacity and availability, which may vary during one's lifetime.

The survey results well represent the ambition and range of objectives pursued by GAS: from an economic impact, to a social and environmental one. GAS activism, however, coincides with gasistas' own lives. Therefore, the study of GAS practice cannot but be a form of "engaged anthropology" (Low and Merry 2010). This consists of tapping into the "cultural intimacy" (Herzfeld 1997) of specific groups, representing the complexity and idiosyncrasy of motives, skills, and relational dynamics that brought solidarity purchase groups from managing their purchases collectively but privately, each in its own group, as I have shown in Chapter 3, to increasingly scaling up, while rethinking at the same time the nature and representational power of their own networks (Chapter 4).

NETWORKS OF NETWORKS

One of the opening remarks at the GAS/DES national assembly of L'Aquila in June 2011, perhaps unsurprisingly, was that individual GAS sometimes lack ambition and do not engender sufficient resources to make solidarity economy real. To do so requires a further passage: from the control of short supply chains to processes of actual governance, sometimes involving local public administrations. Hence the need for solidarity economy networks, whose aim should be to create synergies and reciprocal trust among a territory's economic, institutional, and social actors who are motivated to create districts of solidarity economy through transparent decision-making processes. Once DES are in place, though, RES should disband themselves, lest a risk of leaderism ensue.[4]

This is just one brief extract of one of the extensive interventions that took place during the three-day assembly of the GAS/DES movement, encamped on one of L'Aquila's hills on a splendid midsummer solstice weekend, not far from the closed-off ruins of the city center, which lay abandoned beyond security fences after the earthquake of April 2009. The all-day schedule included lectures, seminars, working groups, debates, summaries, and small-group meetings: activities ran well into the night. The biggest gatherings took place under tents, with plastic chairs arranged in circles, or in a theater-like fashion for plenaries. Small-group meetings happened all around, under olive trees, on the slopes of the abandoned terraced gardens, or even in the children's playground. A screen and PowerPoint projection facility was rigged up for the plenaries, but most discussions took place by the long-established Lilliput technique: a moderator would explain the agenda, would attend to turn-taking, and would keep written track of the main points of the discussion on big paper posters with colored felt-tip pens. The mental maps of the group's brainstorming would be kept available on panels for everyone to see, and a rapporteur would relate the group's deliberations and proposals to the plenary (Figures 5.1, 5.2, 5.3). I had become acquainted with this technique for inclusive, though in-depth debate at the previous assembly of the GAS movement in Osnago near Milan, the year before. It was also used during the foundational meetings of ReteGasBergamo, before and after the September 2010 debacle.

Figure   5.1 L'Aquila, June 2011. Gasistas visit the Basilica di Collemaggio, gravely damaged by the 2009 earthquake. Photo by Cristina Grasseni.

Figure 5.2 National Assembly GAS-DES, L'Aquila, Parco del Sole. A working group under the tents of the assembly. Photo by Cristina Grasseni.

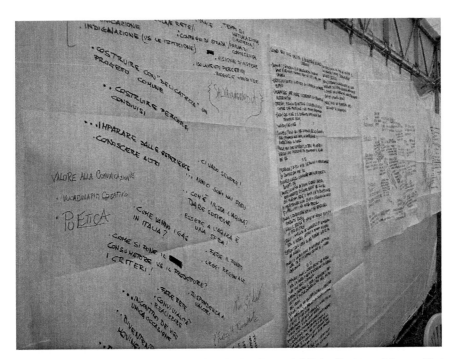

Figure 5.3 National assembly GAS-DES, L'Aquila, Parco del Sole. Posters of the working groups line the inside of the assembly tent. Photo by Cristina Grasseni.

At L'Aquila, T-shirts worn by the assembly participants featured statements such as "Bolivarian movement for New Colombia," "Water is a Common," "Sweet evasions. T-shirts from jail," "No research no future," "Libera" (the anti-mafia association), "Equosud Fair Self-Production," and "Black Sheep." The most commonly worn clothes were unbleached cotton shirts and trousers, and flowing gowns. It was a festive event, with children and families, and a colorful market with temporary stands selling fresh foods, wine, drinks, crafts, and documentation about solidarity economy, environmentalism, degrowth, global justice, transition towns, pacifist activism, DIY, and philosophy. At one of the plenaries, explicitly devoted to moving beyond food, one of the speakers noted how exactly ten years had elapsed since the Genoa Social Forum.[5] In 2001, this self-summoned meeting of global justice activists had been scheduled to take place at the same time and place as the twenty-seventh G8 meeting. The forum, which according to contemporary news attracted up to three hundred thousand demonstrators, was never allowed to meet the representatives of the G8. After some of the demonstrations degenerated into extensive property destruction, the gathering was infamously drowned in violence by the Italian police, during riots that left one demonstrator dead, several hundred arrested, and thousands injured. Three people went into a coma as a result of police beatings, including British journalist Mark Covell. At L'Aquila ten years later, the word *Genoa* was an emotional reminder for most of us, who had either lived the violence and the fear in person or had witnessed it incredulously, trying to distil meaningful information from Milan's People's Radio or from the Internet, as the national TV headlines and most of the press accused the Social Forum of having attracted organized violent demonstrators to the scene.

Unfortunately, that distant sunny weekend of July 2001 saw many more Italians crowding summer sales than demonstrating in support of the desperate calls for solidarity coming out of Genoa. Much later, twenty-five policemen were convicted for perjury, abuse of power, mistreatment, and physical lesions of ninety-three demonstrators, who, among other humiliations, were allegedly forced to sing and parade giving the fascist salute to their guardians, while incarcerated in the Genoa prisons. Beyond these juridically established facts, though, the audiovisual documentation still publicly available online gives a cogent sense of the extent of the violence, the devastation, and the wantonness of it all.[6] It felt safe, under the makeshift auditorium of L'Aquila 2011, to bet that most of those present, and old enough, had been somehow crying out their anger and despair ten years before, as their trust in the democratic state, the media, and civic solidarity was being beaten into silence, while everyone else went on shopping as usual.

Rete Lilliput was one of the 1,187 associations that adhered to the Social Forum. Of these, 86 were based in Genoa, 1,015 in Italy, and 172 were international—ranging from the steelworkers' trade unions to missionary nuns, from the Communist Workers Recreational Association to the Humanist Party.[7] After the Genoa beatings, an ex-Social Forum friend told me, it was commonly understood that the network would devise other ways of responding to global issues—that is, on a more local and pragmatic basis. If raising the issue of inequality and injustice in public demonstrations meant being crushed by state violence, then everyday practice and family foraging would become the main political weapon. Critical consumers would organize themselves into networks in order to exercise their political agency through the economic system. Networks of networks (of associations, Fair Trade shops, ethical banks, producer's cooperatives, etc.) would circulate not only ideas but also money, goods, and services, thus de facto liberating the economy from capitalism. The agenda of going "under the radar," as reported to me in conversation by my anonymous friend, was a post-Genoa strategy for actually building "another economy" instead of asking for it.

This finds explicit resonance in activist literature as well as in calls to withdraw from the indecency of global economy.[8] Davide Biolghini, co-founder of the Italian working group on solidarity economy networks, Tavolo RES, states clearly that the social actors of the Italian solidarity economy have been influenced by the global justice and pacifists movements through the Social Forums, since the end of the 1990s: "This has led to a specific integration, within Solidarity Economy, of scenarios for alternative economies, not simply to correct the capitalist market but seeking methods and tools for *another economy*" (Biolghini 2007: 22). In fact, the years following Genoa saw a booming of solidarity purchase groups. From the two GAS existing in the city of Genoa in 2001, for example, sixty-five developed.

Back to L'Aquila, we were reminded it was now time to move beyond food. We had debated this issue already at the 2010 national assembly of GAS at Osnago near Milan, where it was agreed that the following assembly of the solidarity purchase groups would also be the assembly of the districts of solidarity economy. At Osnago, in small working groups dispersed between a community center built in perfect brutalism style and a concrete school's gym, amidst the sticky heat of a humid June afternoon in the middle of an anonymous metropolitan sprawl of the Lombard flatlands, we discussed how to promote new agriculture for food sovereignty. Projecting our imagination beyond the tarmac and concrete that was all there was in sight, we debated how to lobby municipal administrations for organic and local food in school canteens or to make use of solar panels mandatory in public buildings. Among the participants of the working group on food sovereignty, we had a representative of the NGO ManiTese and activist Blandine Sankara from Burkina Faso, who talked about the role of women in establishing cooperative models of sustainable, local agriculture and how this can and does expose local activists to direct political violence. We sketched ideas on how to establish collaborative paths toward farmers' self-certification through participated guarantee systems.

At L'Aquila, we further considered how to develop other economies as a way to respond to the economic crisis—already biting in the summer 2011—in a context that combined the economic challenge with that of the local reconstruction after the earthquake. A significant advancement was perceived in the capacity of gasistas to act as selectors of self-proposed, self-declared ethical producers by asking for evidence of fiscal transparency, disclosure of price-making mechanisms, and respect of workers' rights. In this process, the traditional construction of corporate social responsibility as a largely self-imposed ethical restraint was being turned into a demand for transparency on the basis of collectively elaborated protocols and questionnaires. Though eventually self-certified (and thus open to fraud), the process of asking questions and obtaining answers was constitutive of a new type of trusting relationship.

At the 2011 GAS/DES national assembly, the theme was specifically how to review and better connect the parallel agendas of GAS (the solidarity purchase groups and their networks) and the districts of solidarity economy (DES). A new charter was developed and approved: the ten columns of solidarity economy were underscored by the GAS national assembly and by the working group for a network of solidarity economy, Tavolo RES, as representative of the districts. This three-page manifesto gave a timely definition of *solidarity economy* as the working of a network: an economy that defends the commons, respects Mother Earth and everyone's good living, and functions collaboratively on the basis of reciprocity, inclusion, and human relationships. An economy that promotes local ties and accepts its natural scale and limits, though aiming to develop through networks and to be transformative of society, defending human rights, and renegotiating the role of the market.[9] To use an expression that had emerged in the meetings of ReteGasBergamo to distinguish between the common gasista and the visionary network activist, at Osnago and further on at L'Aquila it seemed that the base and the avant-garde of the movement were finding a common ground.

In between the two yearly assemblies, several kinds of cross-network collaborations had flourished, with reciprocal enrolments across different working groups. I was aware of many of them, though not a first-person participant. Mailing lists of working groups, direct knowledge of some of the activists, and later my own professional collaboration with Tavolo RES to design and carry out the survey of GAS contributed to my understanding of the movement. Already at Osnago, in May 2010, several open calls for GAS-supported initiatives were taped to the assembly wall: for instance, a proposal to launch a national campaign for a drastic decrease in meat consumption, limiting meat production to organic only, with traceability across the spectrum and more humane living conditions in animal breeding. Or, a strategy to co-produce a GAS-led information network to bypass the interest-driven mass media via a Lilliputian-diffused network of news scouters, writers, and bloggers, clustered around locally known and credible activist groups. A third manifesto called for action directly in the arena of political representation, quoting the example of the Solidarity Civic Pact in Caltanissetta, Sicily, or the municipal "Civic List," which gained 9.6 percent of the votes in the town of Concorezzo near Milan in 2009.[10]

Beyond these ambitious calls, some small-scale projects evolved out of GAS working groups on key issues such as farmers' self-certification. For instance, discussed at Osnago under the agenda of food sovereignty, a system of participated guarantee (SPG), called Pedagogia della Terra (Pedagogy of the Land), began its experimental phase in Lombardy in 2012 thanks to funding from a Regional Bankers' Foundation, Lombardy's Cassa di Risparmio delle Province Lombarde (CARIPLO). The project was prepared by the well-established cooperative Short Circuit (Corto Circuito) in Como (probably the most advanced gasista achievement in Lombardy in the area of management, jobs creation, and coordination of GAS suppliers) in partnership with the district of solidarity economy of Brianza, which pioneered the relocalization of food supply chains with its project Spiga & Madia (see Chapter 2). Within a nationwide network of solidarity economy activists, every successful experience is capitalized upon and functions as the stepping stone for further projects. In turn, these can bring together like-minded networks that are geographically far apart. Thus, Corto Circuito was present in most of the main discussions and projects of solidarity economy in Lombardy: from the critical discussion of a regional law to normalize GAS economic activities, to active participation in local governance (one of the cooperative members being a representative in the municipal council of the town of Como). Corto Circuito also organizes the yearly fair of solidarity economy, Fa' la Cosa Giusta (Do the Right Thing), which increased attendances by 30 percent in 2011.

DES Brianza is respected nationwide for Spiga & Madia and other following and further-reaching projects, such as Dental Health for Everyone, Co-Energy, and Change Band (Cambia Banda). The latter was launched in 2007 as a collaboration with Livecom, reportedly the first nonprofit telecommunications provider in Italy. A social cooperative integrating recovering addicts and differently-abled workers into its staff, this Padua-based company offers DES Brianza an advantageous contract for telephone services via VOIP (through an Internet server). After preparatory debates at Osnago and L'Aquila in 2010 and 2011, the Co-Energy project was launched at the end of 2011 in the name of all the Italian GAS and districts of solidarity economy, as a contract between the Co-Energia Association and Trenta Spa, a publicly controlled green energy producer in Trento, at the foot of the Dolomites, generating mostly hydroelectric but also photovoltaic energy and investing on developments in natural gas provision. In 2012 the Co-Energy project further evolved with interest from and involvement with the populous Milanese GAS network InterGAS, which funded a solar panel energy production plant to be set up on the roof of one of the GAS network's providers. The plant was provided by a social cooperative, Retenergie, which has the ambition of covering the national territory through local nodes. Explicit and metaphorical reference to the network model is recurrent in these projects: nodes and light networks are supposed to synergize in order to reach wherever the service is needed, maintaining each one's identity but interlinking with whatever potential collaborations become available.

The common characteristic of these agreements, which are open to public inspection on the web site of DES Brianza, is that the commercial operator binds itself to donating 2 percent of the gains to a solidarity and development fund for further projects of the district of solidarity economy.[11] It is especially in the latest, most ambitious projects that DES Brianza was finally able to foreground its social and solidarity-driven vocation, after years of foundational work on carefully planned and budgeted projects. The initial projects eventually benefitted from a deeply motivated but relatively small number of adherents who contributed to set it up. The dentistry project, A Smile for Everyone (Un sorriso per tutti), offers dental services to DES members at reasonable market prices and the income thus generated feeds a 3 percent solidarity fund that the dental practice can use to subsidize services to the elderly and the unemployed of the Monza and Brianza area (whether they are, or are not, registered members of the DES[12]); that project is a collaboration of two social cooperatives that serve the local community.

I was well aware of DES Brianza as a driving force of solidarity economy in Lombardy since the 2009 meeting to set up the GAS network of the Bergamo area. At the October foundational assembly, minutes from a March 2009 meeting were transparently circulated by the Charon group—the working group in charge of ferrying the fragmented scenario of Bergamasque solidarity groups to a more coordinated, networked existence. A member of DES Brianza had been invited by Charon to the first preliminary meeting with twenty-nine GAS referents from the Bergamo area to discuss the creation of a network. According to the minutes circulated, the DES representative had been adamant about a clear distinction between a network of GAS and a district—in fact, in Brianza, as later in Bergamo, a two-track system was immediately to emerge: the GAS network would be flexible, light, potentially open to any new GAS at any time, and as wide as possible. A district would have to enlist committed members who would work on promoting committees, presiding over associations, and eventually signing legally binding contracts for commercial services. Nevertheless, it is apparent that what was called Retina dei GAS della Brianza (that is, "the small network," a diminutive that connotes lightness as well as smallness) would not only favor and enable the exchange of information among solidarity purchase groups but also organize collective purchase, promote new groups, and have a representational role as regards administrations and media. It was the base supporting the ambitious projects of the district activists. After the initial downturn and much consensus-building, this was the model followed by ReteGasBergamo. Already in 2009, the Retina GAS of Brianza had been able to bid for regional funding to start up a cooperative for the distribution of GAS products to its members. Project PIDOS (Piccola Distribuzione Organizzata e Sostenibile, or "small, organized, and sustainable distribution"), in collaboration with the local artisans association, had bypassed the issue of storage through same-day distribution with vans.

While in Bergamo much debate was devoted to whether GAS activism should be political or not, DES Brianza declared its political nature from the start: the promoting group of the district was the result of a collaboration between the political and cultural association La Mondolfiera and the local node of the Lilliput Network, in 2004, to set up a district of solidarity economy following the model proposed by Brazilian activist Euclides Mance. La Retina dei GAS della Brianza was, from the beginning, one of the actors for the development and promotion of the district. A DES project in other words does not take place in a political vacuum. Apart from providing economic support and a pool of participants from a network of solidarity purchase groups, its mission is to interconnect other social, economic, and institutional actors. Thus Fair Trade, the local Time Bank, two social cooperatives, and two municipalities were among the first interlocutors of DES Brianza. The steering group made its first steps within the framework of project Equal "New LifeStyles" (NuoviStilidiVita), whose aim was to monitor and support the first networks of solidarity economy in Lombardy. In 2006, the first territorial experiments began: one devoted to the short bread supply chain (Spiga & Madia) and the other to telecommunication (Cambia Banda). At this point, the DES was established as an association for social promotion with the name Toward a District of Solidarity Economy of Brianza. Partners in the association are two consortia, one cooperative, Slow Food, and the GAS network of Brianza.[13]

This brief foundational history highlights the diversity in the organizational capacities of gasista political activism between neighboring provinces, especially as compared with the fifteen-month stalemate of ReteGasBergamo and the very slow growth of DES Val Brembana (Bergamo and Brianza are two provinces in the Lombardy region, and they are no more than fifty miles apart). It also shows the intimately political agenda of food activism, which needs to be understood and engrained in territorial, institutional, and economic networks. Finally, the geometry of the networks of networks was apparent here in its involvement with more than one project at the same time, while leaving various degrees of participation and support available to the different layers of participation.

In the light of these contextual diversities, the Lombard project Participated Guarantee Systems (PGS) moves beyond the immediate objective of providing proximal and organic fresh bread to gasistas and tries to find a coordinated response across networks and districts to a global issue: the ever-increasing market pressure on small, marginal, and de facto sustainable farming. To certify one's products as organic, farmers incur heightened bureaucracy and costs, only to meet marketing needs. DES and GAS activists consider this instrumental to a global corporate strategy on organic farming, engendering land grabbing and peak soil. These issues have been independently explored and denounced by a number of agencies such as Transition Towns, Guerrilla Gardens, and the well-respected Toblacher Gespräche, co-organized by Wolfgang Sachs of the Wuppertal Institute for Energy, Environment, and Climate, one of the authors of the "Third Assessment Report of the Intergovernmental Panel on Climate Change."[14] The Lombard PGS project makes its first steps as I write, capitalizing on the expertise accumulated through local short supply chain projects on bread production, such as Spiga & Madia.[15]

Bread-making has important symbolic undertones in the choice of the food supplies that are being reappropriated by GAS activists. The Christian prayer that states "give us this day our daily bread" has an immediate resonance within Italian society—both because the daily diet is historically founded upon cereals and because various traditions of bread-making have existed in peasant society, with a diversity of cereal crops such as durum wheat and rye used to produce loaves designed to last for several days, sometimes months (Papa 1992). In fact, it had surprised us to find out, through the CORES report, that bread was the item that Bergamo's gasistas bought least: less than 10 percent of them. GAS bought both fresh and dry products: more than 90 percent of the groups bought fruit, cheese, oil, pasta, and flour. Less than half of them bought also fruit juices (42%), clothes (35%), sweets (24%), or poultry (23%). The absence of bread from the basket of GAS products can either be explained by home-production or by preference for fresh rolls bought at the corner shop.

Home bread-making is one of the activities on which activists in Bilanci di Giustizia[16] and the de-growth movement insist, as a basic task, to be reappropriated, together with one's time, dignity, and balance. In Bergamo, over the year 2011, forty-four GAS groups have organized activities that are in line with this agenda: fourteen groups organized collective fruit or vegetable picking at the farmer's fields, nine ran a workshop on home bread-making, six produced preserves and jams together, and five groups signed contracts with their producers to commit to buy out their entire crops (Osservatorio CORES 2013: 7–16). Home bread-making, once organic flour is bought through GAS (mostly every six months, as in the case of rice, maize, etc.) would in fact be much easier than reintroducing a short supply chain for fresh bread, as the DES Brianza did, which involves bakers, millers, and wheat farmers. It was something we discussed in the Mapping Group for ReteGasBergamo, and apart from the old age of the only organic mill-owner in the Bergamo area the idea of a newly formed network creating a short supply chain for bread sounded too much like "battling against windmills." Funding such a project would not be easy[17] and would probably run against the efforts of the Bakers Association to sensitize its members on the issue of access to bread for large families. In 2011, the bakers' association (Associazione Panificatori) engaged in a successful campaign to engage Bergamo's bakers to offer plain fresh bread at 1 Euro per kilogram instead of producing smaller and smaller rolls of very diverse types for discriminating but wealthy customers. In the present context of crisis, it made perfect sense for gasistas not to compete against an artisanal association that was openly working toward restoring some food access and equity through popularly priced bread.

Both the Kuminda conference in October 2011 and the solidarity economy fair L'Isola che c'è in September 2011 devoted specific attention to GAS-supported experiences of short supply chains and in particular to bread-making. Kuminda is a yearly public event organized in Milan by Terre di Mezzo, the independent publisher and promoter of the fair Do the Right Thing (see Chapter 2), together with ACRA, a 1968-founded NGO working in developing countries. Kuminda gathered about 3,500 participants in 2012[18] and is consistently seeking a public recognition from institutional stakeholders in the running up to EXPO 2015, scheduled to take place in Milan on the theme of "Feeding the Planet". By 2012, the GAS movement had gained the moral authority to invite the EXPO Milan Functionary on Sustainability to the certainly not grand premises of a restored farmstead on the outskirts of Milan to enquire about Milan's institutional engagement in green procurement and to boast GAS results in supporting local supply chains. Local authorities were reminded that consumers are not only individuals and families but also public administrations and institutions. Solidarity purchase groups and districts of solidarity economy were teaching their own governors a lesson in grassroots sustainability, self-help, and moral improvement.

Kuminda 2012 also hosted an international section: 130 delegates from twenty European countries met within the framework of the Urgency network. This was the first Europe-wide meeting of self-defined forms of community supported agriculture or CSA, which was described in Urgency's e-mails in the run-up to the event as "homologous to our GAS." As the Urgency website explains, three international symposia preceded this occasion, in Aubagne (France) in 2004, in Palmela (Portugal) in 2005, and again in Aubagne in 2008, in concomitance with the World Social Forum. Building on the experience of the French AMAP, the symposia wanted to connect different types and forms of "local and solidarity based partnerships existing in the world (CSA, ASC, Teikei, AMAP, Reciproco, etc.)."[19] Furthermore, "food, sustainable agriculture, agricultural politics, access to land, young farmers' training and installation, land settlement, ecology etc." were all clearly identified as political issues, which public institutions and partners would be invited to discuss. Among other initiatives, Urgency's international committee proposed a common definition for "local and solidarity based partnerships between producers and consumers." The Urgency network, which plans a California meeting in 2013, states:

> URGENCI brings citizens, small farmers, consumers, activists and concerned political actors together at global level through an alternative economic approach called Local Solidarity Partnerships between Producers and Consumers. Some well-known examples are: CSA (Community Supported Agriculture) in the Anglo-Saxon countries (US, UK), Teikeis in Japan, AMAP (Association to maintain small-scale family farming) in France, GASAP (Solidarity-based Purchasing Groups for small-scale family farming) in Brussels, GAS (Solidarity-based Purchasing Groups) in Italy, ASC in Quebec, and Reciproco in Portugal.[20]

In the e-mails that circulated in the run up to the Kuminda event, it was explained that this was not just an occasion for reciprocal knowledge but one of coordination and agenda-setting on food sovereignty. Kuminda hosting a Milan gathering of Urgency is one example of how a small number of solidarity economy activists are busy planning ahead and keeping abreast of the many possible alliances and developments, nation- and worldwide. Nevertheless, I would disagree with a simple equation of solidarity purchase groups being the equivalent of community supported agriculture because the former are largely consumer-driven while the latter are often producer-driven, and this may lead to quite different dynamics in terms of participation, communication, and decision-making. Considering the range and diversity of the local solidarity partnerships existing across the globe, one should understand that international coordination tends to be a loosely knit fabric, connecting tighter nodes of distinctive activists' networks, focusing on a wide variety of projects: from active citizenship, to social inclusion, to sustainable green economy. This loose network is far from a scaled-up version of a single solidarity purchase group. First, even within the GAS movement, the practice of solidarity purchase is interpreted in many different ways. Second, solidarity economy experiments are very diverse worldwide and may well focus on workers' cooperatives rather than on consumers' provisioning or sustainable agriculture. Last, with GAS there is no coordination from above nor an elective delegation mechanism in place but rather a spontaneous nomination of spokespersons to forums, which leaves the ground open to debate and sometimes controversy, as we saw ethnographically in the case of ReteGasBergamo.

There exist more than one international network of solidarity economy. Besides Urgency, which insists on producer/consumer partnerships and sustainable agriculture, RIPESS (Réseau Intercontinental de Promotion de l'économie sociale solidaire), defines itself

> as an intercontinental network that connects social and solidarity economy networks throughout the world. As a network of networks, it brings together continental networks, that in turn bring together national and sectorial networks. RIPESS believes in the importance of global solidarity in order to build and strengthen an economy that puts people and planet front and center. From Lima to Quebec, from Dakar to Luxembourg, RIPESS organizes global forums every four years and is a nexus for learning, information sharing and collaboration.[21]

Denomination and mapping are key activities for solidarity economies. Thus for Urgency, finding a standard denomination is fundamental for reciprocal acknowledgement, for external recognition, and for achieving global standing. For RIPESS, the first priority is to map, voice, and theorize economies that would otherwise remain uncharted. Its mission is thus reminiscent of feminist geographers Gibson-Graham's auspice—to voice and represent diverse economies that are congruent with a variety of concrete and contextual politics, practices, and affects (Gibson-Graham 2006).

What strikes in this fluid second-order networking fervor is not only the capacity for reciprocal support (for instance, accommodation for Urgency delegates at Kuminda was offered by fellow gasistas in the Milan area) and the fluidity of enrolment (with activists engaged simultaneously in different kinds of projects) but also fragmentation. Above all else, activists maintain a pragmatic rooting in their own contexts. The gasistas who set up short supply chains in the Milanese metropolitan sprawl are consciously playing the role of the independent citizens who Robert Putnam commended for the flourishing of democracy (1993), building up a wealth in social capital by engaging associatively in civic development. Notably, network activists situate themselves at the furthermost outposts of an archipelago of critical groups, associations, and circles, strategizing to bring about what Sidney Tarrow and Douglas McAdam have defined as "scale shift": "the process through which contention at one level is transposed to a higher (or a lower) one" through either "diffusion" or "brokerage" (2003: 1). This process is neither seamless nor uncontested. For example, the Urgency event at Milan's Kuminda was not underscored by the Tavolo RES—effectively the only grassroots coordination table for the promotion of networks of solidarity economies in Italy. Among other issues, Tavolo RES' informal nature prevents it from receiving funding from, formally adhering to, or representing associates in a project. DES Brianza instead has a formal profile as an association with a statute and a board of administration. In other words, the often-debated preference between a loose and inclusive coordination that does not take the form of delegation and a formal mechanism of representation is still an open issue in the GAS world.

Tarrow and McAdam remind us that "transnational framing and coalition-building must bridge broader cultural chasms than their domestic equivalents" (2003: 3; Snow and Benford 1999) and that "the objects of transnational contention are far broader, and less easily targeted than the national state" (2003: 3; Tarrow 2002). Scholarly engagement and activist scholarship, in the case of community and solidarity economies, seems key in doing the work of bridging frameworks and setting forward-looking agendas—for instance, on the topic of mapping and charting solidarity economies.[22] So far we have seen how districts of solidarity economy and networks for solidarity economy are actively engaged to make proximal, healthier, and more responsible commodities known, available, and logistically attainable. In doing so, they may well start from individual and family needs, providing for themselves and the network's associates, but this may then benefit society at large. In this, the family orientation of so much discourse and practice in GAS activism is far from familistic. Investing in short food supply chains, participative certification, and mapping the producers are deliberate and concerted actions that aim to increase the general knowledge about viable alternatives to mass consumption. However, gasistas' styles of consumption should not be taken as being representative of the average Italian family. In this section, I have provided a bird's eye view of the advancement and connectedness of some of the most successful projects and networks, such as DES Brianza. In the next section, I return to my first-hand experience and involvement in the Bergamo area, where some of the key actions in stepping up from GAS activism to a network of solidarity economy were the creation of so-called citizenship markets as well as participation in the nationwide reflection of the GAS movement to step beyond food, through a local working group on sustainable and solidarity driven textiles and clothing.

CROSSCUTTING COUNTER-EPISTEMOLOGIES

While the Brianza GAS network (Retina Brianza) was born roughly at the same time as the district of solidarity economy of the same area (DES Brianza), in

Bergamo the evolution of solidarity economy followed a different path. The only district, DES Val Brembana, was a local project whose members had found inspiration and support within the study group Sustainable Citizenship and the association Market & Citizenship. These two entities, in turn, collaborated with the GAS movement and specifically with ReteGasBergamo (in fact, most of its members were gasistas themselves), but they did not coincide with it. On the contrary, they constituted a reservoir of resources, inspiration, and expertise for what later took the name of network of solidarity economy (RES) of the Bergamo area. According to activists' theorization, it is usually GAS groups and their networks that provide the social and organizational base upon which second-order networking initiatives take rooting (Tavolo RES 2010). Nevertheless, in the case of Bergamo it was through Sustainable Citizenship and Market & Citizenship, rather than ReteGasBergamo, that a wider number of social actors and associations, already present and active in the Bergamo context, managed to synergize and bring about a number of cultural, economic, and political projects.

Sustainable Citizenship (Cittadinanza Sostenibile) originated as a "study group on critical consumerism" following a one-day symposium organized in December 2007 by sociologist Francesca Forno at Bergamo University. The conference, Shopping for Human Rights, was inspired by the Swedish political scientist Michele Micheletti, who was guest of honor, and her theory of Sustainable Citizenship. This is a "sustainable action on the part of individual consumers" who collectively influences policies and practices to remedy environmental and social injustice.[23] Crucially, the workshop summoned the main actors of Bergamo's fragmented scenario of civic and religious associations to a roundtable discussion of the perspectives of critical consumption. It was possibly the first time that such a varied spectrum of political and socioeconomic representatives met on neutral grounds: the Ethical Bank, the Time Bank, and anyone dealing with consumption and its critique, from Fair Trade to the antimafia movement Libera!, from Catholic missionary groups to the Communist Recreational Circle, from Bilanci di Giustizia to Legambiente, to socially inclusive agricultural cooperatives, to the farmers' trade unions.[24] What ensued in the immediate aftermath was a free seminar hosted at Bergamo University for all those wishing to continue reading and discussing on Sustainable Citizenship. Volunteers, activists, and NGO representatives became fixtures of the monthly seminars, which culminated in a second conference in November 2009, dedicated to critical consumption as a form of antimafia resistance: *Legalità è partecipazione. Il consumo critico come nuova frontiera della lotta alle mafie* (Legality is participation. Critical consumption as a frontier of anti-mafia resistance).[25]

The minutes of all the meetings of Sustainable Citizenship since 2007 are available online. By the end of 2009, each meeting averaged a dozen people. This tight-knit group won funding from a bankers' foundation,

CARIPLO (which traditionally funds projects for social and institutional development), to further expand its activities with a project tellingly entitled Not-OnlyFood. They organized a citizenship market, a map of solidarity economy, and a training initiative for NGOs. It helps to think of this working group as a network of networks of the type explained in the previous section. The first diagrammatic representation of Cittadinanza Sostenibile (Figure 5.4), in fact, pictures it as an ensemble of nineteen entities that are involved and represented in activities spanning seminars, projects, and co-research. A social housing institution, Fair Trade cooperatives, the Ethical Bank and the agency for ethical finance Mag2, Bilanci di Giustizia, a citizens' committee for Bergamo's agricultural park, socially inclusive agricultural cooperatives, cultural and environmental associations, the Bergamo Time Bank and Slow Food, the de-growth movement, an independent radio station, and a small farmers trade union were all represented in Cittadinanza Sostenibile, together with ReteGasBergamo.

Sustainable Citizenship is defined as a free and open network, but through its visibility, transparency of action, and consistency over time, it took the shape of a networking committee, wherein individuals would act as referents and gatekeepers for associations, whether formally or informally represented. In other words, this was an important meeting ground for people who had

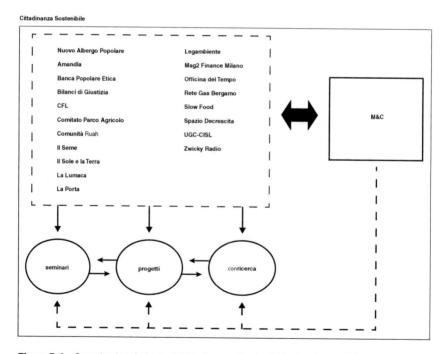

Figure 5.4   Organizational chart of Cittadinanza Sostenibile. Courtesy of Francesca Forno.

motivation, knowledge, and expertise—not only as individuals but also because of their own participation in other circles, associations, or activities.
Acting as an unambitious self-training and discussion group, Sustainable Citizenship was unhindered by the crippling debates about representation and
delegation that were halting the development of ReteGasBergamo. An important turning point was the establishment of a formal association, Market &
Citizenship, in March 2010 to support and serve the operational needs of
Sustainable Citizenship projects. Setting up a development agency was a crucial step for participating in funding calls and developing partnerships. This
separation of roles left Sustainable Citizenship free to maintain an open profile as a network and a discussion group, while Market & Citizenship could be
operational with projects defined through such open discussions. Sustainable
Citizenship, in turn, decided to shed the definition of study group and took
the name of Bergamo network for solidarity economy (Rete di Economia Solidale della Bergamasca).

Since its debut in 2011, Market & Citizenship has organized a fortnightly
citizenship market, under the name Mercato Agricolo e Non Solo (Farmers'
Market and Beyond). The market stands feature seasonal and local fruit and
vegetables, as well as local cheese, fruit preserves, salami, corn flour for po-
lenta, honey, wine, and the occasional Fair Trade products. Nevertheless, in
setting up citizenship markets, the Market & Citizenship project spelled out
its principles of food sovereignty, food democracy, food justice, food responsibility, and food quality, thus setting them apart from generic farmers' markets and specifying the political meaning of proximal foods.[26] Admission to
the market is granted by a self-evaluation protocol according to the following
principles: degree of environmental and health preservation, engagement in
social work, local provenance and food miles, degree of involvement in a relational economy, and participation in the activities to foster and diffuse the
mission of a citizenship market.[27]

As is clear from these premises, Market & Citizenship's strict standards
set citizenship markets aside from the plethora of public events show-
casing local products, variously advertised as *nostrani*,[28] certified by geographical indications, or promoted as typical.[29] In fact, the convergence of
conviviality (food and wine tasting), market (buying produce), and fair (show-
casing the same and other produce and projects) is a well-rehearsed formula in the many commercial events that are made to coincide with the old
and new *Sagre* (popular festivals) that mark topical moments in the agrarian and religious calendar. May fairs, summer hay-making feasts, fall trans-
humance processions, All Saints vigils, Christmas markets, and spring/
Carnival festivals are often sponsored by local municipalities, ethnographic
museums or eco-museums, folklore associations, and also by Slow Food,
especially in conjunction with the promotion of presidia products. The

rhetoric surrounding these events is difficult to distinguish, on the surface at least, from that of GAS: solidarity with the peasants, conservation of the environment, relocalization of food production, respect for the landscape, and virtuousness of the customer-producer relationship.[30] Slow Food uses the expression *co-production* to mark especially the latter, explicitly following the GAS example and, with its latest stress on good, clean, and just foods, it is aligned on the same principles of the solidarity purchase groups. Local collaborations on specific projects often ensue: the working group of Market & Citizenship for instance counts a well-known leader of a local Slow Food *Condotta* among its ranks. Citizenship markets may well include Slow Food presidia products and guided tastings but are at once wider in scope and more ambitious in their intentions. After negotiations with the Bergamo municipality for a public space in the town center, the fortnightly markets were inaugurated right outside the town's urban center, in the presence of local authorities, in April 2012. This first edition hosted a presentation of Bergamo University research on consumption in Bergamo, a Sustainable Citizenship initiative, a public aperitif with M&C products, street theater and children's entertainment, and the free distribution of a map for the critical consumer, *Bergamo eco-solidale*.

A key step in this strategy of synergic and public visibility was in fact the map of services and producers (*mappa per il consumatore critico*), which Sustainable Citizenship and Market & Citizenship produced in 2012. The map aimed to chart green and solidarity economy actors in a participatory way. The call requested that providers subscribe to a charter of principles, including the centrality of people, transparency and equity, workers welfare, environmental preservation, and active communication.[31] The map, distributed both on paper and online, works as a directory of services. Mapping solidarity economies was effectively co-producing them—similarly to what Kevin St. Martin argues of New England fisheries as commons: the act of charting them contributed to bringing them into existence (2009). It was the very act of mapping that contributed to bringing solidarity economy to the fore of the media and institutional attention in Bergamo—despite a long-term presence of GAS groups throughout the area. First, locating reliable, quality producers was not only a primary need for GAS groups but also an opportunity for local farmers to sell directly in protected markets. The protocol of self-evaluation for the citizenship market also served as a guideline to farmers wishing to access GAS customers. Through the self-evaluation protocol and by connecting at the market, producers learned how to communicate and share their profiles with GAS consumers. Thus, relational and cognitive strategies were deployed and developed on both sides. Second, mapping producers also meant facilitating the creation of networks among them by making them aware of each other's existence. Third, these actions brought both producers and GAS to the attention of local institutions and administrations. The university responded by publicizing the mapping initiative at a well-attended open day, while Bergamo municipality made a space available for the market right in the center of town (probably expecting that the market would attract tourists, too).

On a sweltering Sunday in July 2012, I attended the Bergamo citizenship market with my family and found out with surprise that all the activities and events, including the Sunday lunch that I had preregistered online for, were being held on the spacious street pavements outside the urban center. The stands of fresh vegetables and preserves were closing down by midday, as most of the customers, about 100 people, were taking turns sitting at the benches under white gazebos, eating the couscous and meat sticks prepared by a cooperative for social inclusion and served on trays. Salami, bean salad, tap water in clear bottles and whole wheat bread were followed by gasistas' homemade cakes. It was the most peaceful and convivial way to reclaim the streets. Eating on the curbside in the middle of the tarmacked town center was actually quite pleasant—partly thanks to the water bombs that the children were playing with. In the humid heat, relaxed conviviality and simple commensality specifically connoted a—by now familiar—sense of community. I knew few people personally, but the sense of a shared understanding was palpable. An understanding of why we were there, when we could have easily been anywhere else, in the shade (Figures 5.5 and 5.6).

Market & Citizenship also organized public seminars and a training course for local associations and NGOs, taught by local activists of Sustainable Citizenship, Market & Citizenship, Bilanci di Giustizia, and ReteGasBergamo. Topics included getting to know the Bergamo GAS experience, how to promote sobriety and ethical consumption, and family budgeting through solidarity principles. The transparent objective was to sensitize the existing civic and religious associations of the Bergamo area to explore potential synergies on the transformation of lifestyles and consumption. While solidarity economy activists could bring a fresh capacity for grassroots mobilization, longer-standing associations and well-established cooperatives could offer a better organization and more resources. The objective was to reach, convince, and train the leaders of existing circles to act on a voluntary basis as network facilitators, precisely in their capacity as managers of local NGOs. In this way, the eco-sustainable Bergamo could widen its ranks, from a privileged elite of discriminating consumers with high education and access to information to wider sectors of the local population.[32]

Through the map, the citizenship markets, and the training program for local NGOs, Market & Citizenship and Sustainable Citizenship were helping to

Figures 5.5 and 5.6 July 2012: moments of conviviality at a citizenship market in the center of Bergamo.

rethink the market, both as a place and as a practice. Beyond an individual-istic conception of economic transactions, they were devising collective ways to monitor, discipline, and moralize the market. They were providing cultural repertoires, political frameworks, and moral authority for restructuring provisioning as a form of active citizenship and environmental stewardship, well beyond consumer's choice. The concept of reinventing the market to turn it into a public space for socialization, transparency, and reciprocity was adopted by GAS on an ad hoc and spontaneous basis. GAS Bazar, for example, was a local initiative of a Bergamo GAS, launched in the name of reducing, reusing, recycling, and then passing on. The idea was to become more mindful about the stuff that we dispose of daily: domestic appliances, tools, toys, clothing, furniture, IT items, and so on. A free market was organized, similar to a yard sale, with the difference being that everything was given away for free. Every item had to be clean, safe, and working. In Italy, fashion and face are important social values. I have never seen yard sales or trunk sales in upscale boroughs. Wearing secondhand clothes is almost shameful and definitely something for the young, radical, or poor. In this context, a free, secondhand market was a bold outing. It tried to couple the reuse and recycle philosophy with the concept of a gift among equals (as opposed to philanthropy or donations to the more disadvantaged), maintaining reciprocal dignity and decency.

While this example was an initiative of a single GAS, more and more groups frequently got together on an ad hoc basis to invent and manage specific markets on the basis of their "unstable hard-headiness," as Luisa put it. One of such projects was the textile market inaugurated in 2010, currently running its fourth edition. The focus of the project was to treat textiles and clothing with the same critical scrutiny that GAS usually devote to food. In fact, it was felt as a major step to move beyond being only an alternative food network. The initiative was inspired by a seminar hosted by Sustainable Citizenship on solidarity-driven price-making in the textile industry. The topic was how to reweave, so to speak, the local conditions for a socially sustainable textile production in light of an established global model of delegating labor-intensive manufacturing to countries with no minimum wage or union rights. The seminar, organized by the Sustainable Citizenship study group in December 2010, explained how even famous "Made in Italy" textile corporations keep only the value-adding aspects of design and product-styling in-house, while counting on a cheap and fast, but polluting and inhuman worldwide logistics based on the exploitation of the weakest labor markets. Delocalization had local consequences: the demise of manufacturing traditions, the pressure on workers' rights, rising social inequalities, or the ungoverned environmental costs of global logistics.

These events were precious for enabling a number of diverse activists to network and compare concrete experiences and ideas. Sustainable Citizenship provided an umbrella organization, Market & Citizenship, the operative working group. The seminar on clean textiles was thus one of the first public events in which a solidarity economy network profiled itself publicly in Bergamo as a coherent movement. This specific event had important reverberation in local debates on governance because of its relevance to the demise of the long-established textile industry in the valleys near Bergamo, especially Val Seriana. In particular, the seminar featured a local campaign against the conversion of a postindustrial textile site in Albino into yet another commercial mall. It hosted one of the local textile entrepreneurs as a guest of honor and presented a case study, Made in No, for the relocalization of artisanal textile production. Supported by a Christian association in the province of Novara, since 2006 Made in No has produced organic and equitable underwear: the customers (mostly GAS groups and Fair Trade shops) guarantee preorders in exchange for a transparent pricing. The project imports organic cotton from a Brazilian workers' cooperative, Justa Trama. The full list of providers is public, and each actor in the production chain contributes transparently to the final price, guaranteeing minimum wage to workers and declaring the costs for sustainable production. The project was initiated by a local tailor, who converted his artisanal manufacturing firm—rapidly running out of business because of international competition—to target a local demand for high-quality but accessibly priced cotton underwear.[33]

As a follow-up to the seminar, a working group set itself up: it was in itself a veritable knowledge bank of solidarity economy in the Bergamo area. The members list included long-term gasistas and GAS founders, local scholars, and delegates of ReteGasBergamo involved in census, training, and communication working groups, as well as influential members of the Bilanci di Giustizia, and agricultural trade unionists. The list continued with the local Time Bank, both of the two Fair Trade cooperatives active in the Bergamo area, and both of the two Slow Food Condotte, as well as DES Valle Brembana. By profession, they were a hospital nurse, a librarian, teachers, unionists, retired factory workers, post office clerks, and a few self-employed. Because of their involvement in various types of local NGOs, they were best positioned to appreciate the successful experiment in Novara and to capitalize on a serious reflection on how to determine price, whether in large distribution chains or in participatory collaborations.

Within six months of the seminar, the working group organized a fair of clean textiles in Bergamo, with a market of Made in No and other organic and solidarity textile makers, as well as sewing and recycling workshops and public demonstrations of handloom-weaving. Fifteen producers form throughout Lombardy and Veneto were present, and the event was widely advertised within and outside the GAS network as a unique opportunity to meet, listen to, and buy from producers who are ecologic, equitable, and transparent about producing clothing: from organically dyed jeans to unbleached cotton, from handmade alpaca wool to the Made in No underwear. Even though only a certain number of GAS groups were actively involved in hosting and organizing the event, it was an important turning point, marking the proactive role of solidarity purchase groups in rethinking the economy.

The transition from food to nonfood as an acceptable topic for GAS engagement would not have been made so swiftly without the facilitating expertise bank of Sustainable Citizenship, which made available literature about successful alternative provisioning networks elsewhere in Italy. The composition of the working group was such that no sector in the variegated world of Bergamo's solidarity economy would feel excluded. This was a particularly important lesson learned in the wake of the ReteGasBergamo debates on the so-called basis/avant-garde divide. The seminar on Made in No sensitized public opinion on the concrete and local issue of what to do with a dismissed textile industry in Albino, but the fact that Market & Citizenship had been active in the same village for almost a year organizing citizenship markets certainly made a difference to the capacity of popular mobilization against yet another shopping mall.

Cittadinanza Sostenibile was perceived by gasistas as a hub and a springboard for a number of seedling initiatives—to adopt their vegetable metaphors. From participating in the meetings of ReteGasBergamo, there is no doubt that at times Sustainable Citizenship was seen as anticipating a more laborious ripening process that the GAS network did not feel ready for as a whole. Nevertheless, it did proactively provide gasistas with a constructive meeting ground, a common discourse, and repertoire of action. This soft networking strategy proved valuable. Environmental, anti-mafia, and social justice activists came together for the purpose of self-training, focusing on food provisioning first (through the citizenship markets) and then on clean textile, and by contextualizing the problems vis-à-vis their own contacts and agenda, they innovated each other's repertoires and collaborated toward doing something new. Vice versa, the nonviolent debating practices adopted by ReteGasBergamo and the GAS national assembly became a valued repertoire of Sustainable Citizenship, which in 2009 decided to respond to the open call of Francesco Gesualdi, the co-founder of Rete Lilliput with Comboni father Alex Zanotelli, to became one of the nodes in his network for a just economy (ideally, a continuation of the Lilliput Network, which was formally operative between 1999 and 2009).[34]

Sustainable Citizenship provides a model for what, I maintain, was in fact happening elsewhere throughout the solidarity purchase groups and their networks and districts, though probably more slowly and with serendipitous outcomes: people of various backgrounds, professions, and associative culture were learning to rethink the fundamentals of economic life by deriving transformative concepts and practices from experience, from local histories, and from each other. The variety of experiments within solidarity economy is a testimony to the richness and redundancy of this process: wherever second-order networks were functioning as meeting grounds for trusted collaborations, a number of what I call *crosscutting counter-epistemologies* were being tested. Overlaps in interests for the relocalization of food production brought together Slow Foodies and gasistas: the former setting up a short chain over red maize; the latter converting the same producer to organic potato farming. The model of the short supply chain was being appropriated by DES activists to push it beyond reterritorialization and squarely challenge the determination of price, whether for bread or for underwear. Interstices and overlaps made potential sites for collaboration across networks about sustainability and ecology. Gasistas learned from Bilanci di Giustizia how to "shift" budgets and how to draft self-test protocols of production.[35] Districts of solidarity economy took this further to substitute participatory guarantee systems for organic certification.

Above all else, from the convergence of anti-mafia, environmentalist, and consumers' rights literature and activists, gasistas learned to rethink the space and function of the market. They invented protected farmers' markets for their providers and made them a tool for "dropping the anchor" in city centers, reappropriating public spaces through citizenship markets and orange landings. They introduced free swapping markets and organized no-food markets and managed to turn them into parties. As one gasista wrote in the public online forum following the Nembro assembly, the difference between Sustainable Citizenship and ReteGasBergamo was that "*Cittadinanza Sostenibile* is a cultural entity, a working table for associations, institutions, and citizens . . . but while *Cittadinanza Sostenibile* connects like-minded people, ReteGasBergamo tries to maintain a dialogue between a variety of people, some of whom have diametrically opposite views." This comment is indeed telling of the fact that the results of three years of collective debate, readings, and self-training within Sustainable Citizenship were being perceived, in 2010, as a like-mindedness that was not there at the start but was nevertheless easier to attain in a smaller, tighter circle of relationships than in a network that aimed to keep together sixty-two GAS groups in harmonious consensus.

Whether in ReteGas or in Sustainable Citizenship, provisioning activists understood that the circulation of skill and knowledge is equally important as the provisioning of commodities and therefore organized study groups, expertise banks, and vocational training across networks. Especially because of its self-organized and nonprofessional nature, training and communication play a very important role in the tool kit of network development. As we have seen, at all levels the actors of the solidarity economy scenario are more often than not self-funded volunteers. They do run the risk of overexposure, which may put their own projects at risk. More organized cooperatives and NGOs, on the other hand, are often criticized within the volunteer circles as they may find themselves bidding for public funds—and even be allocated spending provisions—for projects that have not been designed locally or in contexts of which they do not have the necessary grounded knowledge. Lack of participatory decision-making is a common criticism that is raised against the third sector (especially large-scale associations and cooperatives) from within the ranks of loosely organized grassroots networks such as GAS, RES, and DES. In fact, scholars of the social and cooperative movements have highlighted how the professionalization of the nonprofit sector, in the long run, has made it ill-equipped to contribute to long-term capacity-building in local communities (Forno 2013a, and Meyer, 1989). On the contrary, GAS self-organization can be read as a sign of societal vitality, a spontaneous process of regeneration of societal ties that prevents dramatic breakdowns by reweaving economic transactions into social links.

Davide Biolghini of Tavolo RES (2009: 170) stresses the role of network animators—that is, facilitators who moderate meetings, keep track of developments, make sure that everyone is on board and on the same page, help redrawing the agenda, avoid personal conflicts, and apply simple turn-tacking techniques in meetings to avoid polarization. Their role vis-à-vis the socioeconomic contexts is also fundamental, in that they provide the contact point for a number of groups and individual entrepreneurs. At the national level, Tavolo RES sees itself as a hub of facilitators, similar to how Sustainable Citizenship played a role at the local level, to enable networking and the development of solidarity economies. For instance, training courses are offered when enough funding and interest can be generated locally. A training course for network developers was organized by Tavolo RES in the Brembana Valley near Bergamo in the winter of 2010. It was described in the promotional leaflet as a *Corso per Animatori di Reti Locali* (Tavolo RES 2010): a training course for facilitators (*animatori*) of local networks or, in the organizers' words, "a tool box to build an alternative to the predominant economic system, based on sustainable local development, network democracy, responsible participation, and active citizenship." This was one of the few solidarity economy events organized on the basis of fee-admissions only and was clearly envisaged as both selective (that is, aimed at people who were already active in the movement) and as a fundraiser. Teaching was organized on a residential basis over three weekends, spanning about three months. Each weekend focused on a specific module: knowledge and imagining solidarity economy, power, communication, and governance, and experiences and practices.[36]

Taught by activists and scholars who were internal to the solidarity economy movement, the seminars spanned the topics of conflict and social change as well as commons, rights, and needs. The practicum hinged on experimenting with alternatives: "using the economic crisis to propose a new political and economic paradigm," outlining the "potentials of critical consumption for social change," and sketching "energy and food crisis scenarios." Lessons in how to promote change through social networks included "ecology of power: how to make decisions in complex systems," "sharing knowledge for community growth and conflict management." "how to communicate alternatives and promote a desire for change," and "how to facilitate a group, manage a process, let interests and presumptions emerge." Experiences and practices included tips on sharing practices, creating a shared memory, and learning from experience. Workshops included "how to plan, produce and distribute goods and services," presenting the most successful projects of the districts of solidarity economy in northern Italy: the cooperative Corto Circuito (Short Circuit) in Como, project Co-Energy in Brianza, and project Made in No. Furthermost, areas of discussion and information concerned "the integration of local DES with public welfare," "self-management of money and credit," "reappropriating the landscape, self-determining food," and introducing "a national and European network of GAS and RES." This format was not devoid of political ambition, hoping to trickle down from network facilitators into forms of more widespread socioeconomic impact (especially through forms of mutual help, peer-training, and self-help).

Social movements scholars warn that "the obsessions of scale-jumping and scaling up local microresistances can also be an academic imposition that misunderstands the actual aspirations and overlooks the limitations of those sustaining place-based projects" (Chatterton and Pickerill 2010: 486). Scaling up at all costs, in the words of Chatterton and Pickerill, does not contribute to an honest "understanding of the messy particularities of activist place projects." Quoting the feminist geographer Geraldine Pratt, this comment suggests that "vanguard tendencies" are rooted in mostly white male academics ambitions to make their activist groups go global, "rather than getting involved in everyday sustenance work" (Chatterton and Pickerill 2010: 486). In the comparative examples of Sustainable Citizenship and ReteGas-Bergamo, we can see two adjacent but noncompeting strategies that eventually fed back into each other's views on how to make themselves relevant to their context (a different and less colonial ambition than that of "scaling up"). We can see how they actually did it in practice in the case of Sustainable Citizenship: through tight-knit self-training, focusing on few ambitious and well-organized events, and by making one's activities and reflections transparently accessible. In the case of ReteGasBergamo, this happened through inclusive, collective, and as wide as possible debate for as long as it was sustainable and finally converging on a value framework and a procedural code that would become binding for anyone subscribing to the network.

Even though I adopted the language and definitions that emerged spontaneously in the debate of ReteGasBergamo in the aftermath of the failed Nembro assembly, depicting Sustainable Citizenship as avant-guard and GAS as basis, one engaged in a fugue forward (*una fuga in avanti*), the others in consensus-building, would be misleading. I do not think that this language choice actually corresponded to a Marxist distinction between an intellectual vanguard and an unself-conscious proletariat; on the contrary, each model was charting its own repertoires and practices, and they probably would not have come to adopt the same tools and resolutions, if they had not mirrored and responded to each other's instigations and needs. Cittadinanza Sostenibile acted as a conceptual reservoir in which novel strategies and projects could be debated and initiated, thanks to the proximity and exchanges among crosscutting repertoires, experiences, and styles of participation: counter-epistemologies that found a common ground in rethinking provisioning.

Likewise, each solidarity purchase group acted as a laboratory within which original and sometimes unique ways of refashioning provisioning were devised. It is unsurprising that they showed resistance to network-wide online orders, after having spent years to each select their own trusted customers and having invented ways of combining collective logistics and accounting with an explosive growth in membership (some through chains and subgroups, others through budding and grafting). Network analysis has shown that proximity and collaboration on concrete tasks are potential channels for spreading and adopting innovative models, repertoires, and ideas (Roger and Shoemaker 1971, Forno 2011a).[37] In seminal reflections on networks as structures of relations, on their generativeness and resilience, Mark Granovetter underlines "the role of concrete personal relations and structures (or 'networks') of such relations in generating trust and discouraging malfeasance" (1985: 490). The daily practice of provisioning and the basic need of procuring food served as a common ground that was easy to share, upon which specific political and epistemic toolkits to move beyond food could be developed, socialized, and disseminated. By comparison with my own ethnographic experience in ReteGasBergamo, observing the success of Sustainable Citizenship and Market & Citizenship was a unique opportunity to see how a partial overlapping of competences, roles, and practices across activist networks, while generating ample ground for debate, eventually facilitated the adoption of best practices across different groups.

Simultaneously, my Bergamo University colleagues of CORES and myself were carrying out the quantitative survey of Bergamo's GAS, contacting all the sixty-two solidarity purchase groups inside and out of ReteGasBergamo. This experience raised both methodological and deontological issues. To an extent, because of my participation in ReteGasBergamo, I was participating in the creation of the very object I was studying. Nevertheless, through the survey I was also gaining precious insights in the movement's perspective on my own academic research. For instance, we presented our research agenda and had a dry run of the CORES survey at one of Tavolo RES training weekends in February 2011. It was a unique occasion to gather fresh insights and critical feedback from long-term GAS activists. About fifty people were taking the training course, all of whom were involved in various networks and districts of solidarity economy across northern Italy. They had converged to Valle Brembana, specifically to the youth hostel of Camerata Cornello, and about twenty of them accepted to fill in our draft questionnaire, after a long and tiring day of seminars and working groups. Over coffees and grappas of a bright and freezing winter night in this deserted mountain village, I and my colleagues gathered reactions to our forty-page questionnaire. Their understanding and specifications were instrumental in helping to calibrate the number, phrasing, and types of questions asked. Once again, we found that only in-depth knowledge of the movement could generate the right questions—for instance about political activism, associative experience, and network analysis.

For example, a crucial question in the CORES survey consisted of asking the 299 interviewees to think of their best five friends and to answer the following three questions: where do they live? (in the same neighborhood? In the same city? In a city close-by? Or in a distant city?); how do you communicate with them? (face to face? via Internet? by phone?); and are they members of a GAS, too? Once reassured about the fact that the point was to establish a degree of proximity in network analysis, not the names of their best friends, most of the gasistas disclosed that their best friends lived in a city nearby or in the same city, and they saw each other face to face. Between 25 percent and 30 percent of their five best friends were gasistas, too. This largely confirmed the idea that GAS practice is learned by exposure and proximity and— as gasistas' language rightly conceptualizes—that the GAS movement grows like strawberries in a field: by overflowing into adjacent turfs.

In the light of recent calls for anthropology to be more concerned with "inclusion, collaboration, and engagement" through social critique (Aiello 2010), this tight collaboration was a positive though somewhat ambivalent experience for me and certainly motivated me to reflect further about the ethics of my own engagement. The epistemological realization that surveying, charting, and mapping actually create our objects of research was, of course, not shocking. This is something that social scientists have somehow learned to live with since

Schroedinger's cat and Heisenberg's indetermination principle. Collaboration and co-research was also prompting a reflexive attitude that most ethnographers are comfortable with. It was not so much in my participation of the survey design as in my participant observation as a gasista that countless opportunities to steer and influence the outcome of important debates arose. With a focus on bridging networks, I was particularly aware of the importance to facilitate or, vice versa, hinder the flow of information that was channeled even through my own person, in my capacity of both a researcher and a delegate of my own GAS in the Mapping Group of ReteGasBergamo.

I never eschewed from participating in decision-making and deliberation within my solidarity purchase group. But at the Nembro meeting of September 2010, seeing the impasse of ReteGasBergamo, I publicly maintained that those who were present were entitled to vote, as the rules of the game had been explained the year before and GAS assemblies are examples of open and direct democracy. As a result, someone suggested that I put my own candidature forward for coordination of the network. I explained that I could not coordinate the very process that I was observing. While naively positivistic in its synthesis, this position in effect drew the line of my own participation. I continued to voice my opinions, contributed to the debate, and possibly influenced some of the discussions. But I did not lead, represent, or speak for the organization. To an extent, this was confirmed later on, as, in one of the following meetings of ReteGasBergamo, ambivalent opinions were voiced about people who are part of the movement "out of their professional engagement," including scholars, trade unionists, and cooperative workers. Even though their time and commitment is volunteered, some perceived a latent conflict of interest, as if there was something to be gained for us at the end of the line: a trade union project, a deal for the cooperative, or a book. Deontological restraint was never assured to a sufficient degree.

Conclusion

Diana, my elder gasista who once offered me cow liver, confessed during a GAS meeting: "You know, I go to the supermarket sometimes. There are a few things I need that I cannot procure through GAS. So I go, and I just buy those items. But I look into the baskets of the other shoppers, and I pity them. I really pity them for what they end up eating, and how." While Europe is swept by yet another food adulteration scandal, which leads one to conclude that horse meat was introduced in large distribution networks at unspecified levels of the supply chain, even for rather costly and discriminating supermarket chains in early 2013, one would conclude in sympathy with Diana and happily eat the free cow liver and tongue that she procured for me through my solidarity purchase group.

In the light of the economic crisis initiated by the financial scandals of 2008, GAS have by now achieved a critical mass in Italian society. Their groups find local connections with Fair Trade shops, environmentalist associations, or ethical banks. We have seen in the previous chapters how they thus create so-called districts of solidarity economy (DES) and networks of solidarity economy (RES), which aim to circulate not only information and ideas but also goods, services, and money. Some DES have been successful in setting up local food chains and reintroducing local breeds and crops, as in the case of the DES Brianza, which sponsored wheat crops for the production of local bread in the Milan area (see Chapter 2).

In gasista activism, while great care is put into making sure that everyone shares the burden of organizing provisioning, even more stress is placed on the fact that solidarity should be driving the provisioning process. In Chapters 3 and 5, I have argued how GAS activism is not only reweaving the fabric of a more sustainable economic practice on a local basis, but it also responds to a pandemic loss of trust in Italian society. On the basis of their provisioning practices, gasistas gain the moral authority and the technical expertise to teach and instruct the institutions that should govern the territory on how to carry out such governance in a collaborative, ethical, and sustainable way. Solidarity economies have thus become the locus of critical reflection and action on core elements of Italian contemporary society: the market, the commons, and the role of the individual as citizen, consumer, and producer.

The literature on political consumerism in Europe and the United States (Allard et al. 2008, Leonini and Sassatelli 2008) shows how several forms of civic consumerism have developed within different frameworks, their efficacy depending on their local rooting in specific cultures of participation, local experiences, histories, and subjectivities. In Chapter 4, I provided a critical description of how solidarity purchase groups may find significant challenges when they try to organize themselves into networks that have a conscious political ambition.

I insisted on the importance of relationality within GAS practice and on the crosscutting counter-epistemologies that travel across activists networks. For instance, Sustainable Citizenship worked as a second-order network for the Bergamo area, providing a meeting ground for diverse types of activism that would otherwise not necessarily intersect and cooperate. Likewise, many grassroots mapping efforts overlapped and synergized over the need of charting the boundaries of the GAS movement: ReteGasBergamo, Market & Citizenship, and my own CORES research group at Bergamo University collaborated to map solidarity purchase groups and nascent solidarity economy districts and networks. Mapping created mutual knowledge and cooperation also at the institutional and entrepreneurial level.

Recent reviews of alternative provisioning in Italy read it as a political phenomenon. Paolo Graziano (2009: 17–20) in particular proposes to envisage GAS as a "pressure movement" of public opinion on local administrations (to increase recycling, for instance, or locally harvested produce in school canteens). My ethnography shows how this is not a spontaneous result of GAS practice: different objectives and subjectivities are developed at different levels—in the individual solidarity purchase group, within GAS networks, and at a nationwide and international level by networks of long-term activists and scholars. While gasistas certainly have by now the numbers to shift significant budgets toward local economies, promoting higher sustainability, the most ambitious projects I described here (such as the citizenship markets or the orange landings) were network projects. It was first and foremost within and across networks that novel political readings of provisioning were conceived and experimented.

I have analyzed the multiple convergences between different forms of provisioning activism: within solidarity purchase groups (GAS), in networks of GAS, in districts of solidarity economy (DES), and in Cittadinanza Sostenibile, as one example of a solidarity economy network (RES). I dwelled on how collaboration on specific projects engendered communication and cross-pollination of practices and discourse, something I called crosscutting counter-epistemologies—between activists and scholars, between gasistas and well-established associations (such as Slow Food), and between different theoretical discourses: that of co-production as postcapitalism, that of solidarity as a form of engaged Christianity, and that of "economies of trust" and "of regard" (Sage 2007, Offer 1996) as a way of re-embedding economic transactions in reciprocity and "affect" (Richard et al. 2009, Roelvink 2010).

GAS provisioning spans many types of short supply chains, including face to face, proximal, and spatially extended to regional areas (Sage 2007: 151–2, based on Murdoch, Marsden, and Banks 2000). Gasistas engage their neighboring farmer as well as the Parmesan dairy or the Sicilian orange-grower, though an ongoing discussion on food sovereignty within the movement favored a shift toward spatial proximity. Co-production is thus also interpreted in terms of a close and personal collaboration with the farmer. If not directly working the fields, gasistas take a personal stake in the farming enterprise in terms of planning the crops, providing financial support in times of crisis, and especially by being faithful customers. Gasistas have progressively learned to not only value organic produce but also invest in local agriculture; to distinguish between the product per se and the complex food system that brings it about. While the charismatic leaders may be motivated by an agenda and awareness of international solidarity networks, higher numbers are nevertheless reached by this systematic reinvention of food at the microscopic scale. My argument is that the ultimate result of solidarity purchase groups is not securing quality-added foods at affordable prices for oneself and one's family (though this is undoubtedly the most immediate result of their practice) but, more generally, establishing reliable and trustworthy partnerships—socially, economically, and politically—in a time of perceived generalized moral bankruptcy and societal fragmentation.

The book raised a number of questions about the refashioning of provisioning within the GAS movement. What is the social role of food when it becomes the object of collective deliberation in a solidarity purchase group? How does the GAS practice of solidarity change ways of sharing food and styles of consumption generally? I described how gasistas manage logistics, seasonality, and ICT—I explained their resistances and capacities for innovation. I questioned the premise that food activism is a privileged middle-class fad and showed how provisioning takes on militant meanings in Italy, especially at a time of economic and societal crisis but also on the basis of a long and diverse history of associative culture and styles of participation. I stressed the capacity of gasistas to inform themselves, debate, and build consensus as they not only refashion supply chains according to their own principles but also reweave economic and political relationships into a gravely dehisced societal fabric.

The immediate reasons for the growth of solidarity purchase groups may well be the impoverishment of the lower middle classes and their retrenchment in networks of kin and friends. Nevertheless, the anthropological interest in this phenomenon lies in the social processes and political results of these groups' progressive exposure to, and appropriation of practices of solidarity economy. This is why an ethnography of GAS cannot stop at an analysis of the management of alternative food networks but necessarily grows into an ethnography of civil society, as gasistas find themselves posing fundamental questions about sustainability and democracy, political ecology and political anthropology.

Why food then? Despite the diversity of Italian food cultures, their communal insistence on conviviality and commensality marks just about everything in Italian society—from gender roles to social status, from religious symbols to festivities, from rites of passage to age group identity (Counihan 2004, Harper and Faccioli 2010). It is no surprise that changing food provisioning styles can be as far-reaching an endeavor as reweaving the fabric of society itself. Food as a total social fact, once changed, can be generative of new sociality, economic circuits, and political participation.

The argument of this book is that GAS collective practice of provisioning is transformative of lifestyles in ways that mere ethical consumption at an individual level would not be. GAS are collective actors: they devise alternative circuits for food distribution; practice mutual help; experiment with a social pedagogy of sustainability; inject trust, reciprocity, and solidarity in the everyday drudgery of food procurement. They may enhance civic engagement, select new interlocutors for governance, and shape a fluid geometry of networks of networks that is, nevertheless, fiercely opposed to hierarchies and delegation. From GAS to RES to DES, the reinvention of provisioning has economic, social, and political implications. As I show in Chapter 4, though, this should not be understood as a predetermined progression: GAS and DES were not conceived of as one the basis of the other, and their convergence is an ongoing process. In fact, not all gasistas may agree with, or even be aware of, the most advanced projects of solidarity economy.

Throughout this book I have maintained a distinction between GAS and DES, as my ethnographic experience shows that it is not at all banal or spontaneous for GAS to form networks and to develop them further into networks of solidarity economy (RES). Vice versa, DES are not necessarily the outcome just of GAS, but, more frequently, they are the result of careful and patient networking among alternative provisioning activists and different types of associations, NGOs, and institutional agendas. Certainly, the philosophy and modus operandi of GAS, RES, and DES have their roots in the seminal reflections on critical consumption of the 1990s and the Lilliput Network experience of mobilizing for global justice before and after Genoa 2001. Beyond the widespread recognition of respected charismatic leaders such as Francesco Gesualdi and Father Alex Zanotelli, though, their trajectories are overlapping but distinct. Solidarity purchase groups propose a popular formula for alternative provisioning that, especially in times of crises, proliferates independently of its founders and has ramifications in the fabric of society, thriving on existing webs and modalities of mutualism between kin, neighbors, and friends. DES provide a systemic reflection to this, proposing further projects and moving beyond food: with short supply chains, participated guarantee systems, and green energy procurement. GAS' new mutualism reweaves the economy when all other instances of delegation prove untrustworthy. DES provide a political direction to this, but without gasistas they would not be grounded in society. Vice versa, many solidarity purchase groups, without the models of the districts of solidarity economy, would be just purchase groups.

Gasistas strive unevenly to regain agency both individually (as citizens and consumers) and collectively (as groups and as a movement). Even at the microscale, though, GAS ethnography shows how reinventing the paramount role that food has in society means, for food activists, moving away from the products of agri-business and mass consumption toward new social strategies for revaluing food as a common good, as environmentally responsible, and as a catalyst for meaningful relationships and lifestyles. Thanks to an ongoing dialogue across and within networks of solidarity, activism, and engagement, in fact, the provisioning practices of gasistas may well turn into something akin to what Marcel Mauss called a total social fact—"at once political and domestic."[1] However ambitious it might sound to recall the Maussian theory of the *fait social total* within this context, it is not a reckless theoretical generalization to emphasize how, within the networks of provisioning activism, diverse aspects of collective and individual motivation and practice become interwoven as part of a transformative experience, which comes to inform and organize what would otherwise remain separate spheres of domestic and social roles, expectations, and fulfillment. It is no surprise that some key reflections on "the other economy" sprung out of a rediscovery of Mauss's theory of the gift.[2]

The solidarity purchase groups I observed and liaised within the Bergamo area flourished because they capitalized on the proximity of marginal farming contexts to postindustrial urban areas. On a local basis, gasistas thus try to reverse-engineer the deskilling of urban consumers by experimenting in new ways of reconnecting rural/urban divides. Their foodscapes do not include only GAS providers, but also citizens' markets, neighborly sharing, gift-based exchanges, or what solidarity economy activists call self-production: *autoproduzione*—that is, growing and producing staple foods at home.

The qualitative and quantitative data harnessed so far have developed over a longitudinal dimension: my Bergamo ethnography extended over more than two years, while survey and network analysis of ReteGasBergamo was carried out at the peak of the expansion of the GAS network in Bergamo in 2011. I participated in one specific solidarity purchase group over an extended period of time, as is a common ethnographic practice, but I also acted as its representative in a nascent network of GAS. A further dimension of this research was opened up with the national GAS mapping project involving CORES and

Tavolo RES, as this allowed us to develop a joint understanding of strategic research questions for the GAS movement. This kind of multisited, multifaceted, and longitudinal research on alternative provisioning networks had not been done before.

The CORES report proved that gasistas increase their intake of organic, seasonal, and local foods, while they decrease their intake of meat and processed foods. Gasistas focus their attention on recycling practices, energy consumption, and water consumption. They have a keener interest for local politics and have a higher self-perception of their social efficacy than the average citizen (Osservatorio CORES 2013). A legitimate question is whether this is a transformative experience for producers, too. From the quantitative and ethnographic findings presented in Chapters 3 and 5 there is evidence that GAS, as a spontaneous and self-organized movement, has encouraged producers' best practices, economically sustaining a growing number of small farmers. There is also evidence that this initiative is in most cases encouraged by consumers and much more rarely by producers. Exceptions do exist, especially among people who have chosen farming as a personal vocation, for political, environmental, or existential reasons, as in the case of the initiator of the Sicilian network of orange producers described in Chapter 3. We have seen how solidarity purchase groups provide a learning environment for otherwise clueless consumers about the infiltration of the mafia in large food supply networks—a crippling condition especially for southern Italian farmers. As we saw in Chapter 5, in times of ecological crisis, when more and more frequent droughts, coupled with heavy rains and landslides, often endanger crops, a direct relationship with proximal customers is often a relational guarantee for smallholders, especially if customer orders and investments have been placed well before sowing. Due to very low crop prices in large distribution chains, small farmers may find more congenial outlets at a retail level: GAS-organized farmers' markets and fairs provide a protected environment where the producers encounter the consumers on the basis of a previous relationship of reciprocal knowledge and trust. From this point of view, GAS establish the necessary reciprocal acknowledgement that is a precondition to potential economic partnership.

While food provisioning occupies the majority of GAS practice, I suggested that solidarity purchase groups, thanks to their cross-fertilization with advanced models of solidarity economy such as the districts of solidarity economy, are increasingly appropriating the idea of moving beyond food. This helps us rethink GAS, and alternative provisioning as a whole, as a serious and potentially global phenomenon, trying to reconfigure local economies in times of crisis. The ensuing theory is that solidarity economy networks function well as second-order networks—that is, as groups of people already affiliated with other relevant networks of volunteer work, civic engagement, or environmental concern, who would not otherwise be readily in touch with each other but find in provisioning activities a meeting ground and a creative reservoir of resources. The issue of food security—which is now relevant to a widespread echelon of Italian society—is not appropriated by these actors as a purely techno-scientific problem but as a systemic issue of governance of the territory and of collective capacity-building—all of which require peer-to-peer help and lifelong self-education.

Might the districts of solidarity economy contribute to social inclusion at large, with enhanced opportunities for employment, equality, and food access for all? This is certainly a genuine hope of the gasistas I know, and there is evidence that some of the most advanced DES projects include specific actions of social solidarity at large, such as the dental care provision of DES Brianza, A Smile for Everyone. Nevertheless, it is an ethnographically observable fact that the solidarity purchase groups I personally acquainted myself with in the Bergamo area seemed to display ethnic and class homogeneity—not because of active selective practices toward outside applicants but rather because new members were more often than not co-opted by friends and family. Ongoing student ethnographies in well-established cooperative networks that participate in DES projects in the Milanese area also contribute to confirm a similar homogeneity, despite the tolerant and egalitarian vocation of these groups. Even within industrial and rural areas in which a high intake of migrants is distinctly visible—both in the demographic statistics and in the numbers of employees in rural activities—the relational ways in which GAS co-produce districts and networks of solidarity economy remain de facto restricted to mainly white circles.[3]

An ethnographic understanding not only of local GAS activism but of how it feeds into networks of networks broadens our understanding of alternative provisioning: it repositions alternative provisioning by foregrounding its political, relational, and epistemic creativity in rethinking the economy and reweaving society. I hope to have provided such understanding, by focusing on GAS' local cultural repertoires, their relational tools, and on how they go about the laborious exercise of networking. By unveiling the workings of their crosscutting counter-epistemologies, we can get an anthropological insight into their constraints and possibilities. My thesis is that solidarity economies rethink the elusively simple act of provisioning on different economic, moral, and social premises. By focusing on solidarity economy networks as situated practices, by investigating their transformative skills, and by mapping their porous borders, I wish to have conveyed the ethnographic evidence of how shared practices and discourse about the economy at once constrain and enable collective deliberation and political imagination. Solidarity economy activists adopt the term co-production to define a collaborative relationship that actively enables production, rather than regulating it through market demand. Thus co-production expresses not only the collaboration between consumers and providers but also the scholars' intervention to map, voice, and theorize economies that would otherwise remain uncharted (Gibson-Graham 2006). My project borrows these and other co-production theories (Van der Ploeg and Renting 2004, Jasanoff 2006) to illuminate how solidarity economy activists reorganize and rethink their mission and practice, as their networks connect and blossom, like strawberries.

Notes

INTRODUCTION

1. The conference program and materials are available at <http://www.venezia 2012.it/convegno-nazionale-g-a-s-e-d-e-s>, accessed December 29, 2012.
2. See <http://www.retegas.org/index.php?module=pagesetter&func=viewpub& tid=2&pid=10>, accessed August 8, 2012.
3. See <http://www.retegas.org/index.php?module=pagesetter&func=viewpub& tid=2&pid=3>, accessed August 8, 2012.
4. Andrea Saroldi, a factory worker and unionist from Turin, has published books on social justice, voluntary sobriety, and solidarity purchase groups since 1997 (Saroldi 2003). Leadership is crucial for the—often laborious—networking activities of GAS (see Chapter 4).
5. A pilot phase was concluded in the Bergamo area in June 2012. Since then, further data were gathered throughout Lombardy. By January 2013, 1,583 gasistas of 204 GAS were interviewed, while 451 active GAS were mapped in Lombardy.
6. See Osservatorio CORES (2013). The data used here are part of a wider research project, Dentro il Capitale delle Relazioni, carried out by CORES under the direction of Francesca Forno, Cristina Grasseni, and Silvana Signori at Bergamo University (www.unibg.it/cores). The study was endorsed by the Italian solidarity economy network (Tavolo RES; www.retecosol.org) and carried out in collaboration with Davide Biolghini and Giuseppe Vergani of Tavolo RES. The survey was conducted through online questionnaires that were filled out by 299 people in the Bergamo area.
7. For numbers of GAS, see <http://www.retegas.org/index.php?module=pagesetter& func=viewpub&tid=2&pid=7>, accessed August 8, 2012. For the interview to Mauro Serventi, see <http://navdanya.radiondadurto.org/2011/11/26/verso-des-garda-incontro-con-mauro-serventl/>, accessed August 8, 2012
8. See <http://www.asca.it/news-Consumi__Coldiretti__spesa_di_gruppo_per_7_ mln__Da_carpooling_a_Gas-1211852-ECO.html>, accessed October 13, 2012.
9. "Gruppi di Acquisto Solidale. Bergamo ne studia l'esperienza," *L'Eco di Bergamo* (September 12, 2012), <http://www.ecodibergamo.it/stories/Economia/ 313482_gas/>, accessed December 29, 2012.
10. Presentation at the conference Food for Living, Energy for Life, Bergamo, November 26, 2010.
11. J.K. Gibson-Graham is a pen name for two authors, Julie Graham and Katherine Gibson, who write together.

CHAPTER 1. ALTERNATIVE PROVISIONING NETWORKS

1. A Time Bank is a free association of citizens who exchange services on a volunteer basis, using a time unit as a measure of the value exchanged. So, for example, any service or activity that takes an hour can be exchanged with any other service or activity that takes an hour.

2. Time banks and GAS originated in very close localities in the province of Parma—the *terroir* of Parmesan cheese but also of an intense political debate on "red" and "white" cooperatives. In 1995, the two then existent Time Banks (in Parma and in Sant'Arcangelo di Romagna) established a national working group: Tempomat, l'Osservatorio nazionale sulle Banche del Tempo, with the mission of supporting new Time Banks and monitoring the existing ones. There are currently about 300 Time Banks in Italy. The principle of the Italian Time Banks is simple: a group of people get together and decide to exchange services on the basis of an equal time unit to satisfy both material and immaterial needs. "Time exchanged is equal for all and time is measured in hours. Hours are made of 60 minutes for everyone, independent of profession, social class or income" (*La regola costituente,* <http://www.tempomat.it/guida.asp>, accessed December 31, 2012).

3. The use of "patrimonialization" is common in scholarly literature in French, Spanish, Catalan, and Italian (from *patrimoine, patrimonio,* or *patrimoni,* meaning at once "endowment" and "legacy"). "Heritagization" appears in English-language literature, especially with reference to UNESCO's campaign to foster and conserve Intangible Cultural Heritage (ICH; see Bortolotto 2009). Nevertheless "heritage" and "patrimony" carry different undertones. Patrimonialization shows more clearly the effects of commodification on "heritage"—in terms of intellectual ownership, reification, competition, and standardization (see Roigé and Frigolé 2011).

4. See <http://resbergamasca.wordpress.com/cittadinanza-sostenibile/>, accessed August 9, 2012.

5. The following literature review owes greatly to the collective effort conducted with Virginie Amilien, Elena Battaglini, Colin Sage, Francesca Forno, Paolo Parigi, Juliette Rogers, Mario Salomone, Silvana Signori, and Laura Terragni to write grant proposals at the European and national level about the significance of alternative provisioning networks for sustainability strategies and for active citizenship in different European countries.

6. As Colin Sage notes, in the current world food system significant pressures on land and water for food cultivation compete with increasing demand for biofuels. Global food demand is projected to double by 2050, due to the increased consumption of livestock products by a population that is set to grow by a further 3 billion and is experiencing a nutrition transition. This jars with the fact that already 1 billion people are currently malnourished. Freshwater scarcity is likely to become more acute while projected oil flows will drop to 60 percent or less of current supplies. These global challenges are important framing issues for understanding the political relevance of alternative food networks, especially given that what we eat has more impact on climate change than any other aspect of daily life (Sage 2011: 3–4).

7. See <http://www.reseau-amap.org/avis-daniel-vuillon.php>, accessed December 30, 2012.
8. The first comprehensive Transition Town project was launched in Totnes, Devon, in 2006 (Hopkins 2008).
9. See my critical review of the idea of community, especially when rhetorically adopted in development projects, including some eco-museum revivals (Grasseni 2011b).
10. Thanks to Oona Morrow and Katherine Gibson for suggesting a radical reframing of language for this phenomenon.
11. In this case, internal conflicts have resulted in the failure to obtain a protected denomination of origin in addition to the presidium status. Elsewhere, as in the case of Bitto cheese, a fierce battle ensued between the Slow Food presidium and the existing PDO consortium, since their production models were at odds (Grasseni 2012c).
12. See <http://ec.europa.eu/agriculture/events/small-farmers-conference-2012_en.htm>, accessed August 9, 2012.
13. On the public role of food in socioanthropological analysis, see the work of Carole Couhihan on food and gender, and food in globalization (Counihan and Williams-Forson 2012).
14. "The biopower that Foucault begins to analyse in the late 1970s is a power exerted over and through the life of populations, not so much in his estimation a power to kill but a power to create and maintain life through health practices, sexual regulation, genetic experimentation, racial policies, medical paradigms, economic systems, and so forth" (Hardt 2011: 31).
15. Notice that 'economies of affect' may facilitate economic transformations either way: Richard and Rudnyckyj (2009) argue that post-colonial subjectivities can be rendered commensurable with neoliberal capitalism, and underline how public discourse about love, sharing, and grief went hand in hand with the dismantling of state welfare and the introduction of neoliberal normativity in Mexico and Indonesia.
16. "Serventi a Radio Onda d'Urto" (November 2011), <http://navdanya.radiondadurto.org/2011/11/26/verso-des-garda-incontro-con-mauro-serventi/>, accessed August 8, 2012.
17. For a brief history of the Lilliput Network, see Chapter 2.

CHAPTER 2. THE REINVENTION OF FOOD

1. I have described the challenges of contemporary living in a small mountain village on the basis of fieldwork in a subsidiary valley of Valle Brembana, Val Taleggio (Grasseni 2009a).
2. See <http://www.nestle.com/brands/allbrands/spellegrino#.ULp9G41y73s>, accessed November 30, 2012.
3. *Pizzo* are racket extortions to shops and entrepreneurs. See the section titled "Solidarity in co-production" in this chapter.

4. See in particular the work of the Museo Etnografico dell'Alta Brianza (MEAB) and its documentary film on local cultivars and agricultural tradition, such as the potatoes of Annone (<http://meab.parcobarro.it/>, accessed August 28, 2012).

5. I am particularly grateful to Michele Corti for his correspondence on the matter of neorurality and for information about farmers' markets in Lombardy.

6. The Italian *prodotti tipici* roughly translate as *produits de terroir*—that is, as "typical" instances of what a certain localized agricultural and culinary tradition can produce in a very specific environment. Hence their protection through geographical indications and protected denomination of origin. Typical here does not denote normality but a singularity that is closely tied to one specific territory and cultural identity.

7. *Il Parco di interesse locale (PLIS) del Molgora (bassa Brianza) ha il 'suo' pane. Un esempio che merita di essere seguito (11.07.09)*, <http://www.ruralpini.it/ Inforegioni11.07.htm>, accessed September 8, 2012.

8. MAG2 is a cooperative specializing in ethical finance. It supports approved projects with funds provided by cooperative members, who invest their savings in the guise of a cooperative bank. MAG2 was one of the founding members of the nationwide Ethical Bank, a bank that provides basic banking services and investment funds to customers who wish to invest in closely monitored projects and transparently managed funds.

9. See <http://www.apprezziamolo.it/>, accessed September 8, 2012. Details of the Spiga & Madia project are described in a promotional video (see <http:// www.youtube.com/watch?v=mQaCbIBq4cs>, accessed September 8, 2012) and on the website of DES Brianza (see <http://des.desbri.org/spigamadia/ progetto-spiga-e-madia>, accessed September 15, 2012).

10. Lucy Long, on the other hand, favorably reviews the online exhibition of Iowa-based foods by American folklorist Rachelle Saltzman (Long 2009): see <http://www.iowaartscouncil.org/programs/folk-and-traditional-arts/place_ based_foods/index.htm>, accessed September 15, 2012.

11. For the agenda of Crocevia and of the International Planning Committee for Food Sovereignty, see <http://www.croceviaterra.it/ and http://www.foodsovereignty. org/>, accessed September 12, 2012.

12. Antonio Onorati, *OK–Il Prezzo non è Giusto! (OK—The Price Is Not Right!!!)*, Unpublished handout, Seminar of the Working Group on Agriculture of the GAS of the Province of Genoa, February 20, 2010, Genoa.

13. Edoardo Gnocchi, "Progetto *Spiga & Madia* per una sperimentazione di filiera corta, locale, solidale, trasparente," Unpublished paper (May 16, 2009).

14. See for instance how users are involved in co-production according to IDeA Community of Practice on Co-production:

    Co-production has become an important reality in public services in the UK and internationally, as we witness greater involvement of service users and communities in the public service chain, both in extent and in intensity of engagement. Indeed, as a recent report by Governance International shows, service users in five European countries are already playing a much bigger role in public services than many professionals in those countries currently realize. (Löffler 2009: 2)

15. See, for instance, the document of the Scottish Community Development Centre, "Community Resilience and Co-Production. Getting to Grips with the Language," Briefing paper, n.d., <http://www.scdc.org.uk/media/resources/assets-alliance/Community%20Resilience%20and%20Coproduction%20SCDC%20briefing%20paper.pdf>, accessed September 16, 2012.
16. Gnocchi, "Progetto *Spiga & Madia.*"
17. See <http://www.osteriabuonacondotta.it and http://www.cuochidilombardia.it/>, accessed September 12, 2012.
18. Kuminda is organized by Terre di Mezzo, the independent publisher and promoter of the fair Do the Right Thing. In the 2011 edition, it gathered about three thousand participants (see <www.kumindamilano.org>, accessed September 12, 2012). The conference on short chain bread brought together the Parco Sud Agricolo of Milan, DES Varese, the Como cooperative Corto Circuito, Piccola Distribuzione Organizzata of Cremona, the organic miller of Cerete near Bergamo, and the GAS network of Brianza.
19. Giuseppe Vergani, private communication, January 2, 2012.
20. This data was circulated at the conference There's Ferment in Milk in February 2010 by Lecco's Chamber of Commerce at the fair Ristorexpo. The conference targeted professional restaurant operators, recommending shorter milk and dairy supply chains to revive local cheese production. Roundtable speakers included myself, Hansi Baumgartner, Giovanni Guadagno, and Matteo Scibilia.
21. On the basis of 2,206 interviewed enterprises in Sicily, a study of the Chinnici Foundation calculated that *pizzo* can range from 32 Euro per month for a tobacconists to 27,000 Euro per month for a supermarket, averaging around 500 Euro per month for a medium-sized shop or firm. The Chinnici Foundation calculates that up to 3 percent of the Sicilian GDP goes to *pizzo* (Maselli 2010).
22. See *Fa' la Cosa Giusta! Fiera Nazionale del Consumo Critico e degli Stili di Vita Sostenibili–Rassegna Stampa 2012,* <http://falacosagiusta.terre.it/sezione04/65/>, accessed September 9, 2012.
23. Italian law n. 96, February 20, 2006, establishes a national framework within which each region legislates specific criteria for ecotourism (*agroturismo*). By definition, this means accommodation and hospitality offered by active farms that either cultivate the land, or keep the woods, or breed animals.
24. There exist several organizations active in Fair Trade in Italy. The Italian Fair Trade Association AGICES (Associazione Generale Italiana Commercio Equo e Solidale) represents 379 organizations, has sales of 103 million Euro per year, and employs 1,900 people (Viganò, Glorio, and Villa 2008).
25. On the Northern League, see Cento Bull and Gilbert (2001), Diamanti (1993), and Dematteo (2011). On Silvio Berlusconi's Forza Italia, see Shin and Agnew (2008). Probably one of the most benign connoisseurs of the Italian sociopolitical system and history is Paul Ginsborg, whose position has transitioned from historical analysis (2004) to political commitment (2010). Ginsborg was among the promoters of a grassroots movement of citizenship awakening (*i girotondi*) and lately founded ALBA (Alliance-Work-Commons-Environment or Alleanza-Lavoro-Beni comuni-Ambiente).

26. Mario (a pseudonym), interview, July 2011.
27. Banca Etica has only fifteen offices nationwide but operates through a network of traveling bankers who meet their clients on an ad hoc basis or through e-mail. It had about 35,000 members by the end of 2010 for a capital of 37 million Euros (figures presented at the conference Voglia di Etica nella Finanza, April 2011, Bergamo University).
28. See <http://www.acli.it/index.php?option=com_k2&view=item&layout=item&id=61&Itemid=72>, accessed September 23, 2012.
29. See page dated January 2, 2000, <http://ospiti.peacelink.it/arena2000/>, accessed September 23, 2012; it lists the associations adhering to Rete Lilliput: Cocoricò, Campagna Chiama L'Africa, Campagna Globalizza-azione dei popoli, Sdebitarsi, Centro Nuovo Modello di Sviluppo, Campagna Dire mai al MAI—Stop Millennium Round, CTM Altromercato, NIGRIZIA, Campagna per la Riforma della Banca Mondiale, Mani Tese, AIFO, Bilanci di giustizia, Pax Christi, Beati i costruttori di pace, WWF, Rete Radiè Resch, Associazione Botteghe del Mondo, Banca Etica, Movimento Nonviolento/Azione Nonviolenta, Peacelink, Associazione Culturale Punto Rosso—Libera Università Popolare, Forum Mondiale delle Alternative, Ass. Italia-Nicaragua.
30. Ibid.
31. See <http://www.padovanet.it/associazioni/padovaifo/lilliput.htm>, accessed December 18, 2012.
32. A complete list of the Lilliput mailing lists is available on line at <http://liste.retelilliput.org/wws/lists>, accessed December 31, 2012.
33. See <http://retecosol.org/modules.php?op=modload&name=News&file=article&sid=20>, accessed September 9, 2012.
34. Ibid.
35. The charter is available on line (in Italian) at <http://www.retecosol.org/docs/CartaRes0703.pdf>, accessed September 9, 2012.
36. See <http://www.retecosol.org/modules.php?op=modload&name=Sections&file=index&req=listarticles&secid=2>, accessed September 23, 2012.
37. "The Republic of the Commons" is freely downloadable (in Italian) at <http://www.democraziakmzero.org/files/2012/07/Democrazia-Km-Zero-La-Repubblica dei-beni-comuni.pdf>, accessed September 6, 2012.

CHAPTER 3. REWEAVING THE ECONOMY

1. *Bilanci di Giustizia* (roughly translatable as "justice through budgeting") is a campaign for radically rebudgeting one's expenses in a choice of voluntary simplicity and nonviolent antimilitarism. The so-called *Bilancisti* are highly respected in the GAS movement. Their objective is to shift a substantial proportion of their family budget away from militarist, colonialist, or environmentally unfriendly economic circuits. They also set high standards for themselves regarding reusing, reducing, and recycling. Their networks of families practice collective purchase,

production of staple foods at home (self-production, or *autoproduzione*), and mutual help. Mario here refers to the existence of a solidarity purchase group, previous to his own, that served exclusively a network of such families.

2. Mario (a pseudonym) via e-mail, September 19, 2012, confirming information gathered in conversation in July 2011.

3. Borzaga and lanes (2011) quote an oral presentation by Felice Scalvini dated 1989 as the first usage of this metaphor, now well established in the organization models of consortia of social cooperatives. I am grateful to Silvana Signori for this information.

4. According to a member of this particular solidarity purchase group, GAS Albino enrolls about 150 families, organized in 9 chains—that is, subgroups with a minimum of 13 and a maximum of 21 participants (Silvana Signori, personal communication, January 2013).

5. See <http://www.comune.milano.it/portale/wps/portal/CDM?WCM_GLOBAL_ CONTEXT=/wps/wcm/connect/ContentLibrary/giornale/giornale/tutte+le+ notizie+new/consiglio+comunale/insediata_commissione_antimafia>, accessed January 12, 2013. Court sentences of February and April 2013 against the Calabria *'ndrangheta* in and around Milan confirm the gravity and diversity of the mafia presence in Lombardy. See <http://edizioni.lastampa.it/novara/ articolo/lstp/40839/> and <http://tg24.sky.it/tg24/cronaca/2013/02/05/ ndrangheta_al_nord_15_ergastoli_milano.html>, accessed April 26, 2013.

6. In Italy, no political party currently has a woman as president or secretary. There has never been a female prime minister or president of the Republic. The gender composition of the parliament in 2012 was 135 women over 630 at the house of delegates and 60 over 320 at the senate. There is no woman in the governing institutions of the National Conference of University Presidents. The National Industrial Association, which represents about 150,000 companies, counts 4 women and 17 men in its top management.

7. On the gendered dimension of domestic foraging, see Rocheleau et al. (1995) and Sutton (2001, 2006).

8. For instance, Equalway.org is a social network project supported by the Italian Ministry for Juvenile Policies, launched in October 2009 in Rome's Città dell'Altra Economia to facilitate a direct link between small farmers and online customers on a national scale. About four thousand certified organic farmers and breeders subscribed. It was designed by Rome gasistas working in information technologies who wanted to make first contact with producers easier and logistics more manageable.

9. The participatory guarantee systems (PGS) were the focus of a workshop at the latest edition of Kuminda in 2012 (see <http://www.kumindamilano.org/>, accessed January 5, 2012) and the project was launched by the DES of Como, Monza-Brianza, and Varese with a public conference on February 16, 2013. PGS are envisaged as a key scaling up action, thanks to funding from a CARIPLO Bankers Foundation project for education about sustainability and staff from a solidarity economy cooperative, Corto Circuito.

10. Nando, e-mail September 24, 2012.
11. Ibid.
12. The website www.peapod.com is a web-based home-delivery grocery store (accessed October 27, 2012). Paying a farmer the same price as would be spent in a supermarket is obviously advantageous to the farmer.
13. On landgrabbing and urbanization, see the online interview with a representative of DES Brianza, <http://www.youtube.com/watch?v=IsOwvZbPs_A>, accessed March 3, 2013.
14. Decreto "Ronchi" (article 23-bis of the Italian law 133/2008).
15. This campaign for shifting family budgets toward just styles of consumption was inspired by Comboni Father Alex Zanotelli and the Catholic priests Albino Bizzotto and Gianni Fazzini. *Bilancisti* are deemed as radical and zealous. Even their self-assigned collective denomination evokes the daily moral obligation of balancing between the truly necessary and the superfluous (Valer 1999, see Chapter 3, note 1).
16. To appreciate how deeply these political divisions run in Italian regional identities and in "red" and "white" political subcultures, see Kertzer (1990) and Shore (1990). A very useful reading on gender relations within left-wing activism is the memoir *Il Manifesto*, about a communist activist and journalist (Rossanda 2005).

CHAPTER 4. NETWORKS IN LABOR

1. I have published extensively on this (Grasseni 2012c, 2011a, 2009).
2. Program and commentary by Michele Corti are available online at <http://www.ruralpini.it/Inforegioni08.04.10.htm>, accessed January 3, 2013.
3. Agricultural production, notably of milk, is regulated within the European Agricultural Policy through a quota system (Regulations 856/1984 of March 31, 1984, 3950/92 of December 28, 1992, and 1788/2003 of September 29, 2003, revised November 18, 2008 by the EU Agricultural Ministers Council). Each registered farmer is allowed a production quota that must not be exceeded to avoid prices crashing on the market. Excess milk production is punished with fines to the producers.
4. "A Rosarno la rivolta degli immigrati,", *Corriere della Sera* (January 7, 2010), <http://www.corriere.it/cronache/10_gennaio_07/rosarno-rivolta-immigrati_4649d878-fbd4–11de-a955–00144f02aabe.shtml>, accessed December 8, 2012. The riots were covered by BBC, CNN, *Guardian,* and *Daily Telegraph.* Radio Popolare of Milan conducted an in-depth journalistic investigation on the events, which included the hypothesis that the riots were fueled by competing mafia-like clans of the local Ndrangheta, battling for the lucrative business of providing indentured labor—at a commission—to local landowners. The connection between local mafia clans and the race riots was disclaimed in a subsequent article on the national press: <http://www.corriere.it/cronache/10_gennaio_12/rosarno-eseguiti-arresti_2b27b3e8-ff45–11de-a791–00144f02aabe.shtml>, accessed December 14, 2012.

5. See <http://www.siqillyah.com/>, accessed December 8, 2012.

6. In the next chapter, devoted to the workings of networks of networks, both lo-cally and at national level, I return in detail to the citizenship markets.

7. See <http://www.retegasbergamo.it/content/laltra-faccia-dellarancia>, accessed December 8, 2012. For a comparable grassroots documentary production on the topic of mafia-free oranges, see *Storia di un'arancia,* video by Clan y Fuoco "La Rupe" (Gruppo scout A.G.E.S.C.I. "Rivoli 2") in support of the SOS Rosarno campaign: <https://www.youtube.com/watch?v=fDQ2zm3_geg&feature=youtube_gdata_player>, accessed December 8, 2012.

8. In brief, the three-page manifesto gives this definition of solidarity economy (*eco-nomia solidale*): 1. it defends the commons (*beni comuni*)—that is, "land, air, water, landscape, energy, knowledge, and genetic patrimony"; 2. it is based on respect of Mother Earth and of everyone's good living (*benvivere,* a transparent reference to Euclides Mance's *Bem Vivir*); 3. it functions through collaborative models based on reciprocity and inclusion; 4. it is based on human relation-ships; 5. it promotes ties with one's territory; 6. it accepts a notion of limit and does not aim to scale up at all costs; 7. it develops through networks; 8. it is transformative of society; 9. it defends human rights; 10. it rethinks the role of the market. (See <http://www.retecosol.org/docs/2011_Aquila_Colonne_v2.pdf>, accessed December 15, 2012.) This is my own synthesis and transla-tion. In Chapter 5, I describe the 2010 and 2011 national GAS assemblies.

9. See <www.ressud.org>, accessed December 8, 2012.

10. See <http://desvalbrembana.files.wordpress.com/2010/09/carta-principides.pdf>, accessed December 15, 2012.

11. Full documentation of the value framework document, its revisions, and the nine zonal meetings is available at <http://www.retegasbergamo.it/content/convocazione-assemblea-generale-annuale-2012–10-giugno-2012-ore-9–13>, accessed December 17, 2012.

12. Source: "Gruppi di Acquisto Solidale. Bergamo ne studia l'esperienza," *L'Eco di Ber-gamo* (September 12, 2012), <http://www.ecodibergamo.it/stories/Economia/313482_gas/>, accessed December 29, 2012.

13. According to the calculations made available on the site retegas.org, each group on average enrolls 25 families of (on average) 4 people; thus each GAS would serve about 100 consumers. A chart of registered solidarity purchase groups is available at <http://www.retegas.org/index.php?module=pagesetter&func=viewpub&tid=2&pid=7>, accessed December 14, 2012.

CHAPTER 5. SEEDS OF TRUST

1. The book-length denunciation of "The Caste" of Italian politicians, by journalists Sergio Rizzo and Gian Antonio Stella of the national newspaper *Corriere della Sera* (2007), made a bestseller in Italy.

2. Eric Wolf and John Cole (1974) found that two adjacent villages in South Tyrol had opposing cultural dispositions despite their identical environmental

context. The Romansch-speaking Tret owed its proclivity to urban migration and employment in trade or wage labor to a Latin inheritance law that divided the land in equal parts among siblings, to the extreme of insignificant portions. The German-speaking St. Felix preserved the inheritance of the undivided homestead, handing down all the assets to the first male born, thus favoring territorial rooting through farming and—later—ecotourism.

3. The ethnographic literature on the anthropology of consumption is plentiful; see, for instance, Miller 1998, 2008.

4. Toni Montevidoni (DES Marche), "Quale Economia Solidale per le Marche: DES ed Empori," Public paper, Assemblea GAS/DES, L'Aquila, June 25, 2011.

5. Deborah Lucchetti (Tavolo RES—Rete di Economia Solidale), "I modelli alternativi di fronte alla crisi," Public paper, Assemblea GAS/DES, L'Aquila, June 24, 2011.

6. The Genoa Social Forum is possibly the first event of mass violence in a democratic country that has been extensively documented by those involved through privately owned audiovisual means and broadcast practically in real time. Several documents are still available online. A search on YouTube for "Genoa Social Forum" brings up 126 hits (accessed December 21, 2012). The facts and the shortcomings of the judiciary process that followed have been condemned by Amnesty International. On the policemen conviction, see "Top Italian Policemen Get up to Five Years for Violent Attack on G8 Protesters. Sentences Suggest Appeal Judges Accept that 2001 Night Raid, When Many Were Savagely Beaten, Was Planned and Covered Up," *The Guardian* (May 19, 2010), <http://www.guardian.co.uk/world/2010/may/19/g8-italian-police-sentenced>, accessed December 21, 2012. The detail of the court of appeal sentence of May 18, 2010 is accessible at <http://www.penalecontemporaneo.it/upload/018ap_diaz_motivazioni[1].pdf>, accessed April 26, 2013.

7. The full list of the associations is on the Social Forum website, which has been closed since October 22, 2001 but is still available at <http://www.processig8.org/GSF/home.htm>, accessed December 21, 2012.

8. Serge Latouche, for instance, insists on de-growth as a moral choice in the face of the "shamelessness" of consumer society (2011: 182).

9. See <http://www.retecosol.org/docs/2011_Aquila_Colonne_v2.pdf>, accessed December 15, 2012. In the text, I offer my own synthesis and translation of the key points.

10. This lies in the province of Monza/Brianza, which hosts the DES-Brianza project, already engaged in reconstructing short food supply chains (see Chapter 2 on the project Spiga & Madia).

11. All the projects of DES Brianza are perusable online. See the dental health project Un Sorriso per Tutti (A Smile for Everyone) at <http://des.desbri.org/sorriso-per-tutti>; Co-Energy at <http://des.desbri.org/co-energia>; and Change Band (Cambia Banda) at <http://des.desbri.org/cambiabanda/progetto-cambiabanda>, accessed December 23, 2012.

12. Note that DES membership only costs 20 Euro. Dental services, incidentally, are covered by the Italian National Health Service through the hospital networks, but the waiting lists are notoriously long and most people pay for private dentistry out of pocket. Private health insurance, thanks to the capillary national service that is covered by general taxation, is practically unheard of in Italy—which makes private medical provision very expensive.

13. This foundational history is made available online by DES Brianza at <http://des.desbri.org/desbri/chi-siamo>, accessed December 24, 2012.

14. See <http://www.colloqui-dobbiaco.it/images/stories/Le7tesi_CollqouidiDobbiaco_2012.pdf>, accessed April 22, 2013.

15. The results and draft protocols elaborated during the funded pilot project were presented at a public meeting on February 16, 2013.

16. See Chapter 3, notes 1 and 15.

17. Spiga & Madia had gained support both from Ethical Bank and MAG2, as well as through the EU funded pilot project EQUAL NuoviStilidiVita 2004–2007, co-ordinated by Davide Biolghini. See the credits at <http://www.youtube.com/watch?v=mQaCblBq4cs>, accessed March 3, 2013.

18. See <www.kumindamilano.org>, accessed December 24, 2012.

19. See <http://www.urgenci.net>, accessed December 24, 2012.

20. See <http://www.urgenci.net/page.php?niveau=1&id=THE%20NETWORK>, accessed December 24, 2012.

21. See<http://ripess.org/ripess-en.html,http://www.ripess.org/mapping-project/?lang=en>, accessed December 26, 2012.

22. See the Community Economies Collective, <http://www.communityeconomies.org, and the RIPESS mapping project http://www.ripess.org/mapping-project/?lang=en>, accessed December 26, 2012.

23. See <http://www.sustainablecitizenship.com/>, accessed April 22, 2013; also see Micheletti and Stolle 2012.

24. The program and list of participants is perusable online at <www.cittadinanzasostenibile.it>, accessed December 27, 2012.

25. The program and the conference materials are available online at <www.unibg.it/cittadinanzalibera>, accessed December 27, 2012.

26. The full project is available online at <http://resbergamasca.files.wordpress.com/2011/08/progetto-mercati-mc 6–3-2012.pdf>, accessed December 26, 2010.

27. The protocol and admission criteria are perusable online at <http://resbergamasca.files.wordpress.com/2011/08/discplinare-mercato-mc-6-3-2012.pdf>, accessed December 26, 2012.

28. Literally "our own." On the rhetoric of *prodotti nostrani,* see Black (2012: 151) and Chapter 3.

29. Presidia are well-established Slow Food agreements to protect foodstuffs and agricultural techniques that are deemed as significant for the cultural heritage and the economic development of their territory. A worldwide map of Slow Food presidia and documentation about its history, numbers, and mission can be

consulted online on the website of the Slow Food Foundation for Biodiversity, listing about 170 international presidia (<http://www.slowfoodfoundation. com>, accessed December 11, 2012) and on the Italian website of Slow Food, listing more than 200 in Italy alone (<http://www.fondazioneslowfood.it>, accessed December 11, 2012).

30. In particular, I have written extensively about the reinvention of cheese and its transformation into food heritage (Grasseni 2011 , 2012a,b,c).

31. The charter and the map are available online at <http://www.cittadinanza sostenibile.it/>, accessed December 26, 2012.

32. The objectives and strategies of the project are spelled out in the publicly accessible document "Non solo cibo. Mercato & Reti per un futuro sostenibile" (Not Only Food: Market and Networks for a Sustainable Future), <www. cittadinanzasostenibile.it>, accessed December 26, 2012.

33. See <http://www.made-in-no.com>, accessed December 26, 2012.

34. The last national assembly of Rete Lilliput took place in Florence in May 2009 and inaugurated a new cycle of grassroots activism; see <http://www. retelilliput.org/>, accessed December 27, 2012.

35. See Chapter 3, notes 1 and 15.

36. The translation is based on the leaflet circulated within ReteGasBergamo and posted on the websites of SCRET (Supporto Connessione Reti Territoriali; www.scret.it), Tavolo RES—Area Formazione e Ricerca (www.retecosol.org) and the e-mail list of Cittadinanza Sostenibile. The original document is no longer online.

37. Roger and Shoemaker (1971), reviewed by Forno (2011a), studied the informal ways in which innovation travels and becomes diffused among farmers in Nigeria, India, and Brazil through network analysis: farmers were asked to name their three best friends, the three most influential people in their community, and the three people who had been most influential in introducing farm innovations. When further asked which person they would organize a cooperative project with, their answers showed significant overlaps between the four sets of people.

CHAPTER 6. CONCLUSION

1. This is the classic definition that Marcel Mauss gives of total social facts: These phenomena are at once legal, economic, religious, aesthetic, morphological and so on. They are legal in that they concern individual and collective rights, organized and diffuse morality; they may be entirely obligatory, or subject simply to praise or disapproval. They are at once political and domestic, being of interest both to classes and to clans and families. They are religious; they concern true religion, animism, magic and diffuse religious mentality. They are economic, for the notions of value, utility, interest, luxury, wealth, acquisition,

accumulation, consumption and liberal and sumptuous expenditure are all present. (Mauss 1966: 76–77)

2. See for instance the *Revue du MAUSS—Mouvement anti-utilitariste dans les sciences sociales,* no. 21 (2003).

3. I am grateful to Silvia Contessi for the insightful exchange of views in this regard, with reference to her participation to the EUPOLIS research on "Heritage localized agri-food systems as a specialized dimension of localized agri-food systems" (2012/2013, Istituto superiore per la Ricerca, la Statistica e la Formazione di Regione Lombardia).

Glossary

Cittadinanza Sostenibile (CS—http://cittadinanzasostenibile.it/). Sustainable Citizenship is the network of solidarity economy of the Bergamo area (*La rete di economia solidale della Bergamasca*). Born as a university seminar on critical consumerism in 2007, Shopping for Human Rights, organized by sociologist Francesca Forno, it developed into an independent network of social, political, and economic actors through its study group and public seminars. CS is represented in the national working group on solidarity economy (Tavolo Nazionale RES—Rete di Economia Solidale).

CORES (www.unibg.it/cores). *Osservatorio CORES—Gruppo di ricerca su consumi, reti e pratiche di economie sostenibili* is the Research Group on Consumption, Networks, and Practices of Sustainable Economies cofounded at Bergamo University by Francesca Forno, Cristina Grasseni, and Silvana Signori.

DES (*Distretto di Economia Solidale*). A District of solidarity economy is a network of associations, providers, and consumers (usually organized in one or more GAS, or solidarity purchase groups) that exchanges goods and services in the name of shared principles of solidarity, which are usually spelled out in a charter or founding document of intents. DES are conceived of as nodes in a network of solidarity economy (RES, or *Rete di Economia Solidale:* http://retecosol.org/).

DESBRI or DES Brianza. The district of solidarity economy of Monza-Brianza, which launched the short supply chain for bread, Spiga & Madia (www.desbri.org).

DES Valle Brembana (Distretto di Economia Solidale della Valle Brembana). A project launched in January 2010 to build a district of solidarity economy in Valle Brembana (http://desvalbrembana.wordpress.com).

GAS (*Gruppo di Acquisto Solidale*). Solidarity purchase group; a group of people who get logether to organize collectively direct provisioning from trusted providers. Retegas.org is the national network that connects and informs those GAS that wish to register with the website. In this book, I refer equally to GAS, solidarity purchase groups, or GAS groups.

Gasista (plural: *Gasistas*). A member of a GAS. In Italian, gasista is what a GAS member calls himself or herself. It is invariant in the female and male version (un gasista, una gasista), whereas the plural, gasisti has a female and a male version (gasisti, gasiste). It is a ubiquitous grammatical convention, in Italian, to use the male plural whenever one refers to a group of people or objects where at least one is male (thus, for instance, 1,000 gasisti may refer to 999 female gasiste plus 1 male gasista). In my own translation, I did not wish to follow this gender-biased convention, and I opted for adding an "s" to gasista to obtain the gender-neutral gasistas.

Mercato & Cittadinanza (M&C).   Market & Citizenship is an association born in 2010 as a development agency of Cittadinanza Sostenibile, to organize, fund, and manage the projects of the CS network. Its main projects are currently the citizenship markets, Mercato Agricolo e Non Solo (Farmers' Markets and Beyond), organized in and around the town of Bergamo, and the R&D project NonSoloCibo (NotOnlyFood).

Province.   An administrative territorial unit, larger than a municipality (*comune*) and smaller than a region (*regione*). For example, Bergamo stands for the homonymous municipality (Comune di Bergamo), hosting about 120,000 inhabitants. It also stands for the homonymous province (Provincia di Bergamo), hosting about 1,100,000 inhabitants (including those of the municipality). The town of Bergamo is thus the seat of the municipal administration as well as of the province administration. Bergamo lies in the region Lombardy, which comprises eleven provinces including Bergamo, for a total of about 10 million inhabitants. Milan is the seat of Lombardy's regional government. In geographical terms, it helps to think of Comune/Provincia/Regione/Stato as a Russian doll system, though the attribution of administrative and political functions to each level does not follow this scheme rigidly. Italy comprises 110 provinces and 20 regions. In this book, when I refer to the Bergamo area, I mean the province of Bergamo.

RES (*Rete di Economia Solidale*).   Network of solidarity economy; a network of associations, providers, and consumers (usually organized in one or more GAS) that carries out actions such as organizing public events and study groups, mapping and connecting solidarity economy actors, initiating pilot projects such as markets and fairs and enabling nascent districts of solidarity economy to connect and thrive. The Italian network of solidarity economy spells out the definition of RES and DES on its website, Retecosol.org

ReteGasBergamo.   The network of GAS of the Bergamo area (or province) that was founded in October 2009 and whose website is retegasbergamo.it.

Tavolo Nazionale RES—Rete di Economia Solidale.   The national working group (Tavolo here means *working group*) for the network of solidarity economy (RES), which promotes, supports, and connects the Italian districts of solidarity economy (DES).

References

Aiello, L. (2010), "Engaged Anthropology: Diversity and Dilemmas," *Current Anthropology* 51(S2): S201–S202.

Allard, J., Davidson, C., and Matthaei, J. (eds.) (2008), *Solidarity Economy: Building Alternatives for People and Planet,* Papers and Reports from the 2007 US Social Forum, Chicago: ChangeMaker Publications.

Amin, A. (ed.) (2009), *The Social Economy. International Perspectives on Economic Solidarity,* London: Zed Books.

Arvidsson, A. (2008), "The Ethical Economy of Customer Coproduction," *Journal of Macromarketing* 28: 326–38.

Baccetti, C. and Messina, P. (eds.) (2009), *L'eredità. Le subculture politiche della Toscana e del Veneto,* Liviana: Padova.

Badii, M. (2012), *Processi di patrimonializzazione e politiche del cibo. Un'etnografia nella Toscana contemporanea,* Perugia: Morlacchi Editore.

Bagnasco, A. (1977), *Tre Italie. La problematica territoriale dello sviluppo italiano,* Bologna: Il Mulino.

Baiocchi, P. (2012), "Il Medioevo prossimo futuro," *Valori* 102(XII): 18–19.

Banfield, E. C. (1958), *The Moral Basis of a Backward Society,* Chicago: Free Press.

Barnett, C., Clarke, N., Cloke, P., and Malpass, A. (2005), "The Political Ethics of Consumerism," *Consumer Policy Review* 15(2): 45–51.

Becattini, G. (2000), *Il distretto industriale. Un nuovo modo di interpretare il cambiamento economico,* Torino: Rosenberg & Sellier.

Ben-Yehoyada, N. (2011), "The Clandestine Central Mediterranean Passage," *Middle East Report* 261: 18–23.

Ben-Yehoyada, N. (2012), "Dead Reckoning, or the Unintended Consequences of Clueless Navigation," *Magazin* 31(16–17): 104–13.

Berlan, A. (2008), "Making or Marketing a Difference?," in G. De Neve, D. Wood, P. Luetchford, and J. Pratt (eds.), *Hidden Hands in the Market,* Bingley: Emerald Group, pp.171–94.

Berlendis, L. (2009), "Un nuovo patto con la terra," *Culture della sostenibilità* 6: 137–46.

Biolghini, D. (2007), *Il popolo dell'economia solidale,* Bologna: Editrice Missionaria Italiana.

Biolghini, D. (2009), "Dai GAS ai DES. La Rete nazionale di Economia Solidale (RES) e i Distretti di Economia Solidale," in P. Graziano, F. Forno, and M. Lepratti (eds), *GASP. Gruppi di Acquisto Solidale e Partecipativo,* Milano: Edizioni Punto Rosso, pp. 166–75.

Biolghini, D., Saroldi, A., Servettini, M., and Castagnola, A. (2008), "Dal consumo critico e dai GAS alla co-produzione e ai distretti di economia solidale," Paper presented at VI Assemblea Nazionale di Rete Lilliput, May 9, 2008, <http://www. retelilliput.org/verona/print.php?news = 1240912909>, accessed December 30, 2012.

Black, R. (2012), *Porta Palazzo. The Anthropology of an Italian Market,* Philadelphia: University of Pennsylvania Press.

Bocci, R., De Santis, G., and Rossi, A. (2009), *Esperienze di innovazione nel sistema alimentare:dai partenariati locali tra produttori e consumatori a nuovi modelli di interazione con le istituzioni,* Convegno internazionale Ettaro Zero. Fare Paesaggio, Costruire Natura, Prendersi Cura del Suolo, Milan, Italy, May 7–8, 2009.

Bortolotto, C. (2009), "The Giant Cola in Gravina. Intangible Cultural Heritage, Property, and Territory between Unesco Discourse and Local Heritage Practice," *Ethnologia Europea* 39(2): 81–94.

Borzaga, C. and Ianes, A. (2011), *Il sistema di imprese della cooperazione sociale. Origini e sviluppo dei Consorzi di cooperative sociali,* Euricse Working Papers, n. 014.

Brunori, G. (ed.) (2007), *Biodiversità e tipicità. Paradigmi economici e strategie competitive. Atti del Convegno di studi (Pisa, 22–24 settembre 2005),* Milano: Franco Angeli.

Cacciari, P. (ed.) (2011), *La società dei beni comuni,* Rome: Ediesse Editore.

Campbell, H. (2009), "Breaking New Ground in Food Regime Theory: Corporate Environmentalism, Ecological Feedbacks, and the 'Food from Somewhere' Regime?" *Agriculture and Human Values* 26(4): 309–19.

Carlini, R. (2011), *L'economia del noi—L'Italia che condivide,* Bari: Editori Laterza.

Carrera, L. (2009), "I Gruppi di Acquisto Solidale. Una proposta solida nella società liquida," *Partecipazione e Conflitto* 3: 89–117.

Carrier, J. (2008), "Think Locally, Act Globally: The Political Economy of Ethical Consumption," in G. De Neve, D. Wood, P. Luetchford, and J. Pratt (eds.), *Hidden Hands in the Market,* Bingley: Emerald Group, pp. 31–51.

Carrier, J. and Luetchford, P. (eds.) (2012), *Ethical Consumption: Social Value and Economic Practice,* Oxford: Berghahn Books.

Castells, M., Caraça, J., and Cardoso, G. (eds.) (2012), *Aftermath. The Cultures of the Economic Crisis,* Oxford: Oxford University Press.

Cento Bull, A. and Gibert, M. (eds.) (2001), *The Lega Nord and the Northern Question in Italian Politics,* Basingstoke: Palgrave Macmillan.

Centro Nuovo Modello di Sviluppo (1996), *Guida al consumo critic,* Milano: Ponte alle Grazie.

Chatterton, P. and Pickerill, J. (2010), "Everyday Activism and transitions Towards Post-Capitalist Worlds," *Transactions of the Institute of British Geographers* 35(4): 475–90.

Clemente, P., Leone, A., Puccini, S., Rossetti, C., and Solinas, P. (1985), *L'Antropologia Italiana. Un secolo di storia,* Bari: Laterza Editore.

Cohen, L. (2003), *A Consumers' Republic: The Politics of Mass Consumption in Postwar America,* New York: Vintage Books.

Cole, J. W. and Wolf, E. R. (1974), *The Hidden Frontier. Ecology and Ethnicity in an Alpine Valley,* New York: Academic Press.

Comaroff, J. and Comaroff, J. (2009), *Ethnicity, Inc.,* Chicago: Chicago University Press.

Corrado, A. (2006), *Soggetti dell'esodo: migrazioni sub-sahariane a Bamako e a Parigi,* Catanzaro: Rubbettino.

Corsìn-Jimenez, A. (2005), "After Trust," *Cambridge Anthropology* 25(2): 64–78.

Corti, M. (2009a), "Il Parco di interesse locale (PLIS) del Molgora (bassa Brianza) ha il 'suo' pane. Un esempio che merita di essere seguito," <http://www.ruralpini.it/Inforegioni11.07.htm>, accessed March 3, 2013.

Corti, M. (2009b), "Filere corte. A Sondrio, Como e Lecco alcune esperienze d'avanguardia ormai consolidate consentono di fare il punto sulle 'filere corte'. Avviata un'indagine dell'Università di Milano," <http://www.ruralpini.it/Inforegioni16.6.html>, accessed January 4, 2013.

Corti, M. (2012), "Prodotti agroalimentari di qualità a valenza identitaria: antica e nuova risorsa dell'agricoltura lombarda," *Confronti* 12(3): 95–115.

Corti, M. and Mastalli, P. (2010), "I caprini di Garzeno 'scoperti' da Veronelli (1968) attendono ancora una valorizzazione," <http://www.ruralpini.it/Inforegioni26.03.10.htm>, accessed March 3, 2013.

Counihan, C. (1999), *The Anthropology of Food and Body: Gender, Meaning, and Power,* New York: Routledge.

Counihan, C. (2004), *Around the Tuscan Table. Food, Family and Gender in 20th Century Florence,* New York: Routledge.

Counihan, C. and Williams-Forson, P. (eds.) (2012), *Taking Food Public: Redefining Foodways in a Changing World,* New York: Routledge.

Davis, J. (1973), *Land and Family in Pisticci,* London: Athlone Press.

De Neve, G., Wood, D., Luetchford, P. and Pratt, J. (eds.) (2008), *Hidden Hands in the Market: Ethnographies of Fair Trade, Ethical Consumption, and Corporate Social Responsibility,* Bingley: Emerald Group.

De Santis, G. (2006) *Spiga & Madia. Promozione di un progetto di resistenza alimentare partecipata. La sovranità alimentare nei Distretti di Economia Solidale. Un progetto possibile per la Brianza,* <http://www.sp.unipi.it/files/4121-Presentazione%20Spiga%20e%20Madia%20SV.pdf>, accessed September 15, 2012.

DeLind, L. (1999), "Close Encounters with a CSA: The Reflections of a Bruised and Somewhat Wiser Anthropologist," *Agriculture and Human Values* 16(3): 3–9.

DeLind, L. (2002), "Place, Work, and Civic Agriculture: Common Fields for Cultivation," *Agriculture and Human Values* 19: 217–24.

Della Porta, D. (1992) *Lo Scambio Occulto. Casi di Corruzione Politica in Italia,* Bologna: Il Mulino.

Della Porta, D. (2004), "Multiple Belongings, Flexible Identities and the Construction of Another Politics: Between the European Social Forum and the Local Social Fora," in D. della Porta and S. Tarrow (eds.), *Transnational Movements and Global Activism,* Lanham: Rowman and Littlefield, pp. 175–202.

Della Porta, D. and Mosca, L. (2007), "*In movimento:* 'Contamination' in Action and the Italian Global Justice Movement," *Global Networks* 7(1): 1–27.

Della Porta, D., Andretta, M., Mosca, L., and Reiter, H. (2006), *Globalization from Below,* Minneapolis: University of Minnesota Press.

Dematteo, L. (2011), *L'Idiota in politica. Antropologia della Lega Nord,* Milano: Feltrinelli.

Deriu, M. (2012), "Democracies with a Future: Degrowth and the Democratic Tradition," *Futures* 44: 553–561.

Diamanti, I. (1993), *La Lega. Geografia, storia e sociologia di un nuovo soggetto politico,* Rome: Donzelli.

DuPuis, E., Goodman, M., and Goodman, D. (2005), "Should We Go 'Home' To Eat? Toward a Reflexive Politics of Localism," *Journal of Rural Studies* 21: 359–71.

Faeta, F. (2011), *Le ragioni dello sguardo. Pratiche dell'osservazione, della rappresentazione e della memoria.* Torino: Bollati Boringhieri.

Filippucci, P. (1996), "Anthropological Perspectives on Culture in Italy," in P. Forgacs and R. Lumley (eds.), *Italian Culture Studies.* Oxford: Oxford University Press, pp. 52–71.

FLAI—Federazione Lavoratori Agricoli Italiani (2012), *Primo Rapporto su Agromafie e Caporalato,* Rome: CGIL—Confederazione Generale Lavoratori Italiani/ Osservatorio Placido Rizzotto.

Flynn, K. C. (2005), *Food, Culture and Survival in an African City,* Basingstoke: Palgrave Macmillan.

Fonte, M., Eboli, M., Maietta O. W., Pinto B., and Salvioni C. (2011), "Il consumo sostenibile nella visione dei Gruppi di Acquisto Solidale di Roma," *AgriRegioniEuropa* 7(27), <http://agriregionieuropa.univpm.it/dettart.php?id_articolo = 851>, accessed December 29, 2012.

Forno, F. (2008), "Nuove reti: consumo critico, legami digitali e mobilitazione," in P. Rebughini and R. Sassatelli (eds.), *Le nuove frontiere dei consumi,* Verona: Ombre Corte, pp. 126–44.

Forno, F. (2011a), *La spesa a pizzo zero. Consumo critico e agricoltura libera, le nuove frontiere della lotta alla mafia,* Milano: Edizioni Altraeconomia.

Forno, F. (2011b), "Social Networks," in D. Southerton (ed), *The Encyclopaedia of Consumer Culture,* vol. 3, London: Sage, pp. 1510–11.

Forno, F. (2013a) "Cooperative Movement," in D. A. Snow, D. Della Porta, B. Klandermans, and D. McAdam (eds.), *Blackwell Encyclopedia of Social and Political Movements,* Oxford: Blackwell, pp. 278–80.

Forno, F. (2013b), "Nuove pratiche economiche e movimenti sociali," in A. De Vita, L. Bertell, G. Gosetti (eds.), *Davide e Golia. La primavera delle economie diverse.* Milano: Jaca Book, pp. 130–46.

Forno, F. and Ceccarini, L. (2006), "From the Street to the Shops: The Rise of New Forms of Political Action in Italy," *South European Society and Politics* 2(2): 197–222.

Forno, F. and Gunnarson, C. (2010), "Everyday Shopping to Fight the Mafia in Italy," in M. Micheletti and A. S. McFarland (eds.), *Creative participation. Responsibility-Taking in the Political World,* Boulder, CO: Paradigm Publisher, pp. 103–26.

Forno, F. and Salvi, S. (2012), *Per una cittadinanza sostenibile: analisi critica dei consumi delle famiglie di Bergamo,* Comune di Bergamo/Cittadinanza Sostenibile, <http://resbergamasca.files.wordpress.com/2011/08/a-rapporto-di-ricerca. pdf>, accessed March 3, 2013.

Friedman, F. G. (1967), "The World of 'La Miseria," in J. M. Potter (ed.), *Peasant Society. A Reader,* Boston: Little, Brown, and Co., pp. 324–36.

Friedmann, H. (2009), "Moving Food Regimes Forward: Reflections on Symposium Essays," *Agriculture and Human Values* 26(4): 335–44.

Fuller, D., Jonas, A.E.G., and Lee, R. (2010, eds.), *Interrogating Alterity. Alternative Economic and Political Spaces,* Farnham: Ashgate.

Galt, A. H. (1991), *Far from the Church Bells. Settlement and Society in an Apulian Town,* Cambridge: Cambridge University Press.

Gambetta, D. (1990), "Can We Trust Trust?," in D. Gambetta (ed.), *Trust. Making and Breaking Cooperative Relations,* Oxford: Blackwell, pp. 213–37.

Gambetta, D. (1993), *The Sicilian Mafia: the Business of Private Protection,* Cambridge, MA: Harvard University Press.

Gesualdi, F. (1990), *Lettera a un Consumatore del Nord,* Bologna: Editrice Missionaria Italiana.

Getz, C. (2006), "What Organic and Fair Trade Labels Do Not Tell Us," *International Journal of Consumer Studies* 30(5): 490–501.

Gibson-Graham, J. K. (2006), *A Post-Capitalist Politics,* Minneapolis: University of Minnesota Press.

Gibson-Graham, J. K., Cameron, J., and Healy, S. (2013), *Take Back the Economy. An Ethical Guide for Transforming Our Communities,* Minneapolis: University of Minnesota Press.

Ginsborg, P. (2004), *Il tempo di cambiare. Politica e potere della vita quotidiana,* Torino: Einaudi.

Ginsborg, P. (2010), *Salviamo l'Italia,* Torino: Einaudi.

Gnocchi, E. (2009), "Progetto Spiga & Madia per una sperimentazione di filiera corta, locale, solidale, trasparente," Paper presented at Apprezziamolo!, Monza, May 16, 2009.

Goodman, D. (2003), "The Quality 'Turn' and Alternative Food Practices: Reflections and Agenda," *Journal of Rural Studies* 19(1): 1–7.

Goodman, D. (2004), "Rural Europe Redux? Reflections on Alternative Agro-Food Networks and Paradigm Change," *Sociologia Ruralis* 44(1): 3–16.

Goodman, D. (2012), "Place and Space in Alternative Food Networks: Connecting Production and Consumption," in M. Goodman, D. Goodman, and M. Redclift (eds.), *Consuming Space: Placing Consumption in Perspective,* Farnham: Ashgate, pp. 189–214.

Goodman, D., DuPuis, M., and Goodman, M. (2012), *Alternative Food Networks: Knowledge, Practice, and Politics,* New York: Routledge.

Graeber, D. (2001), *Toward An Anthropological Theory of Value: The False Coin of Our Own Dreams,* Basingstoke: Palgrave Macmillan.

Granovetter, M. (1985), "Economic Action and Social Structure: The Problem of Embeddedness," *American Journal of Sociology* 91: 481–510.

Grasseni, C. (2003), "Packaging Skills: Calibrating Italian Cheese to the Global Market," in S. Strasser (ed.), *Commodifying Everything: Relationships of the Market,* New York: Routledge, pp. 341–81.

Grasseni, C. (2004), "Communities of Practice and Local Development: The EU Agricultural Policy Seen from a Mountain Community," in P. Messina (ed.), *EU Enlargement. Borders, Boundaries and Constraints,* Padova: CLEUP, pp. 133–49.

Grasseni, C. (2006), "Slow Food, Fast Genes: Timescapes of Authenticity and Innovation in the Anthropology of Food," *Cambridge Anthropology* 25(2): 79–94.

Grasseni, C. (2007), "Conservation, Development and Self-Commodification: Doing Ethnography in the Italian Alps," *Journal of Modern Italian Studies* 12(4): 440–49.

Grasseni, C. (2009a), *Developing Skill, Developing Vision. Practices of Locality in an Alpine Community,* Oxford: Berghahn Books.

Grasseni, C. (2009b), *Luoghi comuni. Antropologia dei luoghi e pratiche della visione,* Bergamo: Lubrina Editore.

Grasseni, C. (2011a), "Re-Inventing Food: Alpine Cheese in the Age of Global Heritage," *Anthropology of Food* 8, <http://aof.revues.org/index6819.html>, accessed March 3, 2013.

Grasseni, C. (2011b), "Cultural Maps and the Marketing of Localities. The 'Observatory of the Landscape' of Valtaleggio," in X. Roigé and J. Frigolé (eds.), *Constructing Cultural and Natural Heritage. Parks, Museums and Rural Heritage,* Barcelona, Documenta, pp. 193–206.

Grasseni, C. (2012a), "Developing Cheese at the Foot of the Alps," in E. Finnis (ed.), *Re-Imagining Marginalized Foods,* Tucson: University of Arizona Press, pp. 133–55.

Grasseni, C. (2012b), "Reinventing Food: the Ethics of Developing Local Foods," in J. Carrier and P. Luetchford (eds.), *Ethical Consumption. Social Value and Economic Practice,* Oxford: Berghahn Books, pp. 198–216.

Grasseni, C. (2012c). "Resisting Cheese. Boundaries, Conflict and Distinction at the Foot of the Alps," *Food Culture and Society* 15(1): 23–29.

Grasseni, C. (2014), "Of Cheese and Ecomuseums: Food as Cultural Heritage in the Northern Italian Alps," in R. Brulotte and M. Di Giovine (eds.), *Edible Identities: Exploring Food and Foodways as Cultural Heritage,* Farnham: Ashgate.

Grasseni, C. (forthcoming), *The Reinvention of Cheese,* Oxford: Berghahn Books.

Graziano, P. (2009), "I GAS: un movimento di pressione," in P. Graziano, F. Forno, and M. Lepratti (eds.), *GASP. Gruppi di Acquisto Solidale e Partecipativo,* Milano: Edizioni Punto Rosso, pp. 11–24.

Graziano, P. and Forno, F. (2012), "Political Consumerism and New Forms of Political Participation: The *Gruppi di Acquisto Solidale* in Italy," *Annals AAPSS* 644: 121–33.

Graziano, P., Forno, F., and Lepratti, M. (eds.) (2009), *GASP. Gruppi di Acquisto Solidale e Partecipativo,* Milano: Edizioni Punto Rosso.

Gudeman, S. (2012), *Economy's Tension: The Dialectics of Community and Market,* Oxford: Berghahn Books.

Guthman, J. (2004), *Agrarian Dreams: The Paradox of Organic Farming in California,* Berkeley: University of California Press.

Hahn, C. (2006), "The Gift and Reciprocity: Perspectives from Economic Anthropology," in S. Kolm and J. Mercier Ythier (eds.), *Handbook on the Economics of Giving, Reciprocity and Altruism,* Amsterdam: Elsevier, pp. 207–23.

Haller, D. and Shore, C. (eds.) (2005), *Corruption: Anthropological Perspectives,* London: Pluto Press.

Haraway, D. (1991), "Situated Knowledges: The Science Question in Feminism and the Privilege of Partial Perspectives," in *Simian, Cyborgs, and Women: The Reinvention of Nature,* New York: Routledge, pp. 183–202.

Hardt, M. (2011), "The Militancy of Theory," *The South Atlantic Quarterly* 110(1): 19–35.

Harper, D. and Faccioli, P. (2010), *The Italian Way. Food and Social Life,* Chicago: University of Chicago Press.

Hart, K., Laville, J. L., and Cattani A. D. (2010), *The Human Economy,* Cambridge: Polity Press.

Herzfeld, M. (1997), *Cultural Intimacy. Social Poetics in the Nation-State,* New York: Routledge.

Herzfeld, M. (2004), *The Body Impolitic: Artisans and Artifice in the Global Hierarchy of Value,* Chicago: Chicago University Press.

Herzfeld, M. (2009), *Evicted from Eternity: The Restructuring of Modern Rome,* Chicago: Chicago University Press.

Herzfeld, M. (2010), "Engagement, Gentrification, and the Neoliberal Hijacking of History," *Current Anthropology* 51(S2): S259–S267.

Hinrichs, C. (2003), "The Practice and Politics of Food System Localization," *Journal of Rural Studies* 19: 33–45.

Holloway, L. and Kneafsey, M. (2000), "Reading the Space of the farmers' Market: A Preliminary Investigation from the UK," *Sociologia Ruralis* 40(3): 285–99.

Hopkins, R. (2008), *The Transition Handbook: From Oil Dependency to Local Resilience,* Totnes: Green Books.

Ingold, T. (2000), *The Perception of the Environment. Essays in Livelihood, Dwelling, and Skill,* New York: Routledge.

Jarosz, L., (2008), "The city in the Country: Growing Alternative Food Networks in Metropolitan Areas," *Journal of Rural Studies* 24(3): 231–44.

Jasanoff, S. (2006), *States of Knowledge: The Co-Production of Science and the Social Order,* New York: Routledge.

Johnston, J., Biro, A., and MacKendrick, N. (2009), "Lost in the Supermarket: The Corporate-Organic Foodscape and the Struggle for Food Democracy," *Antipode* 41(3): 509–32.

Juris, J. (2008), *Networking Futures. The Movements Against Corporate Globalization,* Durham, NC: Duke University Press.

Kawano, E., Masterson, T., and Teller-Elsberg, J. (2010), *Solidarity Economy I: Building Alternatives for People and Planet,* Chicago: Lulu Press.

Kertzer, D. (1990), *Comrades and Christians: Religion and Political Struggle in Communist Italy,* Cambridge: Cambridge University Press.

Kirwan, J. (2004), "Alternative strategies in the UK Agro-Food System: Interrogating the Alterity of Farmers' Markets," *Sociologia Ruralis* 44(4): 395–415.

Kneafsey, M., Cox, R., Holloway, L., Dowler, E., Venn, L., and Tuomainen, H. (2008), *Reconnecting Consumers, Producers and Food. Exploring Alternatives,* New York: Berg.

Lamine, C. and Perrot, N. (2008), *Les AMAP: un nouveau pacte entre producteurs et consommateurs?* Gap: Éditions Yves Michel.

Langer, A. (1996), "Un piccolo potere da prendere sul serio,"in Centro Nuovo Modello di Sviluppo, *Lettera a un Consumatore del Nord,* 2nd ed., Bologna: EMI.

Latouche, S. (2005), *Come sopravvivere allo sviluppo,* Torino: Bollati Boringhieri.

Latouche, S. (2011), *Come si esce dalla società dei consumi,* Torino: Bollati Boringhieri.

Lave, J. (1988), *Cognition in Practice. Mind, Mathematics and Culture in Everyday Life,* Cambridge: Cambridge University Press.

Lave, J. (2011), *Apprenticeship in Critical Ethnographic Practice,* Chicago: University of Chicago Press.

Laville, J. L. (1994), *L'Economie solidaire,* Paris: Descleé de Brouwer.

Leonini, L. and Sassatelli, R. (eds.) (2008), *Il consumo critico. Significati, pratiche e reti,* Bari: Laterza Editore.

Lepratti, M. (2009), "I GAS come nuova forma di economia solidale," in P. Graziano, F. Forno, and M. Lepratti (eds.), *GASP. Gruppi di Acquisto Solidale e Partecipativo,* Milano: Edizioni Punto Rosso, pp. 59–70.

Lewis, O. (1969), "Culture of Poverty," in D. P. Moynihan (ed.), *On Understanding Poverty: Perspectives from the Social Sciences,* New York: Basic Books, pp. 187–220.

Littler, J. (2011), "What's Wrong with Ethical Consumption?," in T. Lewis and E. Potter (eds.), *Ethical Consumption. A Critical Introduction,* New York: Routledge, pp. 27–39.

Löffler, E. (2009), *A Future Research Agenda for Co-Production,* LARCI Commissioned Summary Report, Governance International, <http://www.rcuk.ac.uk/documents/innovation/larci/LarciCoproductionSummary.pdf>, accessed April 17, 2013.

Long, L. M. (2009), "Iowa Place-Based Foods. Review," *Journal of American Folklore* 122(483): 95–97.

Low, S. and Merry, S. (2010), "Engaged Anthropology: Diversity and Dilemmas: An Introduction to Supplement 2," *Current Anthropology* 51(S2): 203–26.

Luetchford, P. (2008), "The Hands that Pick the Fair Trade Coffee: Beyond the Charms of the Family Farm," in G. De Neve, D. Wood, P. Luetchford, and J. Pratt (eds.), *Hidden Hands in the Market,* Bingley: Emerald Publishing, pp. 143–69.

Luhmann, N. (1990), "Familiarity, Confidence, Trust: Problems and Alternatives," in D. Gambetta (ed.), *Trust. Making and Breaking Cooperative Relations,* Oxford: Blackwell, pp. 94–107.

Lyons, S. (2011), *Coffee and Community: Maya Farmers and Fair Trade Markets,* Boulder: University Press of Colorado.

Lyons, S. and Moberg, M. (eds.) (2010), *Fair Trade and Social Justice: Global Ethnographies,* New York: New York University Press.

Mance, E. (2001), *A revoluçãao das redes. A colaboração solidária come uma alternativa pós-capitalista à globalização atual,* Petròpolis: Editora Vozes.

Marsden, T. (2000) "Food Matters and the Matter of Food: Towards a New Food Governance?," *Sociologia Ruralis* 40(1): 20–29.

Marston, S., Jones, J. P., and Woodward, K. (2005), "Human Geography without Scale," *Transactions of the Institute of British Geographers* 30(4): 416–32.

Marte, L. (2007), "Foodmaps: Tracing Boundaries of 'Home' Through Food Relations," *Food and Foodways* 15(1–2): 261–89.

Martin, B. and Mohanty, C. T. (1986), "What Home Got to Do With It?," in T. de Lauretis (ed.), *Feminist Studies/ Critical Studies,* Milwaukee: University of Wisconsin Press, pp. 191–212.

Maselli, P. (2010), *Storie di Resistenza Quotidiana,* DVD, distributed with F. Forno (2011), *La spesa a pizzo zero,* Milano: Altraeconomia.

Mauss, M. (1966), *The Gift. Forms and functions of Exchange in Archaic Societies,* London: Cohen & West.

Maxey, L. (2007), "From 'Alternative' to 'Sustainable' Food," in D. Maye, L. Holloway, and M. Kneafsey (eds.), *Alternative Food Geographies. Representation and Practice,* Amsterdam: Elsevier, pp. 55–76.

McAdam, D., Tarrow, S., and Tilly, C. (2001), *Dynamics of Contention,* Cambridge: Cambridge University Press.

McFarland, A. S. and Micheletti, M. (eds.) (2010). *Creative Participation: Responsibility-Taking in the Political World,* Boulder, CO: Paradigm Publishers.

McMichael, P. (2009), "A Food Regime Genealogy," *Journal of Peasant Studies* 36(1): 139–69.

Meyer, R. N. (1989), *The Consumer Movement. Guardians of the Marketplace,* Boston: Twayne.

Micheletti, M. (2003), *Political Virtue and Shopping. Individuals, Consumerism and Collective Action,* Basingstoke: Palgrave Macmillan.

Micheletti, M. and Stolle, D. (2012), "Sustainable Citizenship and the New Politics of Consumption," *ANNALS of the American Academy of Political and Social Science* 644(1): 88–120.

Miller, D. (1998), *A Theory of Shopping,* Ithaca, NY: Cornell University Press.

Miller, D. (2008), *The Comfort of Things,* Cambridge: Polity Press.

Mohanty, C.T. (1997), "Women Workers and Capitalist Scripts: Ideologies of Domination, Common Interests and the Politics of Solidarity," in M. J. Alexander and C. T. Mohanty (eds.), *Feminist Genealogies, Colonial Legacies, Democratic Futures,* New York: Routledge, pp. 3–29.

Morgan, K., Marsden, T., and Murdoch, J. (2006), *Worlds of Food. Place, Power and Provenance in the Food Chain,* Oxford: Oxford University Press.

Movimento 5 Stelle (2013), *Programma Elettorale per la Regione Lombardia. Elezioni Regionali 2013,* <http://www.beppegrillo.it/listcciviche/liste/lombardia/comunicati_stampa/PROGRAMMA%20REGIONE%20LOMBARDIA%20V.02.pdf>, accessed February 27, 2013.

Murdoch, J., Marsden, T., and Banks, J. (2000), "Quality, Nature, and Embeddedness: Some Theoretical Considerations in the Context of the Food Sector," *Economic Geography* 76(2): 107–25.

Murdoch, J. and Miele, M. (2004), "A New Aesthetics of Food? Relational Reflexivity in the 'Alternative' Food Movement," in M. Harvey, A. McMeekin, and A. Warde (eds.), *Qualities of Food,* Basingstoke: Palgrave Macmillan, pp. 156–75.

O'Neill, O. (2002), *A Question of Trust,* Cambridge: Cambridge University Press.

Offer, A. (1997), "Between the Gift and the Market: the Economy of Regard," *Economic History Review* 50(3): 450–76.

Orlando, G. (2012), "Reflections on Neoliberal and Organic Food Values in Europe," Paper presented at the 12th EASA Biennial Conference, Nanterre, France, July 10–13, 2012.

Osservatorio CORES (2013), *I GAS nella provincia di Bergamo: indagine osservatorio CORES in collaborazione con il Tavolo Nazionale RES*, CORES Working Papers, no. 1, Università degli Studi di Bergamo, http://hdl.handle.net/10446/28934

Palumbo, B. (2003), *L'UNESCO e il campanile,* Rome: Meltemi.

Palumbo, B. (2009), *Politiche dell'inquietudine. Passioni, feste e poteri in Sicilia.* Firenze: Le Lettere.

Papa, C. (1985), *Dove sono molte braccia è molto pane. Famiglia mezzadrile tradizionale e divisione sessuale del lavoro in Umbria,* Perugia: Isuc.

Papa, C. (ed.) (1992), *Il pane. Antropologia e storia dell'alimentazione,* Perugia: Electa Editori Umbri.

Parasecoli, F. (2010), "The Gender of Geographical Indications: Women, Place, and the Marketing of Identities," *Cultural Studies/Critical Methodologies* 10: 467–78.

Paxson, H. (2013), *The Life of Cheese: Crafting Food and Value in America,* Berkeley: University of California Press.

Paxson, H. and West, H. (eds.) (2012), "Naming Cheese: Essays by the Cheese Scholars Collective," Special issue, *Food, Culture, and Society,* 15(1).

Peristiany, J. G. (ed.) (1965), *Honour and Shame. The Values of Mediterranean Society,* London: Weidenfeld and Nicolson.

Peters, J. D. (1997), "Seeing Bifocally. Media, Place, Culture," in J. Ferguson and A. Gupta (eds.), *Culture, Power, Place: Explorations in Critical Anthropology,* Durham, NC: Duke University Press, pp. 75–92.

Petrini C. (2005), *Buono, pulito e giusto,* Torino: Einaudi.

Pitkin, D. S. (1992), *La casa che Giacomo costruì. Romanzo antropologico,* Bari: Dedalo.

Pitt-Rivers, J. (ed.) (1963), *Mediterranean Countrymen,* The Hague: Mouton.

Pitt-Rivers, J. (1954), *The People of the Sierra,* Chicago: University of Chicago Press.

Polany, K. (1968), *Primitive, Archaic, and Modern Economies. Essays of Karl Polany,* New York: Anchor Books.

Pratt, J. (2007), "Food Values. The Local and the Authentic," *Critique of Anthropology* 27(3): 285–300.

Purcaro G. (2010), "Cibi di qualità e a basso prezzo. Così noi battiamo la crisi," *Il Giorno/ Bergamo* (April 3, 2010) 2.

Putnam, R. (1993), *Making Democracy Work. Civic Traditions in Modern Italy,* Princeton, NJ: Princeton University Press.

Putnam, R. (2000), *Bowling Alone. The Collapse and Revival of American Community,* New York: Simon & Schuster.

Ragusa, S. (2010), *A Tutto GAS. Come Aprire un Gruppo di Acquisto Solidale e Vivere Meglio,* Milano: Terre di Mezzo Editore.

Raynolds, L. T. (2004), "The Globalization of Organic Agro-Food Networks," *World Development* 32(5): 725–43.

Richard, A. and Rudnyckyj, D. (2009), "Economies of Affect," *Journal of the Royal Anthropological Institute* 15(1): 57–77.

Rivera, A. (2012), "Uccisi dal profitto, oscurati dale primarie," *Micromega,* <http://temi.repubblica.it/micromega-online/uccisi-dal-profitto-oscurati-dalle-primarie>, accessed December 9, 2012.

Rizzo, M. (2011), *Supermarket Mafia. A Tavola con Cosa Nostra,* Rome: Castelvecchi Editore.

Rizzo, S. and Stella, G. A. (2007), *La casta. Così i politici italiani sono diventati intoccabili,* Milano: Rizzoli.

Rocheleau, D., Thomas-Slayter, B., and Edmunds, D. (1995), "Gendered Resource Mapping: Focusing on Women's Spaces in the Landscape," *Cultural Survival Quarterly* 18(4): 62–68;

Roelvink, G. (2010), "Collective Action and the Politics of Affect," *Emotion, Space and Society* 3(2): 111–18.

Roigé, X. and Frigolé, J. (2011, eds), *Constructing Cultural and Natural Heritage. Parks, Museums and Rural Heritage,* Barcelona: Documenta.

Rosenkrands J. (2004), "Politicizing Homo Economicus: An Analysis of Anti-Corporate Websites," in W. van de Donk, D. Loader, P. G. Nihon, and D. Rucht (eds.), *Cyberprotest. New Media, Citizens and Social Movements,* New York: Routledge.

Rossanda, R. (2005), *La ragazza del secolo scorso,* Torino: Einaudi.

Rubino, M. (2012), "Spesa di gruppo, è boom. 7 milioni di Italiani nei 'Gas'," *La Repubblica* (October 29, 2012), <http://www.repubblica.it/economia/2012/10/29/news/spesa_di_gruppo_boom_7_milioni_di_italiani-45427020>, accessed October 31, 2012.

Sage C. (2007), "Trust in Markets: Economies of Regard and Spaces of Contestation in Alternative Food Networks," in J. Cross and A. Morales (eds.), *Street Entrepreneurs: People, Place and Politics in Local and Global Perspective,* New York: Routledge, pp. 147–63.

Sage, C. (2011), *Environment and Food,* New York: Routledge.

Sandon, M. (2009), "Associazione Bio Rekk, Padova," in P. Graziano, F. Forno, and M. Lepratti (eds.), *GASP. Gruppi di Acquisto Solidale e Partecipativo,* Milano: Edizioni Punto Rosso, pp. 134–44.

Saroldi, A. (2001), *Gruppi di Acquisto Solidali. Guida al consumo locale,* Bologna: Editrice Missionaria Italiana.

Saroldi, A. (2003), *Costruire Economie Solidali,* Bologna: Editrice Missionaria Italiana.

Scammell, M. (2000), "The Internet and Civic Engagement: The Age of the Citizen-Consumer," *Political Communication* 17(4), 351–5.

Servettini, M. (2008), *Dai consumatori responsabili ai co-produttori. Scritto per il Consiglio di Europa, gennaio 2008,* Rete Lilliput/ L'isola che c'è/ Distretto di Economia Solidale di Como, <www.mag4.it/rete/azioni/materiali.html?download = 1140%3Aservettini>, accessed March 3, 2013.

Shin, M. and Agnew, J. A. (2008), *Berlusconi's Italy. Mapping Contemporary Italian Politics,* Philadelphia, PA: Temple University Press.

Shore, C. (1990), *Italian Communism: An Anthropological Perspective,* London: Pluto.

Signorelli, A. (1990), "Il pragmatismo delle donne. La condizione femminile nella trasformazione delle campagne," in P. Bevilacqua (ed.), *Storia dell'agricoltura in età contemporanea,* vol. II, Venice: Marsilio, pp. 625–59.

Signori S. (2010), "Exploring Ethical Investors' Motivations: The Case of the Tomasoni Organic Dairy," Paper presented at the 23rd Annual Conference of the European Business Ethics Network (EBEN 2010 AC), 9–11 September 2010, Trento.

Slow Food Italia (2010), *Le conseguenze del piacere. Documento del Congresso 2010-2014,* San Mauro Torinese: Stargrafica.

Solinas, P. G. (1993), "Ciclo di sviluppo familiare e ciclo della vita nelle famiglie contadine del Senese," *La Ricerca Folklorica* 27: 35–42.

Spaargaren, G. and van Vliet, B. (2000), "Lifestyles, Consumption and the Environment: The Ecological Modernisation of Domestic Consumption," *Environmental Politics* 9(1): 50–76.

St.Martin, K. (2009), "Toward a Cartography of the Commons: Constituting the Political and Economic Possibilities of Place," *Professional Geographer* 61(4): 493–507.

Stille, A. (2006), *The Sack of Rome,* London: Penguin Press.

Strasser, S. (2003, ed.), *Commodifying Everything: Relationships of the Market,* New York: Routledge.

Strathern, M. (ed.) (2000), *Audit Cultures,* New York: Routledge.

Sutton, D. (2001), "Introduction," in *Remembrance of Repasts: An Anthropology of Food and Memory,* Oxford: Berg, pp.73–102.

Sutton, D. (2006), "Cooking Skill, the Senses and Memory: The Fate of Practical Knowledge" in E. Edwards, C. Gosden, and R. Phillips (eds.), *Sensible Objects. Colonialism, Museums and Material Culture,* Oxford: Berg, pp. 87–120.

Tarrow, S. and McAdam, D. (2003), "Scale Shift in Transnational Contention," Paper prepared for the conference on "Transnational Processes and Social Movements" at the Villa Serbelloni, Bellagio, Italy, July 22–26, 2003, <falcon.arts.cornell.edu/sgt2/contention/documents/ST scaleshift jun04.doc>, accessed March 3, 2013.

Tavolo per la Rete Italiana di Economia Solidale—RES (2010), *Il Capitale delle relazioni. Come creare e organizzare gruppi d'acquisto e altre reti di economia solidale,* Milano: Altraeconomia Edizioni.

Trigilia C. (1986), *Grandi partiti e piccole imprese. Comunisti e democristiani nelle regioni a economia diffusa,* Bologna: Il Mulino.

Trigilia, C. (2005), *Sviluppo Locale. Un progetto per l'Italia,* Bari: Editori Laterza.

Tullio-Altan, C. (1974), *I valori difficili. Inchiesta sulle tendenze ideologiche e politiche dei giovani in Italia,* Milano: Bompiani.

Tullio-Altan, C. (1995), *Italia: una nazione senza religione civile. Le ragioni di una democrazia incompiuta,* Udine: Istituto Editoriale Veneto Friulano.

Vaccaro, I. and Beltran, O. (2009). "Livestock Versus 'Wild Beasts.' Contradictions in the Natural Patrimonialization of the Pyrenees," *Geographical Review* 99(4): 499–516.

Valer, A. (1999), *Bilanci di giustizia. Famiglie in rete per consumi leggeri,* Bologna: Editrice Missionaria Italiana.

Van der Ploeg, J. D. (2006), *Oltre la modernizzazione. Processi di sviluppo rurale in Europa,* Soveria Mannelli: Rubettino.

Van der Ploeg, J. D. (2007), "Diversità delle forme di impresa e sviluppo rurale," in G. Brunori (ed.), *Biodiversità e tipicità. Paradigmi economici e strategie competitive,* Milano: Franco Angeli, pp. 184–208.

Van der Ploeg, J. D. and Renting, H. (2004), "Behind the 'Redux': A Rejoinder to David Goodman," *Sociologia Ruralis* 44(2): 233–242.

Van der Ploeg, J. D, van Broekhuizen, R., Brunori, G., Sonnino, R., Knickel, K., Tisenkopfs, T., and Ostindie, H. (2008), "Towards a New Theoretical Framework for Understanding Regional Rural Development," in T. Marsden and J. D. van der Ploeg (eds), *Unfolding Webs. The Dynamics of Regional Rural Development,* Assen: Royal Van Gorcum, pp. 1–28.

Venturelli, L. (2009), "Le banche tagliano il credito: il caseificio salvato dai clienti," *L'Unità* (February 27), p. 33, <http://archiviostorico.unita.it/cgi-bin/highlight Pdf.cgi?t=ebook&file=/edizioni/20090227/pdf/NAZ/pages/20090227_33_ 27ECO33A.pdf&query=>, accessed April 17, 2013.

Viganò, E., Glorio, M., and Villa, A. (2008), *Tutti i numeri dell'equo,* Rome: Edizioni dell'Asino.

Whatmore, S., Stassart, P., and Renting, H. (2003), "What's Alternative About Alternative Food Networks?," *Environment and Planning A* 35(3): 389–97.

White, T. (2013), "Seeds of A New Economy: How Community Supported Agriculture Promotes Diverse Economic Activity," PhD diss., University of Massachusetts.

Wilk, R. (1995), "Learning to Be Local in Belize. Global Systems of Common Difference," in D. Miller (ed.), *Worlds Apart. Modernity through the Prism of the Local,* New York: Routledge, pp. 110–33.

Wolf, E. (1969), "Society and Symbols in Latin Europe and the Islamic Near East: Some Comparisons," *Anthropological Quarterly* 42: 287–301.

Zinn, D. (2001), *La Raccomandazione. Clientelismo vecchio e nuovo,* Rome: Donzelli.

Index